SUMŪD

SUMŪD

Essays, memoir, fiction, poetry, and art from the *Markaz Review*

A New Palestinian Reader

EDITED BY
MALU HALASA AND
JORDAN ELGRABLY
FOREWORD BY
SALEEM HADDAD

SEVEN STORIES PRESS
New York ∗ Oakland ∗ London

SEVEN STORIES PRESS
140 Watts Street
New York, NY 10013
www.sevenstories.com

LIBRARY OF CONGRESS
CATALOGING-IN-PUBLICATION DATA
is on file.

College professors and high school and middle
school teachers may order free examination
copies of Seven Stories Press titles.
Visit https://www.sevenstories.com/pg/
resources-academics
or email academic@sevenstories.com.

PRINTED IN
United States of America

9 8 7 6 5 4 3 2 1

FRONTMATTER ART

p. i: Haneen Nazzal, *Against*, 2022,
detail. Fine art archival paper, 310 gsm,
75 x 55 cm. Courtesy of the artist
and Zawyeh Gallery.

p. ii: Haneen Nazzal, *We Will Never
Leave*, 2021, detail. Digital illustration,
36 x 51 cm. Courtesy of the artist.

p. iv: Heba Tannous, *Fida'i*, 2022, detail.
Digital illustration. Courtesy of the artist.

Contents

v

Foreword

How do you imagine a future when the present is being obliterated before your eyes?

This is a question I have considered, both as a Palestinian and a writer, in the wake of the apocalyptic violence unleashed on Palestinians after the Hamas attacks of October 7, 2023. In the months that followed, it was impossible to look away as Israel reduced most of Gaza to rubble. The magnitude of the brutality meant there was no limit to the blood and gore, the lifeless children and soot-covered bodies pulled from their destroyed homes. The algorithm was more than happy to serve an endless conveyer belt of death into my feed, in what one of South Africa's lawyers at the International Court of Justice described as "the first genocide in history where its victims are broadcasting their own destruction in real time, in the desperate, so far vain hope, that the world might do something."

And yet within this stream of unimaginable cruelty, I found hope in the creative resistance of Palestinians during the darkest moments of violence: a video of a young boy growing corn and onions outside his family's tent, a makeshift taboon cooking system using coal in order to make mana'eesh, a family building a home out of the parachute material used in aid drops, the clowns and jugglers of the Free Gaza Circus entertaining crowds of displaced Palestinians, fifteen-year-old Hussein Al-Attar creating a gadget to power lights in his family's tent in Rafah using wind energy, a man in a displaced camp making a meal in the style of TikTok cooking videos, a recipe composed of "ninety-five percent aid package contents, five percent love and resilience."

These are examples of Palestinian sumūd.

The Anishinaabe critic and writer Gerald Vizenor articulated the Native American concept of "survivance" to refer to the continuation of Native American stories and cultures as not just an act of survival—a response to violence—but one of active resistance, endurance, and regeneration. In Vizenor's words, survivance is simultaneously reactive, active, and proactive, "a standpoint, a worldview, and a presence."

Likewise, sumūd, the process of steadfastness, of survivance, is not just a project of survival but also one of remembrance, record-keeping, and revitalization. It is the immediate and stubborn insistence on holding on; it is the shared process of bearing witness and collective remembrance, an enraged and engaged act of love; and in what are arguably the darkest hours Palestinians have ever lived through—with the world's most powerful countries hell-bent on their annihilation, with nearly all of Gaza's hospitals, homes, universities, and museums reduced to rubble, and with its people trapped and starving inside it like a concentration camp—sumūd is a call for a radical and daring act of imagination.

Here, art and culture play a crucial role. The thinker bell hooks once said that the function of art is not just to tell things how they are but to also "imagine what is possible." In this vein, the compilation and release of *Sumūd: A New Palestinian Reader*, amidst unspeakable and almost unfathomable violence, is more than just an act of bearing witness—it is also a space to showcase the creativity of both Palestinian steadfastness and the solidarity of those who stand alongside them. As Saeed Taji Farouky writes in his piece for this collection, "Culture is a crowbar with which we can pry open the prison gate and smash the windscreen of the limousine when our politicians pull up to the Wyndham Grand Hotel in Manama for the next normalization summit."

Culture is a tool for the creation of counterhegemonic narratives. Through storytelling, poetry, and art, we imagine the contours of a future beyond the barbed wires, fortified walls, and visa regimes of colonial empires. In this sense, the steadfast project of imagining a liberated Palestine is the first step toward a much larger liberationist project: that of imagining a better, more sustainable, and freer world. The centeredness of Palestine in the global project of liberation has never seemed more prescient. In the words of the Palestinian poet Rafeef Ziadah, "Palestinians wake up every morning to teach the rest of the world life."

The poetry featured in this collection builds on this sentiment of survivance. In Eman Quotah's generous, expansive review of Fady Joudah's poetry collection, she writes, "Words, language, are never adequate, but whatever future we look back from, we will have a large body of poems and other writings composed by Palestinians, both inside and outside of Gaza, during this time of genocide and attempted erasure." Reflecting on Joudah's poem "Sunbird," a symbol of Palestinian freedom and hope, Quotah writes: "The poem moves across all directions of the land, 'Fresh east to salty west, / southern sweet // and northern free.' Finally, it swoops, 'From womb / to breath, / and one with oneness / I be: / from the river / to the sea.' "

"From the river to the sea," the much maligned and purposefully misunderstood chant, is itself a rallying call for radical imagination. With this call, Palestinians are imagining a return to the peaceful coexistence that characterized earlier times in Palestine's history, a time that seems so far gone but is not really, because I can see it in the memories of my grandmother, who recalled with perfect clarity a childhood in Haifa where Christians, Muslims, and Jews lived side by side as equals. To preserve our forebears' memories and transform them into imagined futures is the political project of a liberated Palestine.

Imagination is not without its risks. There is the danger of self-delusion and, even worse, the threat of self-destruction. I am acutely aware of this myself, as I write these words on the eve of a planned invasion of Rafah, the last vestige of land upon which Gaza's trapped population has taken refuge, in the same moment when global solidarity for Palestine has never been greater, with more people than ever calling for Palestinian liberation. It is not lost on me that, during this knife-edge moment between liberation and annihilation, every word I write could in a moment feel outdated, irrelevant, or hopelessly naive. Ilan Pappé, in his essay in this collection, posits a question of why, despite impossible circumstances, "are so many of us still convinced that the struggle is not over, and justice will prevail?"

But I take my courage from those at the forefront of the violence. In the harrowing dispatches from Gaza written by the cofounder of Theatre for Everybody Hossam Madhoun and published in this collection, Hossam recounts a conversation his wife Abeer has with a nine-year-old boy she encounters on her way from Al Wafa hospital to the market in Gaza. Abeer asks the boy what he thinks will happen, and he replies that the Israelis will keep destroying and killing until they push out or kill every Palestinian from Gaza. "And what do you think we should do?" Abeer asks. "Do what we do now," the young boy replies. "Stay and live."

The scale of destruction is inconceivable. A recent UN report estimated it would take nearly eighty years to rebuild Gaza. And yet sumūd asks us to train our imagination as a necessary precursor to visualizing liberation.

To stay and to live.

In the end, Palestine will be free.

SALEEM HADDAD, May 2024

Introduction

The Arabic word *sumūd* often translates as "steadfastness" or "standing fast." It is, above all, everyday resistance in the face of Israeli occupation. As the Palestinian author and human rights lawyer Raja Shehadeh writes from Ramallah, sumūd is

> practiced by every man, woman and child here struggling on his or her own to learn to cope with, and resist, the pressures of living as a member of a conquered people. *Sumūd* is watching your home turned into a prison. You . . . choose to stay in that prison, because it is your home, and because you fear that if you leave, your jailer will not allow you to return. . . . It is developing from an all-encompassing form of life into a form of resistance that unites the Palestinians living under Israeli occupation.[1]

Despite the constant oppressions imposed on Palestinians, sumūd is both a personal and collective commitment.

Of the thousands of books published about Palestine and Israel, comparatively few explore the relationship between culture and resistance. During times of conflagration and war, violence often obscures. Yet poetry, literature, and art are the very spaces, even during difficult, extreme times, in which people reveal cherished aspects of their existence and the ideas and philosophies that underpin real and imagined lives.

On the history of sumūd, Palestinian activist and physician Dr. Mustafa Barghouti offers: "While pain and struggle are universally

---

1 Raja Shehadeh, *The Third Way: A Journal of Life in the West Bank* (London: Quartet Books, 1982), viii.

present in Palestinian experiences, sumūd also allows for other experiences and expressions, including a deep-felt joy and appreciation of Palestinian culture."[2]

As promised by its subtitle, *Sumūd* is a *new* Palestinian reader. By featuring memoir, poetry, fiction, reportage, literary and arts criticism, art, posters, and illustration, the anthology explores creative defiance by Palestinians and others who stand beside them—people who believe in the Palestinian right to self-determination and a homeland. Much of the material has been drawn from the *Markaz Review*, the Arab and Middle Eastern literary arts publication. Some of it was published before October 7 and explores issues and ideas long associated with Palestinian life and culture. Since the reader has been compiled and edited amidst Israel's day-in, day-out bombing of Gaza, one can sense an urgency to the more recent contributions. At the time of writing, more than 41,455 Gazans have been killed, with an estimated 147,333 dead, reported missing, or wounded. A study published in the journal *Lancet* warns that the true death toll at this point could be more than 186,000 people.

Since October 7, theater-maker Hossam Madhoun has been posting real-time capsule accounts from Gaza's killing fields—that is, when he can find a solar-power supply to charge his mobile phone and laptop and when he's not completely overwhelmed by desperation and the deaths of people he loves.

The melancholy beauty of life, an eye to detail, and the will to survive—coupled with a determination to understand and capture the uniqueness of what it means to be Palestinian—are themes that echo in the poem "Palestine A–Z," by Mosab Abu Toha. He is one of eight poets featured in *Sumūd*. Poetry has always held a special place in Palestinian literature and the Arab psyche. It has also been one of the best tools in the Palestinian arsenal to counter Israeli oppressors. This was acknowledged by Israeli general Moshe Dayan, who once "likened reading one of Fadwa Tuqan's poems to facing twenty enemy commandos."[3]

---

2   Alexandra Rijke and Toine van Teeffelen, "To Exist Is to Resist: Sumud, Heroism, and the Everyday," *Jerusalem Quarterly* 59 (Summer 2014): 95.
3   Lawrence Joffe, Obituary: "Fadwa Tuqan," *Guardian*, December 15, 2003.

At the theoretical heart of the reader is Ilan Pappé's essay and book review of Tahrir Hamidi's *Imagining Palestine: Cultures of Exile and National Identity* that explores the relationship between culture and resistance. In it, Pappé cites Edward Said's refusal to separate the artistic and cultural from the political, theories that predate the Boycott, Divestment, Sanctions movement. However, there is no doubt after October 7 that sharply articulated Palestinian creative expression has been considered threatening because of the international effort, from the US to Europe, to silence it. Karim Kattan addresses this in his timely essay "At the Threshold of Humanity: Gaza Is Not an Abstraction." Olivia Snaije documents another kind of concerted erasure, in this instance of Palestine's ancient past, as she describes the destruction of heritage sites by the Israeli Defense Forces and the looting of archaeological treasures by Israeli soldiers, in an essay originally published in *New Lines Magazine*. Physician and journalist Ahmed Twaij deconstructs Israel's twinning of ISIS with Hamas, which has been used to justify the severity of the Israeli military campaign in Gaza, in his contribution, "Mosul versus Gaza from a Medical and Humanitarian Standpoint." A humanitarian aid worker in Iraq, he never witnessed the bombings of hospitals and ambulances by the US and allied forces. In "Palestine and the Unspeakable," *Markaz Review* senior editor and essayist Lina Mounzer believes the ferocity of the campaign of bombing early in the war on Gaza was a clear indication of Israel's intent all along.

The reader's foray into literature begins with a sci-fi short story. "Application 39," by Ahmed Masoud, about a dystopian Gaza's bid to win the Olympics, first appeared in *Palestine +100: Stories from a Century after the Nakba*, edited by Basma Ghalayini. By contrast with Masoud's darkly humorous approach, there can be no mistaking the raw emotion in Noor Hindi's poem "Fuck Your Lecture on Craft, My People Are Dying."

Supporting facts are provided by *Sumūd*'s coeditor Jordan Elgrably in his essay "They Kill Writers, Don't They?", an examination of Israel's assassinations of Palestinian literary figures and media workers—yet another clear indication of the threat that literature and reportage pose to occupation authorities. Palestine's greatest public intellectual, Edward Said (1935–2003), was well aware of the power of words. Kuwaiti novelist and academic Layla AlAmmar considers his role as an inspirational figure for Middle Eastern writers everywhere.

The inclusion in the reader of literary essays and book and art reviews allows for a deeper, more critical appraisal of important creative expression and ideas. The Saudi American novelist and literary critic Eman Quotah provides an overview of the potency of Palestinian poetry—many of the poets she writes about have been included in this anthology—in her review of the latest poetry collection by Fady Joudah. A physician and translator, Joudah brought Maya Abu Al-Hayyat's poems about memory, loss, and motherhood to English-speaking audiences.

Activist Ahed Tamimi grew up in the West Bank village of Nabi Saleh, which fought the seizure of its only spring by Israeli settlers and the IDF. In "Childhood," she writes, with Dena Takruri, about being radicalized at the tender age of eight. Both occupation and war pose grave threats to Palestinian families. The fact that, according to the UN's Office of the High Commissioner for Human Rights, nearly 15,000 children have been killed and misidentified during this war on Gaza[4] is the distressing subject matter of Zeina Azzam's poem—"Write My Name" went viral, with people all over the internet reciting it. The possibility of losing an entire generation is brought home by Diane Shammas's recollections about her years teaching in Gaza and the promise shown by some of her students. The sense of present and future loss resonates in the memory of those who came before, which informs filmmaker Saeed Taji Farouky's hybrid script and essay "More Photographs Taken from the Pocket of a Dead Arab."

In the *Sumūd* anthology, memoir and first-person accounts hold a special place. Raja Shehadeh takes readers on a bike ride, immediately after the 1967 war, in "Road to Jerusalem, Then and Now." In her essay

---

4   "Some parents in Gaza have resorted to writing their children's names on their legs to help identify them should either they or the children be killed."— CNN, October 22, 2023.

"Shylock in the Promised Land," originally published in the *Jewish Quarterly*, Jo Glanville finds a Shakespearean antisemitic stereotype given an unexpected reading in Jerusalem's Old City. She's teaching a Palestinian teenager the English version of *The Merchant of Venice*, since the play in Arabic was banned by Israeli authorities. Her encounter is the polar opposite of the one recounted in a prose poem by poet, journalist, and activist Mohammed El-Kurd, "Sheikh Jarrah Is Burning," in which Israeli settlers and the IDF seize Palestinian homes in his East Jerusalem neighborhood. Another kind of meeting between allegedly opposing sides takes place between the co-CEOs of Combatants for Peace, Rana Salman and Yonatan Gher—one Palestinian, the other Israeli—as they come together to commemorate the anniversary of the Nakba, or the 1948 "catastrophe," modern-day celebrations of which are outlawed by the Israeli state.

The experience of Palestinians at home on their own land makes compulsive, if not disturbing, reading. Fadi Quran's tweet turned essay, "Driving in Palestine Now Is More Dangerous Than Ever," again reveals Israeli settlers and the IDF as the root of the problem. Research, writing, and publishing the news from Palestine comes with its own set of trials and tribulations, as detailed by French journalist Chloé Benoist in her first-person account "Unembedded Reporting from the West Bank."

Unsurprisingly the oppressive atmosphere of these articles and essays often explodes into violence. Brett Kline reports on a water-tanker delivery in a West Bank village in "Water-Deprived Palestinians Endure Settler Rampage while Army Punishes NGO Protesters." Violence lurks everywhere, as Mohammed El-Kurd testifies in the poem "Elderly Woman Falls Asleep on My Shoulder," about their bus ride together and her subsequent interrogation at a checkpoint. The figs—not "storms / and bombs and blows"—that the old woman carries in her heavy plastic bags are a reminder of a historic fruit, rich in taste and symbolic meaning. For his 2019 album *Bellydancing on Wounds*, El-Kurd had recorded a longer version of this poem, accompanied on classical oud by Clarissa Bitar, under the title "Figs, Bitch!" Acclaimed Bethlehem chef Fadi Kattan continues the food theme, offering intriguing history (*mansaf* and Battle of the Chicken) alongside recipes (*fatteh ghazawiya*), ingredients (*mouloukhiya*), and kitchen desire in "Culinary Palestine." However, not everything sourced locally is good for the system, as seen in Raja Shehadeh's second essay for *Sumūd*, about *wasta*—nepotism and corruption—in the Palestinian Authority's Diplomats' Quarter.

*

Art was and still is perceived as a threat to Israeli authorities. In the West Bank and Gaza in the 1970s and 1980s, there were no official galleries, and artists showed their work in schools, churches, and town halls. The popularity of these exhibitions among ordinary Palestinians also drew an unexpected audience—the IDF. Artists have always been a front in cultural resistance. Forced to apply for permits to exhibit work, painters and sculptors found their artwork censored. Israeli soldiers even conducted studio visits.

Before the 1993 Oslo Accords, some artists were imprisoned because they dared to incorporate the colors of the banned Palestinian flag—red, white, black, and green—in their artwork. A brief opening up occurred thereafter until renewed tensions, phobias and prejudices, and bloodshed restored draconian Israeli measures. In 2022, for example, Israeli police attacked the funeral procession of slain Palestinian American journalist Shireen Abu Akleh (1971-2022), nearly causing mourners to drop her coffin as the authorities seized Palestinian flags. Now, as algorithms erase Palestine from the internet, the watermelon, which was used in the past to represent the flag, has emerged once again in hundreds of thousands of visual permutations. Occupation and violence have provided opportunities not so much for older and somewhat clichéd art of the martial variety—the clenched fist or Kalashnikov rifle—but for work that's smart, oftentimes snarky, and always modern, in a way that Marcel Duchamp would appreciate.

In the reader, Jerusalem-born writer and translator Taline Voskeritchian introduces the veteran Palestinian artist Vera Tamari, who's had her own iconic run-in with the authorities. For the 2002 installation *Going for a Ride?*, the artist arranged cars crushed by Israeli tanks during that year's invasion of Ramallah on a piece of tarmac on a school football field. From across the street, where she lived, she watched Israeli reactions, and she said in an interview: "A whole cohort of Merkavas turned up, and the tank commanders got out and discussed what to do. Then they got back into their tanks and ran over the whole exhibit, over and over again, backwards and forwards, crushing it to pieces. Then, for good measure, they shelled it. Finally, they got out again and pissed on the wreckage."[5]

Hazem Harb, whose father was arrested, tortured, and then finally released during the war on Gaza, writes about creating art during genocide. These experiences turned him "upside down and back to zero." He has returned to charcoal and gauze, materials he used as a young man making art and growing up in Gaza as one of eight children. Gauze is particularly poignant, since the English name for the raw silk fabric, شاش or *shash* in Arabic, is said to have originated there. Harb is a collector of historic artifacts from Palestine. His circular acrylic collage of a watermelon, taken from a fresco in a villa in Nazareth, appears on *Sumūd*'s back cover.

Other artists contribute conceptual work, photography, drawings, and linocuts, all of which amplify the syntax of Palestinian experience. Khalil Rabah drives nails into an Oxford desk dictionary. Taysir Batniji commissions a photographic series on Israeli watchtowers despite being banned, as a Gazan, from entering the West Bank. Samir Harb animates the Israeli attack on Rafah to the sounds of actual bombing. Architect Heba Tannous sees the spirit of the *fida'i* (*fedayeen*) as integral to the Palestinian psyche.

Understandably, the distant past casts an unmissable pall over the present. Steve Sabella lives in an abandoned 1948 house for *38 Days of Re-Collection* and photographs its contents, encapsulating loss and erasure in fragments of stone and plaster. In his *Metamorphosis* series, he subverts and undermines barbwire and its meaning of "keep out, this is mine."

---

5   William Dalrymple, "A Culture under Fire," *Guardian*, October 2, 2002.

His art on the reader's front cover in many ways captures the essence of the anthology.

However, not all Palestinian art is outwardly critical. In self-portraiture, Raeda Saadeh weaves her eyelashes into dreadlocks adorned with tiny gold keys, in effect blinding herself. The editorial cartoonist and artist Mohammad Sabaaneh reacts to the war on Gaza and his own imprisonment by the Israelis with expressionistic brush-pen and ink drawings and linocuts. Rehaf Al Batniji's social documentary photographs reveal Gaza's unbowed fishermen, who face changeable weather and an aggressive Israeli navy.

The political poster has always been an art form that flourishes during times of strife, and *Sumūd*'s art editor, West Bank curator Nadine Aranki, writes about its rise in popularity during this war. Like artist-activists during the 2011 Syrian revolution and the 2022 Iranian "Woman, Life, Freedom" revolution, Victoria García and Haneen Nazzal belong to online groups—in their case Artists Against Apartheid and Art Commune, respectively—that post visual material for demonstrators to download, print, and carry on pro-Palestinian marches. Works by Nazzal, Dyala Moshtaha, and the Lebanese singer Khaled El Haber have been featured, among others, in the *Posters for Gaza* exhibition at Zawyeh Gallery in Dubai. Long before the current situation, anonymous collectives such as Protest Stencil and Visualizing Palestine have been producing posters and infographics that challenge stereotypes and change the public's perceptions.

For more established art practitioners, a single image is enough to unravel a history of pain. In charcoal and acrylic, Sliman Anis Mansour reveals the penning of Palestinians at their myriad checkpoints in *Homeland*. The series *Shoreless Sea*, by Palestinian's preeminent painter Tayseer Barakat, denotes hardening international attitudes toward the increasing numbers of Arabs who, like the Palestinians, have become refugees.

Some art derives its power because it is situated in a specific time and place; for example, Rula Halawani among the fallen on the streets of Ramallah during Israeli's violent 2002 incursion. Documentation of an ancient olive tree on the West Bank, by South African photographer and activist Adam Broomberg, with Rafael Gonzalez, comes with additional information pinpointing its whereabouts—in part to ward off Israeli settlers.

Filmmaker and writer Nora Ounnas Leroy advances visual criticism from the local to the global in Montpellier, the editorial home of the *Markaz Review*, when she posits this important question after seeing an exhibition of exiled art: "Where Is the Palestinian National Museum of Modern and Contemporary Art?"

Major collections of Palestinian art are invariably stored away, like the one at the Institut du Monde Arabe, in Paris. Occasionally they are brought out and exhibited until a war deems them too dangerous to be seen—then the exhibitions are canceled, and the artwork is packed up and returned to its place in the basement.

In the stream-of-consciousness poem "Beirut," poet Ahmad Almallah captures the diasporic apprehensions of traveling with his daughter from the US to "home" in Palestine. His thoughts oscillate from conflicting feelings toward his father to sexist gibes from Israeli border guards about "hot" Haifa Wehbe as the two make the difficult crossing from Israel back into Lebanon to the continual problems posed by translation. Yet displacement has been a fertile ground for some, as the excerpt from Maurice Ebileeni's book, *Being There, Being Here: Palestinian Writings in the World*, explores the literary heritage of the Palestinian diaspora. But this, of course, depends on where one is and who's in charge. In "Memoirs of a Militant: The Arrest," Nawar Qasim Baidoun details her life under Israeli occupation in southern Lebanon before she was incarcerated in a notorious prison.

The poet Noor Hindi again reveals a disheartening Palestinian American experience in "Pledging Allegiance." Meanwhile, *Markaz* columnist and Palestinian citizen of the world Jenine Abboushi makes her own pilgrimage to Hebron, Jenin, the north, and Jerusalem in the poignant travelogue "Israel's Intimate Separations"—only to be mistaken for Jewish on the plane back to Detroit.

Still, many Palestinians don't have the luxury of travel or leaving.

In "The End of the Palestinian State? Jenin Is Only the Beginning," Yousef M. Aljamal recounts the history of the city and its refugee camp, under occupation since 1967, as a flashpoint between Israeli forces and Palestinian resistance groups. From December 2023 onward, the camp has experienced an increase in air strikes and raids. Jenin's legendary Freedom Theatre, which is located there, was vandalized by Israeli soldiers, and its producer, Mostafa Sheta, was arrested and imprisoned without charge. Journalist Hadani Ditmars reports on the ongoing assaults against the theater company, founded in 2006 by the controversial figure Juliano Mer-Khamis and nominated for a Nobel Peace Prize in 2024 for its years of peaceful resistance to the Israeli occupation.

These are the kinds of essays and reportage the *Markaz Review* aimed to publish when the online journal was founded in 2020 by editor in chief Jordan Elgrably, with a global group of activists, writers, artists, and concerned individuals. They wanted to bring more Arabic-language writing into English translation and provide a home for voices and stories overlooked or purposely ignored by mainstream Western media.

With this in mind, the reader examines the prisms through which Palestinians and their experiences are viewed and oftentimes misjudged. In "Response to *Gaza: Mowing the Lawn*, 2014–15," social justice activist Tony Litwinko reacts to an exhibition of paintings by Los Angeles artist Jaime Scholnick. Noted academics Sara Roy and Ivar Ekeland analyze the ramifications of Israeli, American, and global policies and assumptions about Palestine, particularly in light of present-day calamities, in the essay "Disrupting the Colonial Gaze: Gaza and Israel after October 7."

The *Sumūd* anthology closes with Hala Alyan's poem "Habibti Ghazal"—part love swoon, part warning. Alyan is an award-winning poet, author, and clinical psychologist. The title of her 2024 opinion piece for the *Guardian*, "I Am Not There, I Am Not Here: A Palestinian American Poet Bearing Witness to Atrocity"[6] references "Tibaq"

---

6   Hala Alyan, "I Am Not There, I Am Not Here: A Palestinian American Poet Bearing Witness to Atrocity," *Guardian*, January 28, 2024.

("Counterpoint"), an elegy for the late Edward Said written by the great Palestinian poet Mahmoud Darwish (1941-2008).[7]

In this article Alyan explores an essential aspect of contemporary Palestinian life. "The idea of sumūd has become a multifaceted cultural concept among Palestinians," she writes. To its usual meaning of stead-fastness, she adds that the word in Arabic is "a derivative of 'arranging' or 'saving up,' even 'adorning.' *It implies composure braided with rootedness, a posture that might bend but will not break.*"[8] (emphasis ours)

*

During the war on Gaza, there have been scores of trophy videos posted on the internet by Israeli soldiers in the Strip. One that appeared on TikTok shows a devastated home; the Palestinian family who owned the property discovered it by chance (having been forced out of the same house months earlier) and sent the short, disturbing film to relatives and friends.

In it, an IDF soldier films his unit. Helmeted and armed combatants yell to each other as they make their way through the debris on the stairs and utterly trashed rooms. Sunlight streams in through the windows. Every now and then the soldier points the camera downward and a family memento, perhaps a framed picture, can be glimpsed among the smashed furniture and detritus strewn across the floor. From the layout of the house and the curved metal banister on the stairwell, it was obviously once a gracious family home.

It's unclear why the film was uploaded in the first place. By the time it arrived in one of our WhatsApp group chats, a comment, in Hebrew, had been posted on the video. It read: "In the midst of battle I see a mirror."

These words seem less triumphant and more self-reflective. One

---

7   "I am from there. I am from here. I am not there and I'm not here. I have two names, which meet and part, and I have two languages. I forget which of them I dream in." See "Mahmoud Darwish reading '*Tibaq* / Antithesis'—Homage to Edward Said," YouTube, posted July 24, 2016.

8   Alyan, "I Am Not There."

could even suggest that the person who made the comment felt ashamed.

In this time of brutal, unassailable war, what is the power of culture? It not only reveals who we are to others but in many ways demonstrates the essentialness of who we are to ourselves.

The elderly Palestinians who owned this house—who brought up their many children and their grandchildren in it—were also shown the video.

Afterward, they said to themselves: "We can fix this, we can do this." All the bombing and deaths of family members had not broken them. They still had the expectation of returning home.

There can be no better embodiment of sumūd.

MALU HALASA and JORDAN ELGRABLY, September 2024

Messages from Gaza Now
HOSSAM MADHOUN

I.

Walking from home to the Nuseirat market, traces of last night's bombing on both sides of the street, houses and buildings completely damaged, destroyed, above the heads of residents. No prior warning. Absolute massacre.

Passing by an olive orchard, poor olives, it is the cultivating season. No one will cultivate the olives this year; olives will fall on the ground, dry and rotten; olive trees will dry out and all the branches will fall and be scattered by the autumn wind. Birds and doves will not find olive branches to build their nests for future generations.

Bombing very nearby, behind the olive orchard. Felt the bombing, the sound is very loud, a wave of hot wind passes over my body, moves me from my place. I stop and get close to the fence of the orchard. After a few minutes I hear screaming, people crying and shouting. I move fast, past the orchard and on the right side of a narrow street. At the end of the street, a house bombed, people pulling bodies out from under the rubble, a small car passes by me very fast, the driver is hooting the car horn, for a single moment I saw a woman in the back seat holding an injured child, a girl maybe eight or nine years old. It was very fast, could not know what type of injury or the exact age of the girl. But I saw blood and dust all over her body.

It is too much, I've had enough, I can't continue anymore, fifty-five years full of violence, blood, death, agony, displacement, poverty, sadness, helplessness, despair. I can't take it anymore, I have no days left in me for such a situation, no more. I want to give up. I mean it. I am really ready to leave.

In times like these days, in war times like these, in 2009, 2012, 2014,

2021, 2022, 2023, when my daughter Salma said she couldn't take it any more I told her to listen to the Peter Gabriel song, "Don't Give Up."

Peter Gabriel helped me a lot before. He doesn't help me now. Sorry Peter, I can't handle it anymore.

II.

Buddy

My dog, Buddy, is a small, white, lovely dog, most of the time playing and jumping around, barking with his soft voice, running after street cats if they dare to enter the home. He is a courageous dog, but not when there is bombing. He has no courage, not at all. He's not a coward. He's afraid of the bombing, who isn't?

He's always able to hear the bombing moments before us. He runs toward me or my wife, Abeer, and hides behind us. If we lay on the bed at night, he jumps over our heads and rounds his body around my head or Abeer's and starts trembling and breathing fast as if he's been running for hours. Nothing can calm him. His body becomes very tense. It's not easy to move him away from my head. I feel helpless and don't know what to do to release his fear.

III.

October 20, 2023

I'm walking toward the market. Abeer's cousin lives there and has internet access. Walking—no fuel anymore in my car, and, of course, no fuel at all in the gas stations as quantities entering Gaza from Israel (like all the goods from Israel) are limited and never enough for more than just one week. It's part of the blockade and collective punishment against Gaza. Walking and trying to find any vehicle to give us a ride.

After ten minutes walking, a big van stopped and took us with him. There was a woman sitting in the back seat. About one hundred meters from the market, near a shelter school on a narrow side street leading to the main road where the market is, a big explosion behind us. A huge black smoke cloud rises to the sky. The van trembles, dust fills it. The driver stops. Many people start to run out of the school. As we get out of the van, another big explosion in front of us, much closer, same wave of smoke and fire, people screaming, shouting, crying, running . . . I don't know where to go, confused . . .

Immediately another explosion to the west side, and much closer to us, rubble above us, many people fall on the ground, some people injured by the flying rubble. I was beside the wall of the school. I could not breathe. Nizar, Abeer's cousin, sells tomatoes and onions in the market. Could not think, ran like hell toward where he was—absolutely stupid move, absolutely not rational. Who is rational in this mad war? Who is rational in this slaughterhouse, yes, it is a slaughterhouse. The Israeli butchers are using every single minute to slaughter like sheep as many Palestinians as possible, before the world wakes up.

The bombing was on a side street off the main market street. Rubble, sand, mud, broken glass everywhere. The dust cloud was still in the sky, making noontime look like sunset, yes, it is a sunset, no light in our life.

Arriving at Nizar's spot, all his merchandise full of dust and sand. Nizar is okay. He has a small cut on his hand. Never mind, he is alive. I thought to call Abeer, so she won't worry and think these bombings are near us. We hear bombing every minute. We have no access to news. We don't know what's happening or where the bombing is taking place. There is no way. That's why Abeer heard the bombing and continued whatever she was doing, as usual.

I decided not to tell her what happened. And went back home, walking. I see these houses much more closely than I can while driving. How buildings of three or four floors are crushed on top each other, ceilings attached to the ceilings below, with people's furniture and belongings spread over the street. Some houses are cut in half. Could see half a bed, part of a kitchen, a bathroom with private clothes all around, books, school bags torn and full of dust.

The majority of these houses were bombed full of residents. Many were brought out dead. Maybe many still are dead under the rubble as there are no machines to remove it and reveal what is beneath. What a way to leave this unjust world!

Finally at home after twenty-five minutes walking. Did not buy anything today from the market. We will manage with what we have at home for today.

Ending this episode with some good news from my daughter, Salma, in Lebanon, where she's studying for her master's degree. The university granted her a full-tuition scholarship.

IV.

October 21, 2023, 3:55 p.m.

Sitting in the street beside the front door of a neighbor who has solar panels. Since arriving in Nuseirat ten days ago, I come to this neighbor, bringing my laptop, my mobile, and a power bank to charge them. He is a very gentle and nice man. In the front yard of his home, he's installed several electricity cables and connections. On the ground you see many phones, small batteries, power banks connected to be charged. All the neighbors in the area bring their devices to be charged every day. He receives people from eight in the morning until sunset. Three of his sons are serving people, receiving everyone, helping as much as they can, very polite. What a wonderful solidarity.

V.

A Young Political and Military Analyst

After a long day at Al-Wafa Hospital, we walked to the market to buy whatever we could find for tomorrow's lunch. As there's no electricity, no fridge, we can't store any fresh vegetables. We have to buy what we need day by day. After a long day, it's a 2.5-kilometer walk home. Sometimes we find a donkey pulling a wooden cart so we take a ride. Sometimes we don't and we walk, carrying our bags with the laptops and whatever we have bought for the next day.

Lucky us, after walking for twenty minutes we found a donkey going to the Sawarha area where we live. The donkey pulling the cart was driven by two children: one around thirteen years old and the other around nine.

They said the fees were three shekels each. We agreed. After a few minutes we heard a huge explosion. It shook us. Abeer said, "It's very nearby."

The young donkey rider, who was very relaxed, said, "No, it's a least one kilometer to the south. It's far."

Abeer said, "How do you know?"

The boy: "I know. You should know."

Abeer: "Why should we?"

The boy: "Is this the first time you witness a war in Gaza? Are you not from here?"

Abeer: "Yes, we are from here."

The boy: "Strange. You should be able to identify the sound of explosions and calculate where they could be. You should also be able to differentiate between rocket and shelling sounds."

Abeer: "What's your name?"

The boy: "Ahmad."

Abeer: "How old are you?"

Ahmad: "Nine years old."

Abeer: "Do you go to school?"

Ahmad: "Not now, as they all became shelters, but sure, I am in fourth grade at school."

Abeer: "And now? What do you do?"

Ahmad: "As you can see, helping my family to get an income after the death of my father."

Abeer: "When did he die?"

Ahmad: "Two weeks ago, when they struck the supermarket at Nuseirat market. He was passing by when it happened."

Abeer: "Do you have brothers?"

Ahmad: "Yes." [Pointing at the other boy] "This is Hasan, my older brother, and two younger sisters at home and my mother."

Abeer: "What do you think will happen, Ahmad?"

Ahmad: "Well, the Israelis' dream is to see Gaza empty by any means. They will keep striking, bombing, destroying, killing until they push us out or kill us all."

Abeer: "And what do you think we should do?"

Ahmad: "Do what we do now. Stay and live."

VI.

November 23, 2023

Yesterday I was at the clinic waiting for my colleagues, the counselors, to hand over their duties and send them to the shelter schools to provide some psychological support for the children. One of them was not there. I asked about him. Someone told me that something happened: two people they host were killed in a bombing. The person we were talking about, I know his uncle, who is my friend. I know that he took refuge at their home. I panicked. I finished with my colleagues and went there quickly to see my friend and find out what happened. I arrived. My friend and my colleague were there, sitting outside the house. Their faces said everything. Their faces told me something terrible had happened.

My friend told me his grandson and his daughter's husband were killed. They were taking refuge at the same home but yesterday his daughter's husband went to see his mother in another home with his extended family. He took his oldest son, Waseem, a six-year-old boy.

The home, a building of four floors hosting thirty-seven people, was bombed. They all died—men, women, boys, girls are dead, all of them.

While he was speaking, his daughter, the one I have known since she was seven years old, was not far away. She was hanging the clothes of her dead child on the laundry line, as if nothing had happened. She washed the clothes of her dead son and she put them out to dry in the sun so when he came back he could put them on.

I looked at her, and I searched for the words that would explain what she feels, what she thinks. I could not find them. What words can describe this? Damn it, where are the words? Why don't words help? Words are weak. Words are disabled. No words can explain what she feels or thinks. She lost her husband and her six-year-old son. The son was found and buried, and the husband was still under the rubble with another fourteen out of the thirty-seven people.

VII.

Sounds

Lay down on the mattress, complete darkness but for the slight light of a poor, small candle. Closing my eyes, hoping to fall asleep, it doesn't work. Two days and nights, not a single minute of sleep.

It is amazing how human senses become stronger and more sensitive when you lose one. Like people who have no eyesight, their hearing becomes sharper. This is what happens to me while closing my eyes.

During the day, lots of noise, lots of sounds, mixed sounds of people, chats, speaking, shouting, bombing, explosions, drones, jet fighters cutting the sky in pieces. All mixed so I can't and don't concentrate on any one sound.

In the dark, in the supposedly complete silence, and while laying down with eyes closed, I started to focus more on the sounds surrounding me: the crinkling of a plastic sheet covering the window that has lost its glass, moving in the night breeze; the breathing and sighs of my mother beside me; my heartbeats; the squeak of the field cockroaches; a bird back late to his nest, or flying out of his nest due to an explosive sound; a little baby crying at the nearby neighbor's home and his mother cradling him; the swish of branches in the trees, moving slightly; a whoop of an owl coming from the distance; street dogs getting crazy and barking when bombs happen; sounds of some cats fighting.

All those sounds mean life, mean hope, mean tomorrow will come despite anything.

Other sounds are coming, over all other sounds, making all other sounds vanish, occupying the air and the atmosphere, invading the silence to say: death is coming. The sound of the military drone, the only other sound that would be similar is the electric shaving machine increased a hundred times, filling the space with its annoying noise that no one can ignore even for a moment. Every living creature is obliged to hear it, at all times. Humans, animals, birds, trees, even stones could crack out of the madness the sound causes. It reminds me of only one thing: the Middle Ages' slow killing by torture.

The passing jet fighters—F-15—F-16—F-32—F-I-don't-know-what—cutting the sky like a knife goes through a piece of butter, carrying death wherever they go.

The sound of the artillery shelling: *Boom!* Each shell makes three sounds, the echo of the sound repeated: *Boom! Boom! Boom!* It starts huge and echoes out three times.

The sound of the rocket strikes, very loud, very sharp. If you hear it, then you're alive. It's so fast that if it hits you, you won't hear it. Anyone in Gaza who hears the rocket immediately knows that it has hit some other people, leaving death and destruction behind it. We all know that by experience; we learned the hard way through several wars against Gaza.

Sitting in the dark, trying to ignore the loud sounds of death and concentrate on the little sounds of life. Not easy, but this is my way to pass the night, hoping to overcome insomnia for a few hours.

VIII.

Yesterday the Israelis bombed a neighborhood inside Jabalia Camp, a whole block. Block 6. Jabalia Camp, one kilometer square, with 115,000 inhabitants, the most densely populated spot on earth. Four hundred people killed and injured within a blink of an eye, vanished, disappeared, do not exist anymore. Four hundred people in one shot. Hundreds injured. No hospital has the capacity to treat them. More than forty houses destroyed completely and many people killed while walking in the streets. It was four a.m. when they were struck with six explosive missiles by the Air Force.

Four hundred people of all ages, fetuses in the bellies of their mothers, lactating babies, little children, boys and girls, teenagers and youths, men and women, elderly people, and people with disabilities. A whole community. Disappeared. Just like that, because someone in Israel believed that he could do it, so he did it.

I was listening to the news on the radio, live, people shouting, screaming, the reporter is speaking loudly to be heard above the noise and chaos around him. One of the reporters who lives there is screaming; his family members are among the four hundred.

My family members around me were talking about it all at the same time. I was the only one who said nothing. What can be said in such a situation?

I left the family downstairs and went up to my room and my mattress. I lay down, close my eyes, tears on my cheeks, and suddenly I am there, in that neighborhood, just a few minutes before the strike.

I am walking in the narrow streets of the camp, lots of children playing, men, women passing by, going out or coming back. I walk and look at these poor houses, houses that were built by the UNRWA seventy-one years ago for the Palestinian refugees who were obliged to leave their houses in their homeland, in what is now Israel. Low roofs, no space between the homes, the street is maximum four meters wide, some other streets just big enough for cars to pass through slowly, with some effort. Windows are at the eye level of an average man. Easy to hear the chat of people inside their homes, on both sides of the walls. Laundry ropes are hung with children's clothes. The streets are sandy, sewage leakage every few meters as there is no sewage infrastructure in the camp. People have dug soakaway wells for the sewage—with time they fill and leak into the streets.

Huge noise coming from the nearby market.

I stop. I open the first door. I enter. I'm invisible, people inside the home don't see me, can't feel I'm there. It's a front yard. A woman of around thirty-seven years old is beside a small gas cooker with a pot on it, she's cooking. There is cabbage in the pot. Nice smile, three children around her playing, a seven-year-old girl playing with a doll and two older boys running after each other, and the mother calling for them to be quiet. On the other side of the front yard, another woman is washing clothes in three buckets, one with soap and the other two with clean water. Another woman is taking the cleaned clothes and hanging them on a laundry rope hung between a window on the right-hand side, all the way across the front yard and then attached to the outside of the home.

In the corner of the front yard, a small room. The door is opened. It is an outside toilet, a man of forty-two comes out, asking: "How long until we eat?" "Ten minutes," the woman answers. "Did you get the medicine for your father?" she asks. "I will get it after lunch. It is not four yet." He moves inside the home. I follow him.

Inside the home, a living room and two small rooms on both sides. In the living room, a line of mattresses right up against each other, an old man lying down, four young men in a corner playing cards. The man went out and closed the door. He continued into one of the rooms. Inside the room, a cradle with a baby sleeping. The man enters quietly so the baby continues sleeping. He changes his shirt. He puts on some deodorant. He moves to the second room. Four men are asleep. He wakes them up, "Food will be served in ten minutes. Get up." Two stir lazily, the other two act as if they don't hear the man. He calls again: "Get up, all of you. It's 3:55 p.m. You can't keep sleeping." With a lazy voice, one of the four answers: "But we only just fell asleep. The bombing and explosions don't let us sleep. All night, all day, bombing." The man leaves. An older man, his father, in the living room asks him: "Did you bring my asthma medicine? I should take it after lunch, not later than four o'clock." "Not yet," his son answers. "I'll go to the pharmacy after lunch, I promise I won't be later than four o'clock, I promise."

Tick tock, tick tock, tick tock . . . Four p.m. *Booooom!*

Let's return to 3:45 p.m.

I leave and go into the next home.

To be continued . . .

IX.

Mother Courage—Not Bertolt Brecht[1]

By the wall of the school, the shelter, many sellers lay out their small amount of merchandise on a small old wooden table or a cardboard box or even on a plastic sheet on the ground. Small quantities of cans of meat, cans of tuna, cans of beans, cigarettes, sugar, rice. Some have quantities worth $200 and others, all their merchandise is worth no more than $30. Trying to make enough profit to feed themselves for a day or two.

Among them a lady, a middle-aged woman with a veil completely covering most of her hair, is busy cooking bread in an oven made of mud. A line of people standing to buy a piece of bread or two or whatever. Calling to her seven- or eight-year-old son from time to time to feed the fire under the oven with some bits of wood—a normal scene in Gaza, mainly around the shelter schools.

I took my place in the line to buy some bread when a journalist approached the lady asking her for an interview. Without looking at him she said, "You can see that I'm busy." The journalist was patient and polite. He asked if he could film her as a part of the market and life in the shelters. She shrugged with a sense of not caring if he did or he didn't. The reporter made a gesture to the cameraman to start filming.

The journalist: "Have you been doing this for a long time?"

The woman: "Cooking bread? One month."

Journalist: "You built the mud oven?"

The woman: "No, I bought it from someone who built it but could not work on it. He was too old for this work."

Journalist: "Are you from here? I mean Nuseirat Camp?"

The woman (while working, putting a piece of dough in the oven, turning it over from time to time using a wooden stick): "No. Not from here." [Talking to a customer] "I haven't change for a hundred shekels. Find some change and come back."

Journalist: "Where did you come from?"

---

[1] This message was compiled from messages filed on December 11 and 18, 2023, and January 8 and 22, 2024.

The woman: "From many places since the twelfth of October."

Journalist: "Like where?"

The woman: "From Beit Hanoun. When they started bombing, my eldest son and father-in-law were killed. The bombing was targeting a neighbor's home. They were all killed." She stopped talking and continued her work. The journalist did not rush her. She raised her head again, looked at the journalist for a second, then turned back to the oven and continued talking.

The woman: "We moved to my family home in Shati Camp, 'Beach Camp.' I was at the market with this little son, when we heard a huge explosion from an air strike. I went home with some vegetables. They bombed a nearby home and my parents and my husband were killed. They were all under the rubble. I recognized my husband from his feet that appeared out from beneath the rubble. He was missing a toe. He had lost it in a work accident in Israel two years ago. He used to work in construction. When the accident happened his boss didn't do anything for him. He sent him home and never allowed him to work again. Of course, no compensation. In Israel they don't register Palestinian workers as a legal workforce, so no one can claim any compensation. They just use us as cheap labor, that's all. My poor husband did not rest until he died." [To her little son] "Enough wood, we're almost finished." [To a customer] "This will cost you four shekels."

She looked at the journalist. He was still there holding the mic toward her; the cameraman was focused on her. The woman: "So we moved to Zahra City, to my sister who is married and lives there. They followed us with the bombing. My daughter and my mother-in-law were killed. We came here: myself and this little boy, my sister's son and my injured sister. We are at this school." She pointed at the school behind her.

Journalist: "How do you manage? Does UNRWA distribute food at the school?"

The woman: "Yes. They come every few days, give each family some cans of food, some biscuits, some soap, food barely enough for one day. Anyway we are still alive."

Journalist: "What about water? Hygiene? Toilet?"

The woman: "This is another story. I wake up at four in the morning to join the line for the toilet. At this time there will be a line of seven to fifteen people. If I'm late, I'll find a line of fifty or sixty. I take my injured sister, her daughter, and my little son. We do our business there and go back to sleep again. They distribute mineral water bottles. I don't use them. I sell them to get some money. Here we are surviving."

Journalist: "What do other women do?"

The woman: "Other women? Yes, there was a pregnant woman. We helped her to give birth inside the classroom. She was lucky; her delivery went smoothly. She did not need a hospital. We care for each other in our classroom. Not like in other classes, all day you hear screaming, shouting, cursing, disputes. We are lucky. They look after my sister and her two-year-old daughter when I'm out."

Journalist: "How do you get the wood for your oven?"

The woman: "It was easy in the beginning. I collected bits of wood from the streets, from the nearby olive orchards. Then I started to buy it from wood sellers. It was 1.2 shekels per kilo to begin with, and then the price rose, like all prices, now it is 3 shekels per kilo. Everyone is using fire now as there is no cooking gas or fuel. Scarcity in everything."

She started to clear up, put out the fire, collect the bits of wood that were not burnt yet, and covered the oven with a piece of material. She carried her son and went toward the school. The cameraman followed her with his camera lens until she disappeared inside the school.

END NOTE

Some entries for "Messages from Gaza Now" came with the dates they were written. The messages were compiled and edited by the actor Ruth Lass and director Jonathan Chadwick from London's Az Theatre, which has a long-standing relationship with Gaza's Theatre for Everybody, cofounded by Hossam Madhoun and Jamal Al Rozzi.

Saeed Taji Farouky, *As usual, I was far away and did not take part in the final farewell*, 2004, detail. Photograph. Courtesy of the filmmaker.

Palestine and the Unspeakable
LINA MOUNZER

This moment, as I'm writing these words, this moment, as you're reading them, Gaza is being ground to dust under Israeli bombardment. At this very moment, people are trying to pull the bodies of their loved ones out from under the pulverized remains of their own homes. Entire families have been wiped from the civil register. It is estimated that some one thousand bodies remain trapped under the wreckage, very likely bringing the death toll to an unfathomable four thousand people. Four thousand people in just over a week. That is an average of over four hundred people a day being killed. It is incredibly cruel math to have to do, but Palestinian lives under Israeli occupation have always been subject to this inhuman calculus.

How many Palestinian lives equal one Israeli life? Many have been asking that question this past week, some with incredulity and horror and some with total seriousness. The answer this time seems to be none, and all. No number of Palestinian lives can avenge the Israeli lives lost. And so all the people of Gaza must be exterminated.

The bombardment of Gaza this time comes in retaliation for an unprecedented attack carried out by Hamas fighters on October 7. A large number of fighters paraglided over or drove through the fence encircling the Strip and went through the kibbutzim and settlements surrounding Gaza, killing military personnel and civilians both, and taking about two hundred others back as hostages. An attack of singular horror for the Israeli people, reverberating through Jewish communities across the world as the nightmare of the past—the past of ghettoes and pogroms and concentration camps, the past that they and the world had vowed would take place "never again"—came roaring awake once more. For the people of Gaza, this latest round of bombardment is just that—the latest round of bombardment—only this time it's crueler and more brutal than anything that has come before.

The editor in chief of *Jewish Currents*, Arielle Angel, tries, in an expansive, brilliant editorial, to grapple with holding these two realities side by side, with how to allow for the resonances of two different generational traumas for two different peoples without having them negate one another, while at the same time acknowledging the crushing actuality of the Israeli occupation, which is not past but cruelly present. "One of the most terrible things about this event is the sense of its inevitability," she writes. "The violence of apartheid and colonialism begets more violence. Many people have struggled with the straitjacket of this inevitability, straining to articulate that its recognition does not mean its embrace."[1] It bears repeating: its recognition does not mean its embrace. At the same time, it must be recognized. An annihilation looms before us. In fact, it has already begun.

In a press conference on October 9, Israeli defense minister Yoav Gallant announced the state's intentions. "We are imposing a complete siege on Gaza," he declared. "There will be no electricity, no food, no water, no fuel. Everything will be closed." And then, as though this wasn't clear from his previous words, from the Bantustans in the West Bank, from the sixteen-year siege of Gaza, from the thousands of shells and bombs dropped on that same besieged population, he decided to drive the point home: "We are fighting against human animals, and we act accordingly."

Such collective punishment is considered a war crime under international law, but of course international law only applies to human beings, not "human animals." The phrase stood, disseminated as is without judgment in the Western media, seen only as a harsh but fitting expression of Israeli anger and, therefore, unquestioned and unquestionable.

---

1   Arielle Angel, "We Cannot Cross until We Carry Each Other," *Jewish Currents*, October 12, 2023.

Anger. Many words have been written this last week about grief and mourning—about which deaths are grievable, about which lives deserve mourning, about mourning and grief as acts of solidarity or the lack of vocal grief and mourning as proof of indifference. Less has been written about anger. About who has the right to be angry, and why, and how anger might be spent when it is an entire people raging, raging about the present but goaded to biblical fury by the ghosts of the past. Israeli anger has always been seen as righteous and historically rooted, while Palestinian anger arises simply out of an innate barbarism without cause. If the recent history of Western warfare has taught us anything it is that if your anger is righteous enough, then any violence born of that anger is righteous too. Thus you may engage in mass slaughter and remain mostly blameless in the eyes of the world. Those who have been slaughtered are not people, after all, but human animals.

There is no safe place in Gaza. No shelter, no reprieve. Hospitals have been warned to evacuate, grievously injured, immovable patients and all. The people of north Gaza were given twenty-four hours to flee south: an exodus of 1.1 million people, all asked to leave their homes within twenty-four hours. Then the routes south they'd been assured were safe were bombed. Entire convoys of people incinerated. There is no more room for the dead in the morgues. There is "no time to dig up the bodies" either, as Ghassan Abu Sitta, a plastic surgeon from Gaza, wrote on X. "When I drove from North Gaza to Shifa last night, the stench of decaying bodies every time you drove by a destroyed building was overwhelming." Social media sites are full of wrenching photos and posts from Gaza: people dead and dying, people wailing and pleading with God, people digging their loved ones out of the rubble with bare hands, people saying their last goodbyes to the world. The last post from Dr. Belal Aldabbour reads: "Soon, the last sliver of electricity and connection will be exhausted. If I die, remember that I, we, were individuals, humans, we had names, dreams, and achievements, and our only fault was that we were just classified as inferior." That was October 11. At the time of writing, nothing since.

The out-of-control depravity of the violence now in Gaza shows us, hard as it is to believe, that in previous bouts of rage the Israeli state remained restrained in its response. The international community, chief among it the US, would always eventually pull Israel back from the brink. After some unstated ceiling to the death toll, the international community would, like an indulgent parent, cluck, "Now, now, that's enough of that." This time there is no such restraint and no such admonishments. The narrative of "Israel has a right to defend itself" remains steadfast, repeated like a mantra. In fact, a state department memo circulated on October 13—already nearly a week into the bombing—warned diplomats working on the Middle East against using three specific phrases in their press materials: "de-escalation/ceasefire," "end to violence/bloodshed" and "restoring calm." In other words, there is no hope of ceasefire, no end to bloodshed, no calm. But it's not just diplomats acting as stenographers for the Israeli state. Many journalists have enthusiastically signed up for the job as well, repeating claims from the IDF without checking facts, twisting themselves into rhetorical pretzels to avoid damning language, referring to the people of Gaza, en masse, as terrorists, all together responsible for the Israeli tragedy, as though they were a single hand wielding Hamas's gun.

Make no mistake: this is a war of words, too. Of foregrounding certain words, certain narratives, and silencing others. The people of Gaza are being gradually cut off from the world as their power goes out. According to Reuters, "The Israeli communications minister is seeking cabinet approval to shut down Al Jazeera's bureau in Israel." Human rights lawyer Noura Erakat relays that CBS News refused to air an interview they'd done with her, while ABC refused to air one with writer Mohammed El-Kurd and CNN with political analyst Yousef Munayyer. The 2023 Frankfurt Book Fair canceled an award ceremony for Palestinian writer Adania Shibli, then lied that she had consented to the decision. Pro-Palestinian demonstrations have been demonized the world over as "celebrations of terrorism" or outright banned.

Since words are so important, so dangerous, then let us call what's unfolding in Gaza, right before the world's eyes, exactly what it is: a genocide. A second Nakba. What else might we call this mass slaughter, this forced expulsion of a people from their homes, their cities, their lives? Israel and the US are attempting to pressure Egypt to take in refugees from Palestine, to build them a tent city in the desert. The Palestinians don't want to leave. They know what happens if they leave, for it has happened before. If they leave, there is no return.

But there are also voices and acts of solidarity. Jews the world over, including in Israel, have been declaring and protesting: "Not in my name." Irish press and politicians have been vocal in their condemnation. The Vatican put out a statement "expressing worry primarily for Gazan civilians while Israel is burying 1,300 people who have been murdered." Yet even this mildest of remarks, which still foregrounds the Israeli tragedy, was deemed "unacceptable" by Israel's foreign minister.

A ground invasion of Gaza is being planned. Settler attacks in the West Bank have increased, with settlers arming themselves further. There has been constant fighting on the Lebanese border between Israel and different factions inside Lebanon, its tenor escalating by the day. Civilians in Lebanon have been killed, including a journalist, who, like Shireen Abu Akleh before him, was clearly wearing a press vest and helmet. There are no sane voices by the powers that be calling for an end to the violence, let alone an end to the occupation. There seems to be no concern either that a regional war is possible, almost imminent, even as we stare down the barrels of its anti-tank missiles and aircraft carriers.

I write this from Beirut, where this morning I received a message from my other embassy—a passport acquired when my family fled from a previous war in Lebanon—advising me to "consider leaving while commercial options remain available." The implication, of course, is that the airport will be the first thing to be bombed, as it was in the 2006 Israeli war against Lebanon, and there will be no easy way out. I have a passport that permits me to leave at a moment's notice. My husband doesn't. We stay and wait, glued to the news, our anxiety drowned out by the absolute horror we are watching befall the people of Gaza.

There is no recompense for all this death, destruction, and ongoing trauma. There are hardly any words that fit its magnitude. But let us at least use the words they don't want us to use: Occupation. Apartheid. Colonization. Forced expulsion. Ethnic cleansing. Nakba. Genocide. Let us keep using them, insisting on them, and let us also hear Palestinian voices, read Palestinian words, understand Palestinian narratives, give grace to Palestinian subjectivity and grief and anger. Give it just as much weight as Israeli subjectivity, Israeli grief, Israeli anger. That is all. Just equal weight, equal grace. Even if it seems the two can't coexist without negating one another. Now more than ever, we must have enough imagination for a different kind of world. For we know exactly what happens when we start seeing human beings—speaking of human beings—as human animals. It is the horror of annihilation. And it has already begun.

October 16, 2023

Palestine Philistine

KHALIL RABAH

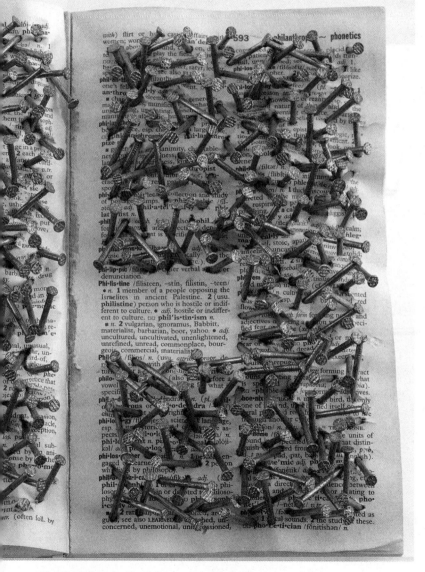

Khalil Rabah, *Palestine Philistine*, 1997, detail. Thesaurus and nails.
Courtesy of Ramzi and Saeda Dalloul Art Foundation.

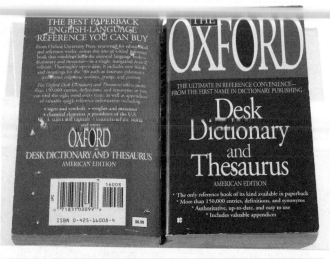

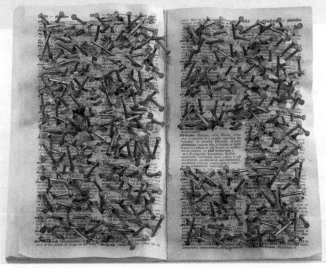

Khalil Rabah, *Oxford Desk Dictionary* (top), *Palestine Philistine* (bottom), 1997.
Thesaurus and nails. Courtesy of Ramzi and Saeda Dalloul Art Foundation.

In his installation, conceptual artist Khalid Rabah draws attention to the
word *philistine*. Of its many synonyms in the 1997 *Oxford Desk Dictionary
and Thesaurus*, "ignoramus" and "barbarian" are more widely known.
As curator Wafa Roz writes for the Dalloul Art Foundation, Rabah "poignantly examines the deep roots of rhetorical violence . . . that connects
a common phrase to the international dehumanization of Palestinians."

Palestine A–Z

MOSAB ABU TOHA

A

An apple that fell from the table on a dark evening when manmade lightning flashed through the kitchen, the streets, and the sky, rattling the cupboards and breaking the dishes.

"Am" is the linking verb that follows "I" in the present tense when I am no longer present, when I'm shattered.

B

A book that doesn't mention my language or my country, and has maps of every place except for my birthplace, as if I were an illegitimate child on Mother Earth.

Borders are those invented lines drawn with ash on maps and sewn into the ground by bullets.

C

Gaza is a city where tourists gather to take photos next to destroyed buildings or graveyards.

A country that exists only in my mind. Its flag has no room to fly freely, but there is space on the coffins of my countrymen.

D

Dar means house. My grandparents left their house behind in 1948 near Yaffa beach. A tree my father told me about stood in the front yard.

Dreams of children and their parents, of listening to songs, or watching plays at Al-Mishal Cultural Center. Israel destroyed it in August 2018. I hate August. But plays are still performed in Gaza. Gaza is the stage.

E

An email account that I used when the power was on, the email through which I smelled overseas air. I used it first to send photos to my aunt in Jordan, who we last saw in 2000.

How easy it becomes to recognize what kind of aircraft it is: an F-16, helicopter, or a drone? What kind of a bullet it was: from a gunboat, an M-16, a tank, or an Apache? It's all about the sound.

F

Friends from school, from the neighborhood, from childhood. The books in my living room in Gaza, the poems in my notebooks, still lonely. The three friends I lost to the 2014 onslaught: Ezzat, Ammar, and Ismael. Ezzat was born in Algeria, Ammar in Jordan, Ismael on a farm. We buried them all under the cold ground.

Fish in our sea that the fishermen cannot catch because the Israeli gunboats care about sea life in the Mediterranean. They once fished at the Gaza beach with a barrage of shells, and Huda Ghalia lost her father, stepmother, and five siblings in June 2006. I walked in their funeral procession to the cemetery. Blood was still fresh on their clothes. They had poured out some perfume to cover the stench. Over time my hate for perfume grew intense.

G

How are you, Mosab? I'm good. I hate this word. It has no meaning to me. Your English is good, Mosab! Thanks.

When I was asked to fill out a form for my US J-1 visa application, my country, Palestine, was not on the list. But lucky for me, my gender was.

H

If a helicopter stops in the sky over Gaza, we know it's going to shoot a rocket. It doesn't see if a target is close to children playing marbles or soccer in the street.

My friend Elise told me hey is a slang word and shouldn't be used. "English teachers would faint at what goes on today in written English," she said.

I

Images on the walls of buildings, a child who was shot by an Israeli sniper, or killed during an air raid en route to school. Her picture was placed on her desk at school. Her picture stares at the blackboard, while the air sits in her chair.

I wake up ill when gloomy ideas about what might've happened to me come in my dreams, what if I had stopped for a few seconds at the window when a bullet from nowhere ripped through the glass.

J

Once I sent a picture of my desk in Gaza to a friend in the United States. I wanted to show that I was fine. On the desk were some books, my laptop, and a glass of strawberry juice.

When I sent that photo, I was jobless. About 47 percent of people in Gaza have no work. But while writing these lines, I'm trying to start a literary magazine. I still don't know what to name it.

K

My grandfather kept the key to his house in Yaffa in 1948. He thought they would return in a few days. His name was Hasan. The house was destroyed. Others built a new one in its place. Hasan died in Gaza in 1986. The key has rusted but still exists somewhere, longing for the old wooden door.

In Gaza you don't know what you're guilty of. It feels like living in a Kafka novel.

L

I speak Arabic and English, but I don't know in what language my fate is written. I'm not sure if that would change anything.

Light is the opposite of heavy or dark. In Gaza, when the electricity is cut off, we turn on the lights, even in broad daylight. That way, we know when the power's back.

M

Marhaba means hi or welcome. We say Marhaba to everyone we see. It's like a warm hug. We don't use it, however, when soldiers or their bullets or bombs visit us. Such guests not only leave their shit, but also take everything we have.

My dad used to prepare milk for us with some qirshalah before school. I was in third grade, and my mother was at hospital taking care of my brother. My brother died in 2016.

N

In 2014, about 2,139 people were killed, 579 of them were children, around 11,100 were wounded, around 13,000 buildings were destroyed. I lost three friends. But it's not about numbers. Even years, they are not numbers.

A nail is used to join two pieces of wood or to hang things on the wall. In 2009, the Israelis targeted an ambulance with a nail bomb near my house. Some were killed. I saw many nails on our neighbor's newly painted wall.

O

Yaffa is known around the world for its oranges. My grandmother, Khadra, tried to take some oranges with her in 1948, but the shelling was heavy. The oranges fell on the ground, the earth drank their juice. It was sweet, I'm sure.

In Gaza, we had a clay oven that our neighbor Muneer built for us. When my mother wanted to bake, I fed it wood stems or cardboard to heat it for the bread. The woody stems were made from dried plants: pepper, eggplant, and cornstalks.

P

A poem is not just words placed on a line. It's a cloth. Mahmoud Darwish wanted to build his home, his exile, from all the words in the world. I weave my poems with my veins. I want to build a poem like a solid home, but hopefully not with my bones.

On July 23, 2014, a friend called and said, "Ezzat was killed." I asked which Ezzat. "Ezzat, your friend." My phone slipped from my hand, and I began to run, not knowing where.

What's your name? Mosab. Where are you from? Palestine. What's your mother tongue? Arabic, but she's sick. What's the color of your skin? There is not enough light to help me see.

Q

We were watching a soccer match. Comments and shouts filled the room. The power was cut off, and everything became quiet. We could hear our breathing in the dark.

Al-Quds is Arabic for Jerusalem. I have never been to al-Quds. It's around sixty miles from Gaza. People who live 5,000 miles away can move there, while I cannot even visit.

R

I was born in November. My mother told me she was walking on the beach with my father. It turned stormy and began to rain. My mother felt pain, and an hour later, she gave birth to me. I love the rain and the sea, the last two things I heard before I came into this horrible world.

S

I like to go to the beach and watch the sun as it sinks into the sea.
She's going to shine on nicer places, I think to myself.

My son's name is Yazzan. He was born in 2015, or a year after the
2014 war. This is how we date things. Once he saw a swarm of
clouds. He shouted, "Dad, some bombs. Watch out!" He thought
the clouds were bomb smoke. Even nature confuses us.

T

In summer, I drink tea with mint. In winter, I add dried sage.
Anyone who visits, even if it's a neighbor knocking at the door to
ask about what day or date it is, I offer them tea. Offering tea is
like saying Marhaba.

They once said Palestine will be free tomorrow. When is tomorrow?
What is freedom? How long does it last?

U

It wasn't raining that day, but I took my umbrella anyway. When
an F-16 flew over the town, I opened my umbrella to hide. Kids
thought I was a clown.

In August 2014, Israel bombed my university's administration
building. The English department was turned into a ruin. My
graduation ceremony got postponed. Families of the dead attended,
to receive not a degree, but a portrait of their child.

V

When we moved from Cambridge to Syracuse, I looked out the
window of the U-Haul van. What a huge country America is,
I thought. Why did Zionists occupy Palestine and still build
settlements and kill us in Gaza and the West Bank? Why don't
they live here in America? Why can't we come here to live and

work? My friend heard me. He was from Ireland. We both loved the Liverpool football club.

In Gaza, you can find a man planting a rose in the hollow space of an unexploded tank shell, using it as a vase.

W

One day, we were sleeping in our house. A bomb fell on a nearby farm at 6 a.m., like an alarm clock waking us up early for school.

In August 2014 after the fifty-one days of Israeli onslaught, the walls in my room had more windows than when I left, windows that would no longer close. Winter was harsh on us.

X

When I was wounded in January 2009, I was sixteen. I was taken to hospital and x-rayed for the first time. There were two pieces of shrapnel in my body. One in my neck, another in my forehead. Seven months later, I had my first surgery to remove them. I was still a child.

For Christmas, a friend gave the kids a xylophone. It had one wooden row. The bars were of different lengths and colors, red, yellow, green, blue, purple, and white. The kids showed it to their grandparents back in Gaza, whose eyes danced while the kids smiled.

Y

Yaffa is my daughter's name. I put my ears near her mouth when she speaks, and I hear Yaffa's sea, waves lapping against the shore. I look in her eyes, and I see my grandparents' footsteps still imprinted on the sand.

How did you leave Gaza? Do you plan to return? You should stay in the US. You mustn't think of going back to Gaza. Things people say to me.

Z

When I was in the fifth grade, our science teacher wanted us to visit a zoo, to see the animals, listen to their sounds, watch how they walk and sleep. When I went there, they were bored, gave me their back. They lived in cages in a caged place.

We use a zero article with most proper nouns. My name and that of my country have an extra zero in front, like when you call overseas. But we have been pulled down beneath the seas, do you see what I mean?

Culture and Resistance in *Imagining Palestine*
ILAN PAPPÉ

Imagining Palestine: Cultures of Exile and National Identity,
by Tahrir Hamdi (Bloomsbury, 2023)

> True,—THIS !
> Beneath the rule of men entirely great
> The pen is mightier than the sword. Behold
> The arch-enchanter's wand !—itself a nothing !—
>
> But taking sorcery from the master-hand
> To paralyse the Cæsars, and to strike
> The loud earth breathless !—Take away the sword—
> States can be saved without it!

So wrote Edward Bulwer-Lytton in his 1839 play *Richelieu*; *Or, the Conspiracy*.[1] Of course, the sword is still needed, and the pen has been replaced by the keyboard, but viewed historically, resistance through writing was done by pens, pencils, and typewriters, and even by graffiti on walls, cartoons, songs, poems, plays, and novels. Nowadays, the internet offers even more inventive ways of expression.

The "Theory of Palestine"

All of these audio, verbal, and visual expressions of the "pen" are part and parcel of the Palestinian resistance since its very inception, but rarely have they been articulated as a theory of resistance, one that helps to unpack the Palestinian experience in a way that feeds back into

---

1   Edward Bulwer-Lytton, *Richelieu*; *Or, the Conspiracy* (Philadelphia: The Penn Publishing Company, 1996), 41.

our understanding of other current struggles by Indigenous peoples, life-seekers, workers, and anyone else victimized by the Global North's economic, political, and moral order. Such a theorization is offered to us here by Tahrir Hamdi in her moving and thought-provoking book, *Imagining Palestine*.

This work is first and foremost a book on cultural resistance. As such, it requires an abstraction that cannot be taken for granted between two concepts: culture and cultural resistance.

In *Culture and Imperialism*, Edward Said commented that there are narrow and expanded definitions of *culture*. The narrow definition relates to the aesthetic and literary assets of a society:

> Culture is a concept that includes a refining and elevating element, each society's reservoir of the best that has been known and thought, as Matthew Arnold put it in the 1860s.[2]

While the latter sees culture as the theater of life:

> In this second sense culture is a sort of theater where various political and ideological causes engage one another. Far from being a placid realm of Apollonian gentility, culture can even be a battleground on which causes expose themselves to the light of day and contend with one another.[3]

In general, the approach to culture in *Imagining Palestine*, and by many of those writers analyzed by Hamdi, is very much a reflection of Said's refusal to accept the separation of the cultural from the political, a ploy that Israel still uses today to preempt initiatives such as the cultural boycott, which is part of the BDS (Boycott, Divestment, Sanctions) campaign, by claiming that the state's intellectuals, academics, and artists—or sports people, for that matter—cannot be targets for being part of its politics of colonization. In 2022, the hypocrisy of this Israeli and Western position was fully exposed: in the name of politics, one could boycott Russian sport, condemn Qatar during the World Cup for its human rights violations, but

---

2 Edward Said, *Culture and Imperialism* (New York: Vintage Books, 1994), xiii.
3 *Ibid.*

push away any attempt to apply the same principle to Israel and its role in the sporting world.

For Hamdi and many of those she surveys, the dichotomy is far less present, and the two are intertwined in what Hamdi refers to as a "theory of Palestine," which means that not only does Palestinian cultural production involve both the narrow and wider Saidian definitions of culture, but it also provides abstraction of culture, resistance, and everything between them that can be applied elsewhere.

The second part of the theorization of Palestine is anchored on the abstraction of cultural resistance. Cultural resistance has become quite a common scholarly reference in cultural studies. As with so many such references, it has multiple meanings and usages.[4] I find Roland Bleiker's one of the most appealing when he conceptualizes dissent and cultural resistance as being "located in countless non-heroic practices that make up the realm of the everyday and its multiple connections with contemporary global life."[5] Cultural resistance underscores how various cultural practices are employed to contest and combat a dominant power, often constructing a different vision of the world in the process.

For Antonio Gramsci,[6] power resides not only in institutions but also in the ways people make sense of their world; hegemony is a political and cultural process. Armed with culture instead of guns, one fights a different type of battle. Whereas traditional battles were "wars of maneuver"—frontal assaults that seized the state—cultural battles were "wars of position," flanking maneuvers, commando raids, and infiltrations, staking out positions from which to attack and then reassemble civil society.

Several features of our time blur national and Indigenous struggles in a way that might be less detrimental to the national project and beneficial

4   Dejan Kršić, "After Brecht," in *The Design of Dissent: Socially and Politically Driven Graphics*, eds. Milton Glazer and Mirko Ilic (Gloucester: Rockport Publishers, 2005).

5   Roland Bleiker, *Popular Dissent, Human Agency and Global Politics* (Cambridge: Cambridge University Press, 2000), 278.

6   Antonio Gramsci, in *Prison Notebooks*, eds. Quentin Hoare and Geoffrey Nowell Smith (New York: International, 1971), 229-39.

to the community on the ground. As Stephen Duncombe[7] remarks, with the immediacy of global media, the local becomes national and at the same time global. Duncombe offers another useful entry point on cultural projects: he sees cultural resistance as a space for developing tools for political action, a dress rehearsal for the actual political act, or as a political action in and of itself, which operates by redefining politics.

Imagining Palestine is thus one of the most comprehensive representations of Palestinian cultural resistance. The analysis transcends the case study of Palestine and touches other people in the world who are still struggling against old and new settler-colonial projects, and who only lately discovered how relevant Palestine is for them, and how cultural, intersectional struggle may now be a crucial part of the way forward.

Hamdi, however, does not employ a deductive approach—namely applying the abstraction and theorization of cultural resistance to the Palestine case study. This is inductive research, where the case study leads to the more general discussion. This is a welcome approach that I recommend to my postgraduate students who like to remain in the comfort zone of deductive analysis. The uniqueness and exceptional realities in Palestine (in particular, the imbalance between Israelis and Palestinians) create a dialectic that is Palestine: full of paradoxes and dichotomies that indeed call for a theory of Palestine alongside, and not instead of, a more conventional approach to its history and present conditions.

Late-Style Resistance

Some of the people we meet in this book are not with us anymore. Whether writers, singers, poets, or artists, they underwent different stages in their struggle against the settler-colonial movement of Zionism and the apartheid state of Israel. Toward the end, whether consciously or unconsciously, and whether they died a natural death or were killed as martyrs in the struggle, they offer a unique perspective

---

7   Stephen Duncombe, "Introduction," in *Cultural Resistance Reader*, ed. Stephen Duncombe (London: Verso, 2002), 1–16.

in what is known as "late style," which Hamdi focuses on in her early chapters in this fascinating book.

Late style is an imagined or real sense of facing the end, which, for instance, in the case of Said, one of the many heroes of this book, led to a certain assertiveness about seeming paradoxes in his life and thought, which he learned to reconcile over the years. Said was constantly challenged for criticizing nationalism in general on the one hand but remaining loyal to Palestinian nationalism on the other. I will come back to the notion of late style when examining the exilic locations of many of the protagonists of this book.

Said is not the only one who navigates as a Palestinian between noble universal values and the existential challenges faced by Palestinians on the ground. In *Imagining Palestine*, Hamdi follows the way Palestinians and pro-Palestinians involved in cultural resistance reconcile various contradictions or seeming dichotomies in a similar way. That similar way is akin to a theorization of the struggle for Palestine, or indeed of Palestine itself as a concept—what Hamdi calls "theorizing Palestine." This is a lifelong process of resignation to the need to coexist with unsolved paradoxes, a fluid situation that Said recognized in his own identity, as Hamdi reminds us when citing the opening sentence of the last paragraph of his autobiography, *Out of Place*: "I occasionally experience myself as a cluster of flowing currents."[8]

As *Imagining Palestine* shows so poignantly, Palestinians who are involved in cultural activity of any sort, and those who support Palestine, are all grappling with dichotomies that are only overcome by a clear realization that culture and resistance go hand in hand when going through what Hamdi calls the "post-catastrophic condition" in which Palestinians exist. In fact, many Palestinians do not regard themselves as living in any postreality, as they refer to this history and present time as the ongoing Nakba, or the ongoing "catastrophe," and at the same time see themselves in a constant struggle for survival, a kind of ongoing *intifada* (resistance).

---

8   Edward Said, *Out of Place: A Memoir* (New York: Alfred A. Knopf, 1999), 295.

Palestinians or people who are immersed in the struggle for Palestine out of solidarity and a sense of justice are aware of the tantalizing shift between despair and hope, oppression and resistance, erasure and rediscovery of Palestine. If your only source of information is main-stream Western academia and media, you may miss the fact that since 1920, Palestinians have struggled individually and collectively for the liberation of their country day in and day out; they have faced daily attempts of dispossession. Even though almost the whole of historical Palestine has been taken over by the Zionist movement, and half of the Palestinians were ethnically cleansed, there is still a sizable presence of Palestinians in historical Palestine, and the struggle continues from within and without. It is an incredible story of resistance because of the power imbalance between Israel and the Palestinians. Israel is supported by a Western international coalition that from its inception has legiti-mized and legalized every stage of the dispossession of the Palestinians. This coalition provided Israel with economic, diplomatic, and military aid that made the Jewish state the most formidable regional power in the Middle East. The Palestinians were, and remain, without a state, a military, or an independent economy and only count on the support of global civil society and that of very few states such as Cuba, Syria, and Iran, along with Bolivia and Venezuela (which do not have an impact as such on the balance of power on the ground).

So how, despite these almost impossible circumstances, is there an ongoing resistance? Why are so many of us still convinced that the struggle is not over and justice will prevail? Hamdi takes us on a journey to one dimension of this struggle, the cultural one, which provides a very inspiring and moving answer to this riddle.

Theorizing an Actual Liberation

Theorizing an actual liberation struggle, nonetheless, is not just an act of abstraction. Seeking the middle ground between a discourse of contem-plation and a conversation with the people themselves is quite a challenge since the language inspired by the works of Said, bell hooks, or Edward

Soja, not to mention Gayatri Spivak, has its own rich vocabulary and phraseology different from the language used by those who are actually the object of such intellectual enterprises—namely the freedom fighters or the very people the intellectuals wish to represent and support.

Some of the intellectuals in the case of Palestine are freedom fighters themselves; hence, the dichotomy is much less acute. Thus, for instance, Ghassan Kanafani is treated rightly in this book as a theorist of liberation and at the same time a freedom fighter, and his cultural production is both a weapon in the overall resistance and a crucial contribution to the discussion of the link between culture and resistance.

Many lesser-known Palestinian artists are also freedom fighters, such as the young Palestinians who draw graffiti on the apartheid walls or wherever they can in public spaces, showing their commitment to the struggle. For many years, such wall paintings were regarded by scholars as the work of youth delinquency, but recent scholarship on this topic, in general, shows much more appreciation for the art of graffiti, and in this new view it represents a means to share values, ethics, and codes of behavior in the locations where, and through the media with which, graffiti is produced.

The same is true of cartoonists, with some more famous than others, beginning, of course, with Naji al-Ali, who was a *shahid* (martyr) as much as anyone killed in the struggle for liberation. Cartoonists are featured in Hamdi's book alongside poets who were freedom fighters in action as well as in writing, dating back to the resistance songs of Nuh Ibrahim, the poet of the 1936–39 Palestinian Revolution, through the poetry of 1948 Palestinians under military rule, all defined together in what Kanafani called *adab al-maqatil* (resistance literature).

Exilic Resistance

Hamdi allocates much space to this discussion on the relevance of theorization to an actual liberation struggle. She identifies closely with intellectuals who refer us to marginal and third spaces as an ideal position from which they could contribute to the almost paradoxical idea of a practical theorization (not dissimilar to liberation theologies, which in their own way grapple with similar challenges). The search for this navigation is the thread that connects an incredibly rich assortment of writers, poets, and artists, examined lovingly and movingly in this book—and one would be heartless not to share Hamdi's admiration and affinity for those she writes about in this book.

Navigation is a place of exile. Readers of this book will discover—and anyone familiar with Palestinian intellectual activism recognizes—this is not merely a geographical exile. Many Palestinians in Palestine are in exile, and many of those in exile feel as though they are under colonization and occupation, as if they were still in Palestine. The exilic space for those involved in cultural resistance is, first and foremost, an epistemological and intellectual space, a notion brilliantly explored by Said in several of his works. Abdul R. JanMohamed found for Said a special term, "the specular border intellectual."[9] There are two border intellectuals, according to JanMohamed: the syncretic and the specular. One may say that in its simplest form the former is an intellectual at home in two or more cultures and thus busy fusing and combining hybrid influences. The latter is not at home with either, although he or she is quite familiar with them, and is thus preoccupied with the deconstruction and critique of both.

We may inject into this definition Said's own typology of intellectuals: first, in the footsteps of Walter Benjamin, the preference for the watchdog of society over the articulator of its truisms; then, the combination of the organic intellectual of Antonio Gramsci affiliated with a grassroots movement, such as nationalism, but nonetheless committed to the purest forms of freedoms of expression and thought, as proposed by Julien Benda.[10]

The centrality of "exile" as an epistemological construct is the

---

9   Abdul R. JanMohamed, "Worldliness-without-World, Homelessness-as-Home: Toward a Definition of the Specular Border Intellectual," in *Edward Said: A Critical Reader*, ed. Michael Sprinker (Oxford: Blackwell, 1992), 96–120.

10   Said, *Representations of the Intellectual* (New York: Pantheon, 1994), 183–4.

product of time, and not only of principle. In his postmortem text, Said focuses on the theme of late style: "the way in which the work of some great artists and writers acquires a new idiom towards the end of their lives—what I have come to think of as a late style."[11] Said was aware he was coming to the end of his life, and this is why his own work was transforming not only idiomatically but also thematically. This is where the discussion of exile is so mature and ripe.

What the latter process achieves, as becomes clear in Said's last interview with Charles Glass, is the maturation of his contrapuntal dialectical approach to harmonious and complementary affiliations and values.[12] He can tell Nubar Hovsepian that he takes a lot of luggage with him because he fears he will never return—a sad reminder of his 1948 experience—and yet he defines exiles like him as fortunate enough, unlike political exiles, to treat home as a temporary base that allows freedom of thought and spirit. As a Palestinian, exile—in the first instance—is traumatic; as a universalist intellectual, it is an asset. At the beginning of the twenty-first century, there was no need to apologize for or to reconcile this contradiction.[13]

But is it a closed circle? Has Said left us with a clear answer of how a society can be both wedded to nationalism and yet secure individual liberties and criticism? Whether coming from a Marxist or a liberal point of view, critics of nationalism produced a dire picture of it; whether they treated it as an ideology, a construct, or an interpretation of reality, they presented it as a reductionist mechanism of identity and interpretation that serves the ambitions of a few at the expense of the many. Said the refugee could not easily allow himself to join in the celebration of demythologizing nationalism. His Palestinianism, so to speak, had to coexist, uncomfortably, with his universalism. Time made this necessary coexistence an asset, not a

---

11 Said, "Thoughts on Late Style." *London Review of Books*, 26, no. 15 (August 5, 2004).

12 *Edward Said: The Last Interview*, interview by Charles Glass, directed by Mike Dibb (Icarus Films, 2004).

13 Nubar Hovsepian, "Connections with Palestine," in *Edward Said: A Critical Reader*, ed. Michael Sprinker (Oxford: Blackwell, 1992), 5–18.

liability, and this in fact was his political legacy for the future: Jews and Palestinians would have to reconcile to a similar existence, as does the national intellectual in exile.

What is so brilliant about this book is that it links the human approach by so many of the Palestinians discussed here to the same paradoxical epistemological and moral questions: navigating between their universal values, unconditional commitment to the liberation of Palestine, and their particular mode of expression. Such navigation is at the heart of the "theory of Palestine."

What makes Hamdi—and Said for that matter—confident that they struck the right balance of making theory relevant is the fact that they are not overtheorizing, so as to make sure that theorization is based on experience, not just abstract contemplation. Theory for Hamdi, therefore, is not necessarily universal but feeds back into the place where similar experiences are occurring.

Hamdi does not idealize the place of exile or margins. As seen from the poems of Mahmoud Darwish and Mourid Barghouti, it can be a dark place—what Barghouti refers to as *ghurba*, which is both absence and alienation—and at the same time a place of creativity. Exile on the margins can happen in a relatively comfortable space, such as Columbia University in New York, but also a very precarious and dangerous spot, such as a refugee camp in Lebanon. But in both locations, the prosecution of cultural knowledge becomes an invaluable contribution to the overall struggle for the liberation of Palestine.

Cultural Resistance for Our Times

In *Imagining Palestine*, a theorization of cultural resistance is inducted from the case study itself. In particular, it is the powerful poetry of Mahmoud Darwish that indicates the link between cultural resistance and actual resistance, and between abstract theorization and concrete experience. As Hamdi shows us, this is clear when one examines more profoundly Darwish's metaphors, which fuse the personal and the political. When, for instance, the poet refers to Palestinians entering their private homes, he also alludes to their entry to their homeland, and this dual metaphoric representation appears in almost every stanza, story, and essay discussed in this book. It goes beyond metaphors as well to the whole attendance to aesthetics—the limited Saidian definition of culture is interlinked with political struggle: the form and the content have the same importance in the wish to be part of the overall resistance. Darwish clarified this when he stated: "No aesthetics outside my freedom." A similar engagement is offered by Barghouti when he wonders in his poetry whether one can oppose oppression with an army of metaphors.

This is a concern for Barghouti, as those involved in cultural resistance do not forget for a moment the other modes of resistance, in particular the armed struggle and the daily, brave guerrilla warfare, which began in 1929 and continues today in what Hamdi calls eastern Palestine (namely the West Bank) and is enhanced by the resilience of the besieged people of the Gaza Strip. As Hamdi shows toward the end of her book, those involved in cultural resistance discussed other modes of resistance available for a liberation movement engaged in one of the longest anticolonial struggles in the world. All the means are justified and discussed, sometimes ambiguously, as Hamdi points to the different but complementary approaches to armed struggle taken by Susan Abulhawa in *Mornings in Jenin*, compared to her other work, *The Blue Between Sky and Water*. In *Mornings in Jenin*, there is a fine discussion about the wish for nonviolent resistance, and yet she is praising the armed resistance in other works. This clear navigation (so Saidian) between the principle universal positions, and the way they can be concretized under oppression, is part of the theory of Palestine. Such navigation will continue to occupy those involved in cultural resistance, as seen with the various attempts to change the harrowing ending of Kanafani's *Men in the Sun*. The helpless death of the men in a tanker, allegedly without any resistance, was not the ending one would find in the film adaptation or the transfer of the story to the year of 1982 by the late '48 Palestinian playwright and director Riad Massarweh. And this is why we met a jubilant Said at the Fatama Gate, between south Lebanon and Israel, hurling stones at the Israeli fence; the same Said who was inspired by the humanism of cosmopolitan Jews in Europe at the turn of the twentieth century.

Cultural Unity and Political Disunity

Thus, cultural resistance is diverse, porous, and dynamic. But on the other hand, it is an antidote to the political disunity from which Palestinians suffer. The cultural resistance reveals unity of conscience as well as of memory. Its symbols are consensual as are its heroes and heroines. Whether it is Bassel al-Araj, who wrote and taught about cultural resistance himself before being assassinated by the Israeli army, or Leila Khaled—long may she live. They are not heroes who necessarily defeated their enemies, but they defeated defeatism, which is one of the *raisons d'être* of the ongoing intifada. This rejection of defeatism enabled Palestinians to challenge the main objectives of the colonizer. As Hamdi reminds us, this was very accurately artic- ulated by Frantz Fanon in *The Wretched of the Earth*: "Colonialism is not satisfied with snaring the people in its net or of draining the colonized brain of any form or subject. With a kind of perverted logic, it turns its attention to the past of the colonized people and distorts it, disfigures it, and destroys it."[14] Moving from one mode of resistance, or from theory to praxis, and from culture to politics, and remaining in between both also applies to the challenge that the theory of Palestine poses to different Palestinian geographical locations and the fragmented existence imposed on the Palestinians by the Israelis since 1948. Therefore, at the end of the book, it becomes clear why Hamdi devotes so much space to discussing whether exiled Palestine and occupied Palestine are the same space: you can be an exiled Palestinian inside historic Palestine, living less than a mile away from your original village that was colonized and Judaized in

---

14 Frantz Fanon, *The Wretched of the Earth*, trans. Richard Philcox (New York: Grove Press, 2004), 149.

front of your eyes, or be in a refugee camp in the Gaza Strip or the West Bank, as well being either occupied or besieged. Whether you are in Sabra or Nazareth, you are denied the right of return, normal life, and liberation.

Thus, cultural resistance overcomes geographical distances, but it also challenges political dissent, since the works of artists unify the Palestinian existence and resistance. In this respect, the book could have also referred to the Palestinian academics who established in recent years a new area of study: Palestine studies. Among their unified contributions was a clear framing of what Palestine is, while politically it is debated by the world and Palestinian politicians. It is not only a whole geographic space; it is one that has always been a coherent geopolitical space. In her book Hamdi illustrates, through ancient olive trees, the indigeneity of Palestine and its long history that since ancient times had only for a short period been partly ruled by Israelites in biblical times, and yet that is the one chapter in history around which the Zionist narrative and the claim for Palestine revolves.

The work of Palestinian historians, a group that is overlooked by Hamdi, has helped to produce a clearer sense of what Palestine means and what Israel does not. Through a committed chronology and genealogy, they showed that Palestine, as a coherent geopolitical unit, dates back to 3,000 BC. From that time onward, and for another 1,500 years, it was the land of the Canaanites. In around 1,500 BC, the land of Canaan fell under Egyptian rule, not for the last time in history, and then successfully under Philistine (1200-975), Israelite (1000-923), Phoenician (923-700), Assyrian (700-612), Babylonian (586-539), Persian (539-332), Macedonian (332-63), Roman (63 BCE-636 CE), Arab (636-1200), Crusade (1099-1291), Ayyubi (1187-1253), Mamluk (1253-1516), and Ottoman rules (1517-1917). Each rule divided the land administratively in ways that reflected its political culture and time. But, apart from the early Roman period and the early Arab period, when a vast population were moved out and in, the society remained—ethnically, culturally, and religiously—the same. Within what we recognize today, this society developed its own oneness and distinctive features.

In modern times, some of the above periods were manipulated and co-opted into a national or colonialist narrative to justify the takeover and conquest of the country. This historical chronology was used, or abused, by the Crusaders and later European colonialists and the Zionist movement. The Zionists were different from the others, as they deemed—as did the powers that be when they emerged in 1882—the historical reference was crucial for justifying their colonization of Palestine. They did it as part of what they termed "the Return" to or "Redemption" of the land, which was once ruled by Israelites; as the historical timeline above indicates, this is a reference to a mere century in a history of four millennia.

Away from the national narrative, we should say that Palestine as a geopolitical entity was a fluid concept since the rulers of the country quite often were the representatives of an empire, which disabled any local sovereignty from developing. The question of sovereignty began to be an issue—one that would inform the land's history and conflict until today—once the Empires disappeared. The natural progress from such disintegration, almost everywhere in the world, was that the Indigenous population took over. Ever since the emergence of the concept of nationalism, the identity of this historical revolution is clearer and more common. Where the vestiges of imperialism or colonialism refused to let go—such as in the case of white settler rule in northern and southern Africa—national wars of liberation lingered on. In places where the Indigenous population was annihilated by the settlers' communities, the settlers became the new nation (as happened in the Americas and Australasia).

The takeover from the disintegrating empires succeeded in a longer process, though so many of the theoreticians of nationalism believe in social and cultural cohesiveness. The liberated land varied in structure and composition: some, having a heterogeneous ethnicity, religion, and culture, found it difficult to become a nation-state, while others were fortunate due to their relative homogeneity, although they had their share of economic polarity, social differentiation, and a constant struggle between modernity and tradition. A liberated Palestine would have belonged to the latter model, which for a while developed in Egypt and Tunisia, and would be less similar to the more troubled cases of Iraq and Lebanon.

These are the deeper organic layers on which Palestinian culture rests, and this sense of continuity and attachment to the land is both theorized and illustrated through culture, not as an act of curiosity but as part of a struggle against erasure.

This uniformity in the cultural struggle explains the recent success in building intersectional and transnational cultural resistance. This new global context for the Palestinian cultural resistance is beautifully shown in Hamdi's book by the various dialogues Indigenous poets and writers had with their Palestinian counterparts. In this way, the massacre at Wounded Knee corresponds with the numerous massacres suffered by the Palestinians over the years. Intersectional solidarity also occurs between Arab poets and writers, as well as famous pop stars such as Roger Waters. Culture becomes enhanced resistance if it is part of a dialogue between people who are still struggling against oppression—living in what Steven Salaita calls the "geographies of pain"[15]— or show solidarity with each other. Hamdi introduces these spaces through diverse literary and poetic sources.

In the end

Between framing the Palestinians as terrorists and Islamists to viewing them exclusively as victims, most of the people who know them—their history, their struggle, and their determination—cannot but admire this nation without idealization but purely on common human and universal values.

Imagining Palestine teaches us something else about the Palestinians: notwithstanding their constant victimization by Zionism, they do

---

15   Steven Salaita, *Inter/Nationalism: Decolonizing Native America and Palestine* (Minneapolis: University of Minnesota Press, 2016), 111.

not see themselves as victims but as people who still hope to win their battle for freedom and justice. Through the works of Palestinian literati, poets, writers, cartoonists, and cultural activists, the agency and resilience of the Palestinians shines through this book. This is not an attempt to idealize a group of very normal people but rather to show how humane the Palestinian struggle for normality is. And there is a good chance that this basic but noble human impulse will direct Palestine in its postcolonial era, when it arrives. In more ways than one, this book chronicles the story of the Palestinian cultural resistance and at the same time becomes part of this resistance.

August 7, 2023

Watchtowers
TAYSIR BATNIJI

Taysir Batniji, *Watchtowers*, 2008. Series of twenty-six black-and-white photographs, inkjet prints on FineArt Pearl paper, 50 x 40 cm (each). Courtesy of the artist and Sfeir-Semler Gallery (Hamburg/Beirut).

Bernd and Hilla Becher's photographs of Europe's postindustrial water towers reminded Taysir Batniji of "the Israeli watchtowers that have invaded Palestinian territory." Born in Gaza, Batniji was not allowed to enter the West Bank. So a delegated, uncredited photographer, at great danger to himself, took the images for the *Watchtower* series "in the manner" of the German photographers. Some of the images, blurred and in poor light, were impossible to aestheticize because of the military context. They symbolize for Batniji "a typography" of oppression.

Taysir Batniji, *Watchtowers*, 2008, detail. Courtesy of the artist and Sfeir-Semler Gallery (Hamburg/Beirut).

At the Threshold of Humanity
Gaza Is Not an Abstraction
KARIM KATTAN

Three weeks ago, in a world that was significantly different from today, I was preparing a keynote speech. I had been invited to talk about my work in Innsbruck, in Austria, at a conference on the French language across borders. Following the Hamas attack on October 7, I received a message from the organizers demanding that I share the title of my speech and that I "refrain from mentioning the current situation and leave the political dimension out of [my] talk to avoid any eruption." I responded that I could not participate under these conditions, my whole practice and life being at stake in what is unfolding in my country. The organizer insisted on calling me so that she could explain that "the current situation"—a euphemism—seemed very confusing and complicated to her, possibly a minefield, and therefore they just wanted to make sure that what I said was appropriate. "I realize," she added, "that you wouldn't say anything horrific. I just want to make sure."

I have been thinking about this conversation in the weeks since, about what it says of the way we Palestinians are considered as living, breathing, writing, political beings. That I did not go to a literary event is a minor, ridiculous consequence of what is happening. But it may suggest a frame, a shape, for that which I still struggle to name for fear it will come true—which is happening now in Gaza and in the West Bank.

"Let us," the organizer suggested over the phone, "find a positive solution." Yet the quandary she created was unsolvable. All possible solutions entailed my silence. The only positive solution available was for me not to exist as I am; to go to Innsbruck and pretend that my country was not being bombed, starved, and devastated. To go and pretend that my life is not defined, as it always has been, by apartheid and colonization. Even if I had wanted to comply with what she demanded, I had no idea how to do it: not only because I am personally affected, as is the very existence of my family and nation, but also because the novel I was to discuss takes place in Palestine.

*

For years we've known that our humanity, as Palestinians, was conditional in the eyes of the world—and even when granted, never fully recognized. We were occasionally given this privilege if we were polite, reserved, almost invisible.

In the weeks since this phone call, we have moved toward something that I find difficult to name. This thing became increasingly clear over the weekend as the West watched with thinly veiled satisfaction as Gaza was cut off from the rest of the world and Israel commenced ground incursions. The ongoing and perfunctory discussions around the need for a "humanitarian corridor" themselves void the word *humanitarian* of its human component; they are discussed as we would discuss the survival of "human animals."

Most Western governments have demonstrated their unflinching solidarity with Israel. Gaza is enduring sadistic collective punishment on a scale we have never seen before. Yet US president Biden, British prime minister Rishi Sunak, and French president Emmanuel Macron flew in, with words of support and eternal gratitude, with promises of funds; they offered firm handshakes and virile hugs and nary a sentence about the massacres in Gaza. The disturbing silence of Western governments is a vicious acquiescence to Israeli exactions. In France, where I live and work, things have been particularly chilling. On October 12, the minister of the interior, Gérald Darmanin, ordered all prefects in the country to ban so-called pro-Palestinian demonstrations due to fears of public disturbance. Although the Conseil d'État later struck down the blanket ban, many prefects have kept them up, often on the flimsiest of pretexts. We could parse, here, the irony of European countries, self-proclaimed bastions of free speech, banning protests, canceling award ceremonies, and demanding to review a writer's planned remarks. But that is not the point.

Those who should be brokers of peace have greeted with disdain calls for an immediate cessation of hostilities. This, in effect, gives a green light to Israel to act with full impunity, exacerbating an unprecedented humanitarian crisis born of seventeen years of siege and numerous major military assaults.

This wanton carelessness and dehumanization are why we feel a compelling urge to document and describe everything, big and small, to make sure that people understand what is at stake: "But *this* was a child," we want to say, "and *this* an adult." Not a thing bound to die a gruesome death in a devastated city but a child who would have grown by the sea, who would have been, perhaps, a good swimmer and bad at math or grown to really love cars or cooking. "And this," we want to say, "was a residential building, this a restaurant on the seashore, this a house with a garden, where someone played or got into a fight in the kitchen, and this is all gone." These are people with names, we want to say, and faces too, and lives, and friends grieving them, if they are not themselves now dead, and cities, cities, entire, whole. Real cities and towns that they call their own and that are now graveyards. Pundits on television, meanwhile, talk of the thousands dead as justified collateral damage—but this, we want to say, is the gleeful obliteration of a seashore, of families, histories, cities.

In the media Gaza is an abstraction, a space designed for the violent death of an abstract people inhabiting it. This death comes at the hands of a natural, impersonal force—not one of the most powerful armies in the world propped up by the most powerful state in the world, with a government, and a people electing this government. It is a convenient framing, one that shifts guilt away from Israel. The destruction comes from above, and those who die are meant to die. All is as it should be. To that, we offer a correction: Gaza is not an abstraction. It is a shore and beaches and streets and markets and cities with names of flowers and fruits, not an abstraction but places and lives and people that are being bombed into oblivion.

٭

We as Palestinians stand at the threshold of humanity. Sometimes invited, but not always. I keep going back to that phone call, to a voice on the phone, hailing from the far and distant land of humanity, where I am a guest until proven otherwise. The voice on the phone, kind, conciliatory, understanding, kept repeating: "Please, Karim, let us find a positive solution." The organizer didn't exactly reject my humanity. It was simply a very inconvenient fact for her that I was a human; she had to contend with it and was very uncomfortable. She suggested that we could talk about things such as "exile, memory, transmission, borders," but, please, without mentioning Palestine. I wondered how I could talk about exile without mentioning the material cause of this exile, which is a history of occupation. I wondered what "memory" consisted of in this context, if not survival in spite of a concerted, century-long campaign to erase all our histories. I wondered, also, if she imagined that it was great fun for me to talk about depressing subjects. Believe me, I would *rather* talk about anything else if I could. But I cannot.

What she was requiring of me was to render every single complication of my political and intimate being palatable and harmless, to stop being a liability to her. These are the contradictions that we are expected, as Palestinians, to solve within ourselves: to exist without talking about why we exist. In a way, she wished, very politely, that I could, very politely, cease to exist. What was I supposed to utter, then, at Innsbruck, if not the consent of my own vanishing? And today I understand what I felt as we spoke. The shadow of things I don't want to name. I was neither angry, nor sad, nor indignant: I was desperate. I kept talking. I couldn't hang up the phone. I couldn't say, "No, I will not come," and hang up. I needed this voice on the phone to acknowledge my humanity. For a few minutes, I was convinced that if we hung up, without this acknowledgement from her, without this recognition of me, I would vanish.

*

These are the facts: no water, no fuel, no electricity. Oxfam warned that the lack of water and the collapse of sanitation services will lead to outbreaks of cholera and infectious diseases. Hospitals, houses, schools, mosques, and churches are bombed indiscriminately (a callous word I am loathe to use, for what is to bomb if not indiscriminately?). As I write, Gaza has been plunged into darkness, all its communications with the outside world cut off. On live feeds and in photographs, explosions light up the skyline. Gaza has become a place designed for death indeed. And we, Palestinians and humanists around the world, wonder: Which will be the horror that will be deemed horrific enough to finally traverse the threshold into universal horror?

It seems there are not enough horrors inflicted upon the Palestinians to prompt the international community to demand, unambiguously, for a cessation of hostilities. The voice on the phone, like much of the world around us, was asking the same thing: please, let us find a positive solution. If only you could vanish, or—easier yet—if only you had never existed at all, and if only you could spare us the horror, the displacements, the bombings, the killings, the starving of a people that you are forcing us to unleash upon you. The world itself echoed in this voice on the phone telling me: there *is* a solution, if only you weren't so stubborn, there is a solution, which is to vanish within the contradictions wrought upon you; if only you could disinvite yourself from the world; if only you did not complicate the world with your existence; if only I did not have to talk to you; if only I did not have to listen to you; if only.

October 31, 2023

Steve Sabella, *38 Days of Re-Collection*, 2014, detail. UNIQUE. 47.8 x 27.4 cm. Black-and-white photo emulsion on paint fragments. Collected from Jerusalem's Old City house walls. Courtesy of the artist. In the collection of Margherita Berloni.

The Past Is Being Destroyed in Palestine— as Well as the Present

OLIVIA SNAIJE

It is nearly impossible today to imagine Gaza as a thriving port on the sparkling Mediterranean, where a rich socioeconomic exchange took place over thousands of years of human history. Yet for millennia, Gaza was an essential stopping point on the overland route between Africa, Asia, and Europe. Rich archaeological treasures found in the area indicate that trading was brisk throughout the Bronze Age— including finds indicating a close relationship with ancient Egypt— until Hellenic and Roman times, and it remained important for both Byzantine and Islamic rulers. Ships loaded with amphorae carrying grains, dried fruit, vegetables, and wine set sail from the ancient port of Anthedon, while caravans bearing incense and myrrh from Yemen and Oman transited through Gaza. Silk from as far away as China and scented woods and spices from India passed by on their way to the Greco-Roman world. Gaza was a unique meeting point between civilizations.

Fast-forward to today, when we see a broken Gaza, its people battered in a cataclysm following decades of continuous tragedy. Since the Hamas attack on October 7, Israel has reportedly dropped more than sixty-five thousand tons of bombs on the 140-square-mile territory, killing over twenty-five thousand Palestinians, with seven thousand still buried beneath the rubble, and injuring over sixty-three thousand. The United Nations estimates that 1.9 million people have been displaced, and more than half of the area's buildings have been destroyed, according to an analysis of satellite data. Infrastructure necessary for daily life has been demolished.

Amid the devastation, an estimated two hundred cultural and ancient historical sites have been damaged or destroyed in this territory that French archaeologist René Elter, who has been working in Gaza since 2001, describes as one "enormous archaeological site." Last weekend a video and stories on Instagram showed that pillaging might be taking place too: Israeli soldiers were rummaging in a warehouse where Elter and his team stored archaeological artifacts.

Elter has been the only archaeologist working in Gaza full-time since he moved there permanently in 2019. He had come at the behest of French archaeologist and Dominican priest Jean-Baptiste Humbert of the French Biblical and Archaeological School of Jerusalem. Shortly after the 1993 Oslo Accords, Humbert began working with the Palestinian Authority and its Department of Antiquities on several excavations in Gaza, which marked the beginning of a relationship between the French Biblical and Archaeological School and Gaza that has lasted until today. Its work in Gaza with local teams has revealed extraordinary sites—most recently a mammoth Hellenistic or Roman necropolis, which was still being excavated in October 2023.

Both Humbert and Elter describe their experience in Gaza as a great human adventure that altered their way of working—what they did went above and beyond field archaeology and became a collective experience shared with the local people.

I met with Elter in Paris following his evacuation from Gaza, via Egypt, having spent a month under Israeli bombs, constantly moving from area to area. Since then, he has been in contact with his team in Gaza every few days, connection permitting, and for the moment what is most important to him is that the entire team is alive.

Long before he and Humbert arrived in Gaza, the British Egyptologist Flinders Petrie had excavated a major site called Tall al-Ajjul, several miles south of Gaza City, between 1931 and 1934, during the British Mandate. His discoveries showed that Gaza had been a northern frontier for Egypt as far back as the third millennium BCE. Petrie's work was halted by the advent of World War II, and excavations only began again after the Israeli occupation of Gaza in

1967. Israeli archaeologists excavating in Gaza between the 1960s and 1980s discovered, among other rarities, fifty unique clay sarcophagi in a necropolis not far from where Petrie had excavated that showed both Egyptian and Phoenician influences. Marc-André Haldimann, former head of the archaeology department at the Museum of Art and History of Geneva and cocurator of an exhibition of Gaza archaeology in 2007, noted in an interview in 2008 that the sarcophagi, among other artifacts, were carted off to Israel, never to be returned.

*

Even though the Gaza Strip is incredibly rich archaeologically, it is relatively unexplored because of the enormous social and political problems it has experienced since 1948. The year the state of Israel was created, nearly eighty thousand Palestinian refugees streamed into the Gaza area, at the time inhabited by fifty thousand people. Gaza has steadily become one of the most densely populated regions in the world, with two-thirds of the population registered as refugees who, for the most part, live in camps. The burden of urbanization and coastal erosion, combined with decades of Israeli occupation, repeated bombings, and the siege, has led to internal political strife, extreme poverty, and overcrowding, which in turn has meant that buildings were often erected on top of historical sites.

When Humbert first arrived in Gaza, he began working on a site near a hospital in the Jabalia refugee camp, which revealed a fifth-century Byzantine church. In 1995 the next important site that he discovered was Blakhiyah, along the coast next to the Al-Shati refugee camp. The famous Hellenistic harbor and city of Anthedon were uncovered there, revealing layers of civilizations such as an Iron Age rampart, Hellenistic houses with painted walls, a Roman water fountain with mosaic decorations, and large Roman houses with Nabataean influences.

This same port of Anthedon, which had been painstakingly exca-vated for nearly thirty years despite damage from both coastal erosion and Israeli bombings, was surveyed just two years ago by the London-based research agency Forensic Architecture (FA), in close collaboration with Humbert.

FA investigates state and corporate violence, human rights violations, and environmental destruction using, among other methods, 3D animations and digital and physical models. Led by the Israeli architect Eyal Weizman, author of the groundbreaking 2007 book *Hollow Land: Israel's Architecture of Occupation*, the team presents their investigations in courtrooms and truth commissions; they are also part of the Technology Advisory Board of the International Criminal Court.

FA's analysis of satellite images revealed a number of large craters and damage to the Anthedon site caused by Israeli bombings in 2012, 2014, 2018, and 2021. In 2022 FA and the Ramallah-based nongovernmental organization Al-Haq called on the prosecutor of the ICC to consider the ongoing Israeli destruction of cultural heritage as amounting to war crimes and "to evaluate their potential contribution to apartheid as a crime against humanity under the Rome Statute."

In an update from December 2023, the Forensic Architecture investigation concluded that most of the Anthedon city and port have been destroyed.

After seeing photographs of Anthedon's destruction, Humbert, who had spent nearly sixty years in the Middle East, told the Lebanese newspaper *L'Orient-Le Jour*, "It appears to have been completely bulldozed in search of tunnels. . . . We prepare ourselves to accept the worst. But this is nothing compared to the genocide of the Palestinian people which is taking place before our eyes." Heartbreakingly the eighty-four-year-old has been recalled to his religious order in France.

There have been attempts to hold Israel to account for the destruction of cultural heritage sites, most recently from Euro-Med Human Rights Monitor, which has claimed that the devastation amounts to systematic military attacks against heritage sites. Fadel al-Otol, who was initially trained by Humbert and has worked extensively with Elter, spoke directly from Gaza on January 23, 2024, in a Zoom webinar organized by the Critical Ancient World Studies Collective and Everyday Orientalism.

The connection was spotty at times, with planes and drones audible and a baby crying in the background. Al-Otol said he hadn't slept for three days since the Israeli army had occupied their storage facility.

"I would need days to talk about all the destruction of the archaeological sites that we are witnessing. We are documenting every form of assault on these sites," he said, adding that he had photographed more than 30 percent of these areas, in particular in the old part of Gaza City.

Back in 1997, Humbert and his team discovered the vestiges of a fourth-century paleo-Christian monastery south of Gaza City. Tell Umm el-'Amr, as it is called, is spread over twenty-five acres of the coastal dune. Sensing that the site could be exceptional, Humbert involved Elter, who had worked in France for twenty years for an archaeological research institute before codirecting a site in Jordan for the French Institute of the Near East.

Very soon after arriving on the Tell Umm el-'Amr site in 2003, Elter and his team discovered a tomb and inscription affirming that the monastery was founded in 329 by St. Hilarion. St. Hilarion is recognized as the father of Palestinian monasticism, and the fourth-century biblical translator and priest St. Jerome wrote about him: St. Hilarion was born five miles south of Gaza, studied in Alexandria, and became a hermit before establishing his monastery, which is considered the oldest in Palestine and is the largest ever found in the Middle East.

*

Field archaeologists work inch by inch; it requires exacting labor, utmost patience and care, and a dedicated team. Gaza kept revealing extraordinary vestiges of the past, and Palestinian workers needed training. Humbert's findings had become so important that an exhibition was organized in 2000 at the Arab World Institute in Paris called *Mediterranean Gaza*, which presented research and artifacts from digs going back to 1994.

In Gaza, Humbert had already begun organizing training for the local people working on the archaeological sites. One day, at the

Anthedon port location, a shy but curious teenager from the nearby Al-Shati refugee camp approached the team and asked if he could work with them. It was al-Otol. Humbert took him under his wing and eventually arranged for him to travel to France and Switzerland to take part in archaeology-related seminars.

Today, al-Otol is in his early forties and has five children. He began working with Elter early on, and over the years they have developed a strong relationship. Elter says of al-Otol: "He is my left and right hand. He is self-taught, and it is he who best knows archaeology in Gaza. He knows how to restore mosaics, metal objects, and do stonecutting. He carries on my work when I'm not there."

Fifteen to twenty years ago, internal Palestinian politics, lack of funding for projects, and the Israeli Operation Cast Lead in 2008 and 2009 slowed excavations on various sites. Funding came in fits and starts, until al-Otol linked up with Jehad Abu Hassan, field coordinator for the Gaza Strip for Première Urgence Internationale, a French nongovernmental organization that helped Gazan farmers, fishers, and people injured by snipers and shelling as part of a broader remit of aiding civilians affected by natural disasters, war, and economic collapse. However, the NGO had never before worked in cultural heritage.

Abu Hassan, a French citizen whose parents were refugees in Gaza, spoke from France, where he had been evacuated with his wife and triplets a month after the Israeli onslaught began. He can cite the exact number of days he has spent under Israeli bombings in the past: eight days in 2012, fifty-one days in 2014, and eleven days in 2021.

It was in 2017 that Abu Hassan learned of a grant from the British Council Cultural Protection Fund. "I thought we could put two and two together, linking the humanitarian aspect with the archaeological heritage," he says.

The proposal, submitted by Abu Hassan for Première Urgence and Elter representing the French Biblical and Archaeological School, which included restoration, training, and public awareness, received a grant for £1,755,000 (approximately $2 million).

Besides professional training, the grant covered two sites: St.

Hilarion and the Byzantine church near the Jabalia refugee camp, which had over four thousand square feet of extraordinary mosaics that needed to be renovated and protected.

Despite obstacles to getting projects off the ground in 2018—obtaining Israeli permission to bring Humbert, Elter, and other specialists to Gaza through the Erez crossing and the nervousness of the French Consulate—local teams eventually began working on both sites. In St. Hilarion, the ecclesiastical complex was restored, with churches, a crypt, a chapel, a baptistery, and accommodation for the monks, as well as a hospice reserved for travelers and pilgrims, which included baths.

The mosaics in the Byzantine church revealed images of shrimp, smoked fish, a string of sausages, a plucked chicken, bunches of asparagus, pigeon eggs, chicken eggs, pomegranates, and an apple from the Garden of Eden. In 2022 a shelter protecting the site was inaugurated, with aerial walkways that allowed the public to visit the vestiges of the church, the diaconicon, the large baptistery, and the restored mosaics. Part of this structure is now thought to be damaged.

Elter developed an entire chain of operations including a learning center with community activities—children could work on a pretend excavation, for example. All the while, a team of forty people was being trained. Elter took care, despite Gaza's traditional society, to have both young men and women learn multidisciplinary crafts necessary for the safeguarding and restoration of the sites. Some learned 3D modeling and recorded 3D images of every excavation—110,000 3D photographs of St. Hilarion were taken. They mastered stonecutting or mosaic restoration to be able to choose the sector that interested them.

"I wanted to encourage team-building and to bring sensitivity and a certain gentleness to their daily life. There is no other team like this in Palestine," says Elter. "Hamas accepted us; there was a feeling of trust, and that meant that we could move forward. It was a win-win situation for everyone."

The ultimate aim was for Palestinians in Gaza to manage the sites.

In 2022, the French Development Agency, linked to the French Foreign Ministry, invested approximately $12 million in St. Hilarion.

The funding, Elter maintains, would have allowed them to work until 2028. That same year, as the ground was being cleared for a housing project in Beit Lahia, near Anthedon, a Hellenistic or Roman necropolis was discovered. Construction on the housing project was halted. The entire team moved over to the burial site, where 150 tombs were uncovered. Nabataean pottery from Petra was found, proving commercial trading within the Arab world, as well as objects in metal and clay, which, Elter explains, can provide information about funerary rites. "It's interesting to compare with other rites in the Roman world or find Egyptian or Eastern influences."

He reveals, "We were so lucky that the cemetery had not been destroyed or pillaged. It was totally intact. What's interesting is that this was not a prestigious burial site; it was the common man's cemetery. There were some more elaborate tombs with sarcophagi that perhaps belonged to wealthy merchants or traders. One grave had painted walls decorated with garlands and wreaths made with laurel leaves."

The team had been particularly moved by the discovery of an adult couple clasped together in an embrace. "We hadn't had an example like this before," Elter says. "It allowed us to talk about it with the team, to talk about feelings with people who are usually very discreet."

*

In October 2023 the Israeli army admitted to damaging the twelfth-century Church of Saint Porphyrius. When asked about the heavy damage to the Great Omari Mosque, a military spokesperson responded that the "target of the attack was terrorist infrastructure which included a tunnel shaft, a tunnel, and Hamas terrorists." The spokesperson added that the army's "actions are in accordance with international law."

There have been numerous reports in the press about the destruction of other heritage sites in Gaza, such as the Hammam al-Sammara and the Qasr al-Basha museum. Elter admits that, while "the heart of historical Gaza has been very severely hit, given the chaos on the ground you have to be very careful about what you see in the media."

He examines the damage from satellite photos but prefers to rely on firsthand accounts from those on the ground. Some of the younger team members have been venturing out to the sites and sending him photographs. For the moment, it seems that St. Hilarion has been spared, and in December 2023 Elter managed to get the St. Hilarion complex provisionally inscribed on UNESCO's International List of Cultural Property under Enhanced Protection.

St. Hilarion's warehouse, however, where the team kept antiquities, supplies, and tools, was robbed by Palestinians who had lost their homes. Elter specifies that people took anything that could be useful for building provisional structures or cooking utensils. They left behind archaeological objects considered unusable, like shards of ancient pottery.

On January 21, 2024, Elter saw his warehouse in a video posted on Instagram by Eli Escusido, the head of the Israel Antiquities Authority. The video shows Israeli soldiers walking around shelves of ancient amphorae or standing in front of opened boxes. In the video, Escusido commented: "Good week, the deputy director of the Antiquities Authority was rushed to Gaza to check a warehouse full of antiquities. Thank you to warrior Moshe Ajami."

It is unclear whether the objects in the warehouse, which come from the St. Hilarion site, are protected under UNESCO's protocol for provisional enhanced protection. This would have given St. Hilarion the highest level of immunity established by the 1954 Hague Convention. The fact that the video was posted by the head of the Antiquities Authority has added to fears about the official attitude toward the theft of heritage.

Surfacing that same day on Instagram were stories posted by Israeli soldiers that showed them holding stone plaques with inscriptions on them from St. Hilarion.

The extent of the looting of Gaza's only archaeology museum also remains unclear. The museum was built in 2008 by Gazan engineer and businessperson Jawdat Khoudary. Recently his daughter Yasmeen had hoped to begin underwater archaeology along Gaza's coast.

In a place where the continuous nature and severity of events have made the struggle for survival a priority, archaeologists in Gaza have diverged from the traditional methods of archaeological teams toward a more inclusive, community-driven approach. This also gives people a reason to be proud of their cultural heritage. During the January 23 webinar, al-Otol said: "Gaza's archaeology is a testament to religious tolerance and human shared culture. I didn't cry over the destruction of my home as much as the complete destruction of the Old City of Gaza."

This profound exchange between archaeologists and the people there provides an impetus to keep working in spite of the destruction. With UNESCO, Elter plans an expert mission for the monuments that he has been responsible for until now.

"But first we need to give people time to recover," he states. They have gone through an incredibly traumatic time and are weak, ill, and wounded. Then "we will adapt to the situation at hand and try to preserve the sites. We will bandage the wounds. Then we'll begin reconstruction surgery." In imagining reconstruction, he cites good examples to follow in Iraq and particularly in Mosul.

There is no question, Elter says. He will not let his team down in Gaza. "We all need to keep moving ahead. I embody for them something that makes them dream and will be there as long as they want to go ahead with this adventure that we created together."

January 25, 2024

END NOTE

Seven months after Elter lobbied to get the St. Hilarion complex provisionally inscribed on UNESCO's International List of Cultural Property Under Enhanced Protection, the complex was officially inscribed on UNESCO's List of World Heritage in Danger.

Art during Genocide
HAZEM HARB

I call *Dystopia Is Not a Noun* and *Gauze* "urgent" works. These were created during the genocide that is now taking place in Gaza. I used to work with collage and archival imagery; I did my research and analysis, took my photographs, and spent time in the making of art. After the arrest and torture of my father and the killing of family and friends in Gaza, what was public suddenly became intensely personal. I don't know how to explain it. I've never experienced anything like this in my life. I was following my family's situation and at the same time dealing with my anger, sadness, and trauma.

I hadn't been drawing or painting for the past ten years. Then suddenly, within a few minutes, I am upside down and back to zero. In what I describe as my "gut drawings" in *Dystopia Is Not a Noun*, I express myself. Charcoal is a material you use with your body, with your hand. With a brush, there is a distance between your hand and the surface.

In *Gauze*, everything is also made by hand. This material is one I worked with in Gaza when I was eighteen or twenty, making my collages, installations, and performance. Both *Gauze* and *Dystopia Is Not a Noun* are *art de l'automatisme*. As an artist and as a human being, you can't escape from the fragility you have inside. There can be a rigidity in sadness but a power too.

I believe art is resistance and that it is also resilience. I had the exhibition a couple of years ago called *Power Does Not Defeat Memories*. Power cannot even defeat art. Being an artist is a huge responsibility. Art should leave behind a legacy—to imagine something of your own individual and collective memories of a country or place.

This is the first time I've dealt with art in a painful way. I've had many different experiences before. I've even worked with some grief. But this time, I went into the work with pain, and the pain comes out in the art.

HAZEM HARB interviewed by **MALU HALASA**
March 29, 2024

(right and next page) Hazem Harb, *Gauze #22*, 2023. Gauze on fine art cardboard, twenty-two works, 48 x 33 cm (each). Courtesy of the artist.

(below left) Hazem Harb, *Dystopia Is Not a Noun #13*, 2023. Charcoal on canvas fine art paper, 180 x 100 cm. Courtesy of the artist.

(below right) Hazem Harb, *Dystopia Is Not a Noun #16*, 2023. Charcoal on canvas fine art paper, 180 x 100 cm. Courtesy of the artist.

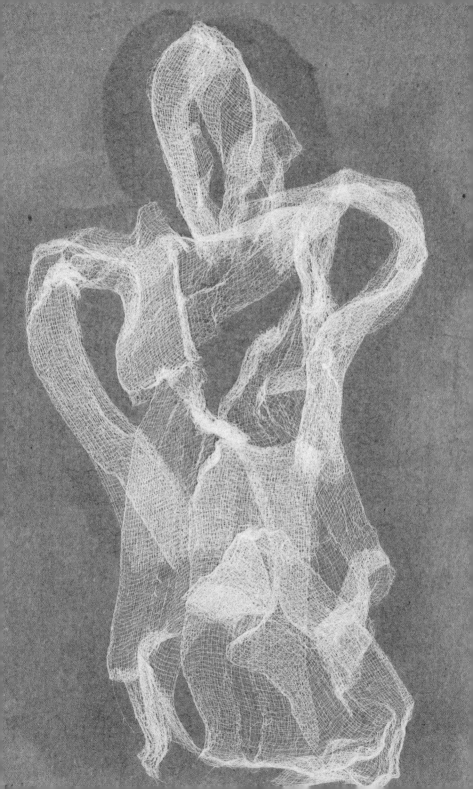

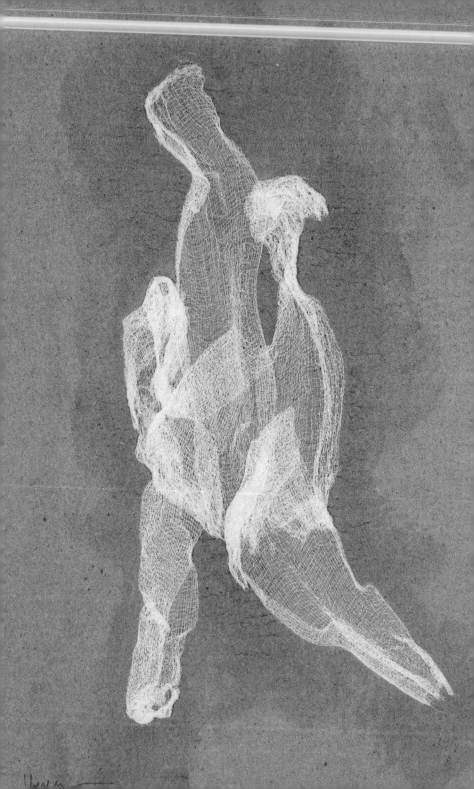

Gaza versus Mosul from a Medical and Humanitarian Standpoint

AHMED TWAIJ

I will never forget the eerie jet-black clouds engulfing Nineveh when its oilfields were ignited by the Islamic State (ISIS), signifying the beginning of the final wave to liberate Iraq from their domination. It was daytime, but the darkness from the smoke created a foreboding sense of gloom. I was a freelance journalist at the time as well as a volunteer doctor. I can recount each waking moment I spent in Mosul, either listening to the harrowing stories of Iraqis living under ISIS's brutal control or tending to the often ruthless wounds sustained by its innocent victims.

And so the more I hear Israel comparing its assault on Gaza to the war on ISIS, the clearer Israel's disinformation campaign becomes.

The images from Israel's attack on Palestinians are now forever etched into our memory. They have been nothing short of brutal, gruesome, and horrific. With the death toll rising into tens of thousands of innocent Gazans, the majority of whom are children; the destruction of entire hospitals; and an ongoing blockade against aid, it is becoming increasingly evident that the Israeli army's claim of being "the most moral army in the world" is mere rhetoric.

Throughout its unrelenting attack on Palestine, the Israeli government has constantly attempted to draw parallels between ISIS and Hamas, despite the two being incomparable. From Prime Minister Benyamin Netanyahu stating, "Hamas is ISIS, and just as ISIS was crushed, so too will Hamas be crushed,"[1] to the promotion of a hashtag on social media sites reiterating that claim (#HamasisISIS) and Israel Ministry of Foreign Affairs's YouTube ads (targeting Western children), all make the parallel explicit. The attempted association between

---

1   "Secretary Antony J. Blinken and Israeli Prime Minister Benjamin Netanyahu After Their Meeting," US State Department, October 12, 2023.

the two is a concerted effort to make the siege on Gaza somewhat more palatable and justifiable to a Western audience, despite such a vicious siege never being deployed against ISIS-held Mosul.

As ISIS was deemed a worldwide threat, with attacks in London, Paris, the US, and elsewhere, a global coalition was set up—garnering vast international support—to destroy ISIS. Israel has preyed on this fear of international terrorism to justify its obliteration of Gaza, along with its civilian inhabitants. ISIS, however, was a transnational organization founded on the ideology of *takfirism* (advocating the killing of anyone who disagrees with your beliefs) versus Hamas, which was created to be a Palestinian nationalist resistance movement. Its means of resistance has landed itself on terrorists' lists worldwide and any loss or targeting of innocent life is deplorable; however, the threat Hamas poses is not the same global threat of ISIS. So unlike what Netanyahu wants the world to believe, Europe will not "be next."

But let us—for a moment—play along with Israel's comparisons. Mark Regev, a senior adviser to Netanyahu, stated, "To get ISIS out of Mosul, there were civilian casualties." And indeed, there were.

Having been present in Iraq during the war against ISIS, as a volunteer medical doctor and freelance journalist, I witnessed firsthand the liberation attempts as well as ISIS's brutal tactics. If Israel wants to compare the current war in Gaza to the liberation of Mosul from ISIS control, then we should do just that.

Both regions have a similar population size. Prior to the war starting, the Gaza strip had a population of 2.2 million (the majority of whom are children under the age of eighteen) and Mosul has a population of around 1.8 million. Much like Gaza, Mosul is a densely populated city, with some almost-impenetrable neighborhoods. Although just one civilian death is too many, in the eighteen months of fighting it took to finally liberate Mosul, between 1,000 and 3,200 civilians were sadly killed by coalition forces. In comparison, as of this writing, 13,300 Palestinian civilians have been killed by Israeli forces in only six weeks. Whole families have been wiped from the civil registry. Not to mention the infrastructural devastation—rendering much of north Gaza uninhabitable—due to the viciousness of the air campaign.

Israel has killed more Palestinians in Gaza since the war began than Palestinians have killed Israelis since 2008, according to United Nations statistics.

The stark difference between Gaza and Mosul is that the Iraqi special forces seemed to place some value on Iraqi life, whereas the Israeli forces lack any concern for Palestinian life, as made clear by Israeli defense minister Yoav Gallant's reference to Palestinians as "human animals."[2]

Iraqi security forces also set up humanitarian corridors to allow the safe passage of innocent civilians out of Mosul prior to and throughout the campaign in Mosul. We witnessed convoy after convoy of civilians braving the harsh route through the Nineveh plains to reach camps of internally displaced persons set up via an array of international charities. On arrival, I saw Mosul civilians finally celebrating a breath of freedom. But despite fleeing their homes, they were guaranteed that they would be allowed to return if they obtained a security clearance.

In contrast, however, no such escape route is available in Gaza. All access in and out of Gaza has been closed off by both Israel and Egypt. All civilians have been stuck inside a strip that is less than a third of the size of the city of Los Angeles and that is increasingly referred to as a concentration camp. Even the humanitarian corridors within Gaza's confines that were alleged by Israel to be safe evacuation routes have been bombed.

Israel has often claimed that the reason the civilian death toll in Gaza is so high is because Hamas has prevented civilians from leaving their homes. No Palestinian has confirmed this claim, despite dozens of journalists being present in Gaza. In Mosul, on the other hand, civilians were actually, sometimes even at gunpoint, stopped from fleeing for safety by ISIS.

---

2   Al Jazeera, Newsfeed, "Israeli Defense Minister Orders 'Complete Siege' on Gaza," October 9, 2023.

With disturbing echoes of the first Palestinian Nakba (or "great catastrophe") of 1948, there has been no guarantee that any displaced Palestinian in Gaza will ever be able to return. Even if they eventually can, what would they be returning to? According to Ynet, a major Israeli news website, over 60 percent and counting of all residential units in Gaza have been destroyed, not to mention schools and hospitals.

In what can only be described as collective punishment, the Israeli government has disturbingly weaponized civilian infrastructure and cut off water and electricity to the strip—which also gives the lie to the claim that Israel stopped its occupation of Gaza when it formally withdrew in 2005.

The restriction of water and electricity was deemed a war crime by European Union president Ursula von der Leyen when Russia did something similar in Ukraine—but now that Israel is doing it, it is supported by Western politicians. The US-led coalition in Iraq never resorted to such collective punishment against the people of Mosul, and access to water was deemed paramount to civilian life. Perhaps it is more apt to consider that it was in fact ISIS that weaponized water and cut off its supply to Mosul's civilians.

The provision of water became essential to helping the city's civilians survive. As a doctor working in the IDP (internally displaced persons) camps outside Mosul, I had access to basic medications, treatment, and, importantly, clean water. We medical staff had to spend nights either in tents or sleeping in our cars, but at no point were we worried about coalition air strikes targeting these safe areas. Medical resources were in constant supply, either via an array of international aid donations or the Iraqi government. Israel, however, has prevented aid from entering Gaza, resulting in a rapid depletion of medication in the strip, and the trickle they finally did allow in from Egypt barely amounts to 10 percent of what Gaza used to receive.

Shocking testimonials reveal that doctors are having to perform lifesaving operations without anesthesia in Gaza. In one heartbreaking video, we see a Palestinian surgeon grieving after having had to perform an amputation on his own son without anesthesia, only for his son not to survive the procedure.

In Iraq, if any critical treatment was required, patients were transported to Baghdad via a short helicopter flight. Gaza, however, has been a no-fly zone for decades now, except for Israel's destructive fighter jets (Gaza International Airport was shut down in 2001). Even in times of no conflict, it is exceedingly difficult for patients to secure a permit to receive critical care outside of Gaza, and when a permit is granted, Gazan ambulances are still not allowed to cross out of the strip. Instead even the most grievously ill or urgently injured patient must endure something called a back-to-back transfer, where they are taken off the ambulance in Gaza and placed onto an ambulance on the Israeli side of the border—a delay that could prove to be the difference between life and death. Like the permit, this needs to be arranged ahead of time, which makes it nearly impossible to provide the timely care that emergencies require.

Over the past few weeks in Gaza, Palestinian ambulances have come under fire from Israeli air strikes. To be perfectly clear: attacks on emergency relief efforts are considered a war crime. In one assault, which left the UN secretary general António Guterres "horrified," Israel attacked an entire convoy of ambulances in an air strike. In Mosul, ambulances were never considered targets by the US-led coalition.

Air strikes in Mosul were far more contained. In order to keep them to a minimum, the Iraqi army would go door to door clearing neighborhoods of ISIS. Only when they found themselves surrounded and unable to proceed would they call in the US coalition for air strikes. In my capacity as a journalist, I often tagged along behind the army, observing their conduct. And I remember the sound of air strikes echoing through the narrow streets of the city. Despite such precautions, the coalition was still (and rightly) criticized for the civilian death toll incurred and were often investigated in the aftermath—and on occasion compensation was provided for victims.

Israel, on the other hand, has been blindly attacking in Gaza, with no effort to minimize civilian causalities, as they supposedly seek to clear out Hamas. Unlike Iraq, for weeks there was no ground approach, only carpet-bombing. In one shocking instance, on October 31, Israel killed at least fifty Palestinians at the Jabalia refugee camp and later claimed, without evidence, that it killed one Hamas commander in the process. Hamas denied this.

These blind carpet-bombings have resulted in the destruction of entire hospital complexes, to the extent that there are no more functioning hospitals in northern Gaza. A desecration of the sanctity of health care facilities is potentially a war crime. A children's cancer unit in Al-Shifa Hospital was obliterated, allegedly using the newly designed R9X Hellfire missile (with its rotating blades, imagine a human meat grinder). At no point has Israel provided evidence of any of these hospitals being used as Hamas bases. And now that the damage has been done and the hospitals have been put out of commission, it is the innocent and most vulnerable Gazans who suffer the most—a reality referred to as a "self-sustaining catastrophe" by Dr. Ghassan Abu Sittah, a British doctor who had been volunteering in Gaza.[3]

In contrast, in Mosul, strikes on health care facilities were kept to a bare minimum and only ever as a last resort—after having confirmed that the buildings were being used as a military base by ISIS. The Iraqi military spent days locked in battle with ISIS fighters inside Mosul's Al-Salam hospital complex; only when they were unable to progress did they request backup from the US in the form of air strikes. And even then, a precision strike was used to specifically target the building housing the ISIS fighters. Israel claims that Hamas has hidden its bases in bunkers below Gaza's hospitals, which begs the question: why would you then destroy the lifesaving facility that is above it?

Like these health care facilities, places of worship have not been safe in Gaza either; even those being used as shelters by civilians. Ancient mosques have been destroyed in what feels like an attempt to erase Palestinian identity. In October, Israel attacked and destroyed the

---

3   Dr. Ghassan Abu Sitta (@dr.ghassan.as) and @thurayyakhldizrk.ink, "In this infographic, Dr Ghassan Abu Sitta (@dr.ghassan.as) explains the current 'catastrophization' of the health system in Gaza . . .," Instagram, November 23, 2023.

twelfth-century Greek Orthodox Church of Saint Porphyrius that was housing Christians and Muslims seeking refuge from the violence. These attacks have caused Gaza's Christians to fear extinction. It is ironic that while Israel has busied itself comparing ISIS with Hamas, it is in fact Israel behaving more like ISIS and threatening the region's indigenous Christian community.

In Mosul, churches were ransacked by ISIS, and Christians were driven out of the city by the militants' *takfiri* ideology. I witnessed churches that had been converted into shooting ranges due to their long and narrow designs. And yet despite these churches becoming known as ISIS military bases, they weren't destroyed by the coalition and are still standing today—despite ISIS's best efforts otherwise.

Likewise, the protection afforded to journalists in each conflict is another point of contrast. Not only has Israel attempted to silence press in Gaza by banning foreign journalists from entering the strip (until recently, they were allowed by Israeli Defense Forces escort only), there have been what appear to be targeted attacks against journalists and their families, with over fifty journalists killed so far. In Mosul, less than a handful of journalists died during the conflict, with all the deaths attributable to ISIS. Journalism was in fact considered globally vital to the coalition's success, and I remember a flood of foreign correspondents landing in Erbil in the days leading up to the assault on Mosul.

If Israel wants to compare Hamas to ISIS, we should examine every aspect of this comparison. Israel claims that its war on Gaza is a war on Hamas, but it's clear to observers that this is in fact a war against Palestine. What we are witnessing is not self-defense at all but a destructive campaign with minimal consideration for Palestinian life. Even during unscripted remarks to an audience in St. Peter's Square, Pope Francis chimed in to announce, "We have gone beyond wars. This is not war. This is terrorism."[4]

---

4   " 'Terrorism': Israel-Hamas Conflict Has Gone 'Beyond War' Says Pope Francis," Al Jazeera, November 22, 2023.

Perhaps it is more accurate to compare ISIS and Israel? While to date ISIS has deplorably killed thirty-three thousand innocents over five years, Israel has, in just one month, devastatingly killed more than a third of that figure. Of course, none of what I have written absolves Hamas of any of its crimes by any means — that is not what is under discussion here—but what we do see is a recurrent pattern of violence conducted by an Israel that continues to act with impunity.

It is time the mirror is held up to Israel. Now really, the question you should be asking yourself is: do you condemn Israel?

November 27, 2023

Application 39
AHMED MASOUD

Smoke drifted out of Rayyan's mouth as he dropped his jaw, turning it into soft concentric circles. Poking his index finger through the middle of them, he turned to his friend, smiling: "It's going to be OK, *wallah*, trust me." His eyes beamed with excitement. Not knowing how else to convince his friend, he leaned forward and embraced him, ignoring his lack of reaction.

"Relax, man. Trust me," he tried again as they began climbing the marble steps of the Gaza City Municipality Building, pausing halfway to look back at the three lemon trees in the square below them. Their leaves looked so dry under that thin layer of dust it could have been autumn. But this was the *khamaseen* season, late spring when the Sinai's sand yellowed the city sky as it passed overhead, carried by the southern wind. At the top of the steps, a large olive wood door greeted them. Rayyan pressed a button and a red laser flickered across his face, before turning green. The door opened and he entered. Ismael, still looking perplexed, followed him just in time before the door purred shut behind them.

Inside the high-vaulted foyer, three long corridors stretched out in different directions. In the first, to their right, video screens lined the walls on both sides, evidently showing live feeds from all over the city. Each screen had a tag: J1 and J2 fed from Jabalia Camp; G1 through G4 covered the major squares of Gaza City. And so on.

The middle corridor seemed to contain only a long series of lifts, with no buttons, just numbers above each one. These Ismael was familiar with. He loved the faint quiver of excitement they sent through you whenever one of them opened its doors, knowing you had chosen it from the micromovements you made yards before. The moment you stepped through you were moving, plummeting downward at a speed given on a small screen on the left-hand wall: usually ten meters per second, before slowing and then surging sideways at ten, twenty, thirty. Lift tunnels like these spiderwebbed deep beneath the old city and beyond, spanning all of what was once called the Strip and linking with another network of tunnels under what they used to call the Bank. If you had the correct entry visa, the lifts would speed you to your destination in minutes. This network had been the collective pride and joy of the independent republics, which had pledged to build them in the so-called New Dawn that followed the collapse of the Oslo Accord and the 2025 invasions, when each major Palestinian city had been forced to declare itself an independent state.

The third corridor ran alongside a series of small meeting rooms. As he walked past, Ismael could see each one was filled with men with mustaches or women with headscarves surrounded by news screens, typing frantically at their desks with each new development. In one room, a hologram of an Indian man in a border-control uniform was giving a presentation on new software that could identify illegal immigrants through facial expressions.

By the time Rayyan reached the room at the end of the corridor, Ismael had caught up with him. They stood still for a moment as a small, hovering drone cam emerged from the wall and performed a retinal scan before the big olive-wood door slid open. The room was crowded; men in suits jostled with others in *jellabiya* and traditional dress. A young woman in a long, flowery skirt and reading glasses that wrapped around her entire head was looking down as they entered. The murmur in the room suddenly stopped.

"Please be seated," the woman said, gesturing toward the bench in front of her. The two of them sat down in silence.

"My name is Lamma El-Rayyes, and I am chairing this emergency session," she began. "Gentlemen, your actions have had considerable consequences across the state, so, if I may, I would like to start by asking you to tell us the facts, as you understand them. We are not interested in the whys of the situation, just in what happened. First, which one of you submitted the application form?"

"I did," Rayyan answered without a moment's hesitation.

"Well, actually, it was my idea," Ismael quickly added.

"As I said, Mr. Ismael, I am not interested in ideas. I just want to establish the facts. I will then report my findings to his excellency, the president of Gaza City, who will talk with his counterparts, the presidents of Khan Younis, Nuseirat, and the others . . ." Lamma waved her hand in the air and a large display screen appeared on the wall behind her. She played around with the bright green buttons on her control pad and a document appeared.

"Is that your signature at the bottom of the page?" she asked, looking at neither of them.

Rayyan and Ismael looked a little bit confused.

"No, of course not," Rayyan started. "This is the signature of our great leader, Mr. Hamad Hamoud, as you know."

"Is this a trick question?" Ismael asked.

"No, it is not," Lamma fired back, fixing her stern gaze on them. "This is not an authentic signature. One of you has forged it."

A murmur of disbelief spread through the room, and a couple of men started heckling.

"This is going to break the peace deal completely," someone muttered.

"We're doomed!" shouted another. "We're heading straight back to the rule of Hamas and Fatah."

"The Israelis won't be happy either," observed an elderly man at the back.

Lamma cleared her throat and the whole room fell silent again. She had an air of natural authority that commanded the room's respect, to the extent that Ismael found himself wondering how far her obvious ambitions might end up taking her.

She raised both hands in the air and continued. "I have to hand it to you; you are a couple of tricksters, it seems." She turned again to the facsimile looming large on the wall display. "So you forge a document, purporting to be from our leader, apply to the International Olympic Committee for the State of Gaza to . . . host the thirty-ninth Summer Olympic Games in 2048."

She turned to face them and the room. "Now, let me ask you," she said, pausing for effect. "Are you out of your minds? This is only eight years from now."

She stared at them for what felt like an eternity. Hearing the contents of the document read out loud felt even more ridiculous than they had anticipated. They both knew the seriousness of the matter, of course. They could be hanged for treason, and the fire in Lamma's eyes seemed to confirm they should expect nothing less. They both fell silent, not knowing what to say. They looked at each other as if comprehending, for the first time, the reality of what they'd done.

The air of confidence that had filled Rayyan on the steps of the building just a few minutes earlier had entirely disappeared, replaced by a sheepish, apologetic look. Ismael's mind wandered from the room, back to a time when they'd both been kids studying together at the UN refugee school. They were only ten years old when the war broke out in 2025. He didn't remember much about how it all started, but he remembered the day the school was bombed as if it were yesterday. Smoke rose in all directions, shrouding the playground like a hood. Ambulance sirens filled the city, as he stood there watching everything unravel around him: all he wanted to do was run back home to his parents' house in Beach Camp. But he was frozen. He wished his father were there to pluck him out of the chaos, people screaming and running in all directions. He wished his teacher were there to shout at him and scare him into snapping out of it and running. But nothing happened: he just froze. The smoke got thicker and closer, until he could see nothing at all, and just as he closed his eyes, Rayyan grabbed him by the wrist and dragged him away.

They ended up in the El Ansar District in Gaza City. Israeli soldiers had already arrived by sea, docking their heavily armored ships at El Mina, Gaza's only port. They were also bombing from the air, using advanced high-speed drones.

The two boys roamed the city for days before eventually settling on a bombed-out residential block on El-Farra Street as their shelter. To their delight, in one of the apartments, they found cans of sardines, hummus, and fava beans, which sustained them for a week until an old woman, a former resident, came looking for her belongings and found them. She brought them back to her new abode in a less bombed-out part of town, where she, her son, and her daughter-in-law raised them as their own. They couldn't return to their families in Beach Camp; the IDF had installed checkpoints everywhere, surrounding and besieging every city, town, and village in the Strip, just as they had done in the Bank. Realizing there was little hope of ever returning to their parents, Rayyan and Ismael stayed with their new adopted family. From then on, they were brothers.

The Palestinian cities, unable to physically connect with each other anymore, declared themselves independent states. Israel had taken control of all the roads between them, and air travel had not been possible since the end of the twentieth century, so the city-states had put everything into tunneling back into contact with each other, starting with shabby old holes Hamas had first dug during its rule—holes that had proved utterly useless in thwarting the invasion when it came.

With time, the city-states grew apart, in outlook and habits, and ever-stricter immigration policies were gradually introduced. On several occasions, tensions slid into open military confrontation, and warring Palestinian cities fired homemade rockets that flew high over the heads of Israeli soldiers, usually landing in the empty fields that acted as buffer zones around each city. The hostilities persisted until a peace deal between the states was signed in 2030, acknowledging the independence of each city-state and the integrity of its borders, even though these borders were very much still under Israeli control, a fact nobody seemed too keen to dwell on.

*

"We could be looking at another war here." Lamma's voice brought Ismael back with a jolt. "Either with Khan Younis, or Rafah, or even Ramallah. Their presidents will all think we didn't consult them in this decision—that the Republic of Gaza City wanted to do this on its own, to steal the limelight. And don't forget Israel! They will no doubt accuse us of breaking our agreements with them on this. Bombs will probably start raining on us because of this—not only on us, but on all the other states. Where will this end?"

All Ismael wanted was to be out of that windowless room and in the open, enjoying the sandstorm. He looked at his friend then mirrored him, staring back down at the floor. It felt like the whole room was watching him. But when Ismael eventually looked up again and caught the eye of one old man sitting at the back, his smile seemed genuine.

The truth of the matter was it had all been a joke, a game of dare that neither party had expected would go this far. Ismael was the first to suggest it and called it "Operation Application 39." Rayyan said he would look after the paperwork, and that was that. They submitted it online, not expecting it would even be read. The two men's day jobs were in the municipality's IT department, positions that gave them enough free time to develop a series of elaborate hacking schemes to entertain themselves in the long hours between reboot requests. At first these consisted largely of hacking into local celebrities' social media accounts and playing practical jokes on their celebrity friends. But they grew bored of this, wanting something more challenging to pass the time. The International Olympic Committee's computer system offered the perfect challenge, and hacking into it even allowed them to look at rival applications from other cities. "Just for research, you understand," Ismael, the better of the two hackers, giggled at the time. "So we don't look like complete fools."

The IOC's reply, dated 12 January 2040, came addressed to the president and read: "The International Olympic Committee feels that the application is very strong and that by hosting the 36th Summer Olympic Games, Gaza City would be able to celebrate and further cement the peace deal signed ten years ago."

"I am sorry, Ms. Lamma, it was just a bit of fun, we didn't think it would actually lead to anything," Rayyan said with pleading eyes. Ismael looked at him with pity, all too aware of how difficult it was for his friend to admit their mistake.

"What do we do now?" interjected someone from across the room.

"We turn it down, of course," another answered.

A woman, who looked in her sixties, stood up. She was smartly dressed and wore a shawl around her shoulders.

"Excuse me, Ms. Lamma. I realize this is a reckless violation by two obviously irresponsible individuals, but we are here now, and, I think, instead of wasting time revisiting how this was allowed to happen, we should instead be thinking of how we could make it work for us, how we can seize it as an opportunity for the whole republic—a chance to show the world how civilized we are. We may actually be able to get the other states to agree . . ."

The room erupted into a cacophony of agreement and dissent. One of the men in suits said the old woman was clearly crazy. "Show some respect, you ignoramus!" a younger woman shouted at him. Rayyan leaned toward Ismael and nodded toward her: "Asmaa Shawwa—she served in the Abbas government in the early 2000s."

"Enough!" shouted Lamma, slamming her fist on the table; the room promptly fell silent. All eyes were now on her.

"I think this is a decision for the president, not us. As I said, I just wanted to establish the facts, and now that I am confident this was not an act of deliberate sabotage, I will take the matter to him and see what he says. Mr. Hamoud will surely have the wisdom to see through this. We will adjourn the meeting and reconvene tomorrow morning. You two are coming to the president's office now, with me."

Rayyan and Ismael stared at each other, terrified. They had never met a senator before, let alone a president; they were just two IT clerks at the municipality.

"Do we have to?" Ismael muttered but didn't wait for an answer.

The room started to empty in silence; people walked out of the main door, each throwing a parting glance toward the two men.

In a soft, slightly robotic voice, Lamma ordered the room's computer to shut down, and as they stepped outside the three of them were met by a small crowd of people waiting in the corridor for their lifts to arrive. A robotic assistant, with a painted-on suit, rolled toward

Lamma, taking her bag and ushering the three of them toward an opening lift. Inside, there was only one button on the wall, which read "The Office of President Hamad Hamoud." Lamma pressed it and within an instant the doors were shut, leaving the boy robot standing outside.

The lift plunged downward and, after a minute or so of sideways acceleration, started ascending again. When the bell rang indicating it had arrived at its destination, a computerized female voice welcomed them to "The Office of President Hamad Hamoud." "If you are carrying a weapon," it added, "you will be neutralized immediately."

"If only we had time for you to hack this motherfucker and de-smug her," Rayyan muttered as they stepped out into the bewildering light of a penthouse office.

As they entered, President Hamoud was busy going through a pile of paperwork behind a huge desk. He looked very tall even though he was sitting down. The two friends felt deeply intimidated by the surroundings and avoided direct eye contact as the president lifted his head up and greeted Lamma.

"*Ahlan*, Lamma, how did the meeting go?" the president said, smiling, before glancing back down at his papers.

"Well, these two idiots are the ones who submitted the application and forged your signature."

"Can you hack her too?" Rayyan whispered. "She's rude." Ismael concentrated on keeping a straight face.

The president stopped reading and looked at the two of them. He stood up and removed his small glasses, placing them carefully on his desk, then stared once more at the two men still refusing to make eye contact.

"I believe you understand the seriousness of your actions?" he asked as he approached them.

"Yes, sir," they answered in unison.

"So, what shall I do with you now? Have you hanged for treason?"

The silence that followed was unbearable. They still couldn't look the president in the eye. They were expecting soldiers to barge through the doors at any moment. Ismael's hands were shaking, and Rayyan could see it.

"Well, Lamma, we are where we are. I have been thinking a lot about this, and I believe we should go ahead and host these games. These two bozos might have actually brought us a gift—"

"But, sir—" Lamma interrupted.

"Let me finish first, please." Mr. Hamoud's tone was serious. "The Republic of Gaza is a thoroughly modern city these days, both in terms of technology and infrastructure. Besides, this could be an opportunity to unite all the Palestinian states together."

"But sir, it could bring about war again, with everyone!" Lamma responded sharply.

"So be it; we will be ready for it." The president's authoritative tone signaled the end of the conversation. He went back to his desk and paperwork. Lamma indicated to Rayyan and Ismael to follow her and, within seconds, they were out the door.

They followed her in silence as she marched back to the lift. The door was already open and, stepping inside, they found themselves instantly transported back to the municipality building, where they were ushered into a small meeting room followed by Lamma's personal assistant, a small robot that glided along on two big wheels.

"It's the thirtieth of March, 2040. This meeting will be recorded and minutes will be sent out directly to you half an hour after it's finished. Please refrain from using offensive language—anything you say will go on your HR profile."

"*Shukran*, Tamir," Lamma addressed the robot, which had moved to her side and started scanning both Rayyan and Ismael.

"OK, well—you are very lucky to be here right now despite the havoc you have caused. I am sure Mr. Hamoud has made a huge mistake, but he is the president, and his wishes must be followed. So . . . tell me, when you submitted this application, did you have the faintest clue how Gaza would actually be able to host these games? How are we going to host a marathon, for instance, when the city's only six kilometers wide? Or the water sports—rowing, sailing, long-distance swimming—when we only have a two-mile-long stretch of coast?"

Lamma didn't sound genuinely angry, more frustrated. She seemed to have accepted the decision, but she looked away as she reeled off her questions, not expecting an answer.

"We could dig more tunnels," Ismael said.

"What?" she snapped.

"The Israelis control all the land between our states; they control the airspace and the sea; only the earth beneath us remains unoccupied. We could build tunnels that circle the city deep underground—2R—that gives us 31.42 km, one and a third laps and you have a marathon!" Ismael said enthusiastically. "We could build football pitches, velodromes—whatever we want down there!"

"What about water sports, wiseass?" Lamma cut him off.

"Well, we have two miles of coast. We can do all the swimming stuff in there, set up lanes going along the coast, backward and forward; all we need to work out is how to stop the waves. I am sure a few rocks will do it. For diving, we can dig under the sea too. Make the seabed deeper. For water polo, we could use one of the new water tanks the World Bank donated to the camps. Why not?"

"So basically what you are saying is that more tunnels and a few rocks in the sea are all we need?" Rayyan asked sarcastically.

"Yes, we know how to dig them, alright! We've been building them since the nineties, so why not now?" Ismael had rediscovered his self-belief.

Lamma watched the two young men and wondered where they would have been if the situation were different, if the war never happened. Her own father had been killed defending Gaza City during the Israeli invasion fifteen years earlier. She'd been sixteen at the time. The day her father never came back was the day she decided to study politics and begin her long, remarkable pursuit of a political career. A lot of people admired her; several unlikely men had even proposed to her, apparently, but to Ismael she looked like someone too smart to jeopardize a career by allowing herself a private life.

*

Thus it was announced that Gaza City was to be the first Arab city to ever host an Olympic Games. Rayyan and Ismael walked out of the municipality building that day feeling elated. They didn't say a word to each other as they walked through the long corridor toward the exit. But as they stepped down onto the street, surrounded by honking cars, the buzzing of delivery drones, and the flickering of advertising screens, they began to laugh. Looking at each other, their laughter grew and for a moment they struggled to catch their breath.

They were through the looking glass now; what had started as a joke had become a new reality, one with the potential to change the whole city's future. After a century of being cut off from the world, now, suddenly, the world was going to come to them. *To pay a visit to this prison*, Ismael thought; *its first ever, in order to watch people running, jumping, and throwing things!*

Neither Ismael nor Rayyan had ever set foot outside of Gaza City. Even getting into other coastal states within the Palestinian federation required a visa and a string of transit permits, which neither of them had ever succeeded in applying for. What they knew of the other states they had all learned from their grandparents. As teenagers they'd dreamt of visiting the Republics of Ramallah and Nablus in the Bank, or to one day hike across the gentle hills of old Palestine, to breathe its fresh air, to take in the scent of olives in the groves that stretched, in their minds, all the way from Bethlehem to Jerusalem.

Collecting themselves from their momentary hysterics, Rayyan and Ismael set off down the hill toward Talatini Street, in the direction of home. As they passed Al Ahli Hospital, an Israeli drone flew low over their heads and landed nearby, only to transform into a bipedal robot. With its oddly doglike face, it began scanning the streets with its dark, translucent eyes as pedestrians looked away.

The dog robot then scanned Rayyan and Ismael, who knew to stand completely still and stare directly at it. Looking away would only get them tasered. On each side of its long, pointed face, just below each camera eye, a screen flashed to life and began scrolling through the two men's vital information: dates of birth, addresses, bank account numbers, professions, etc. Across its chest stretched the blue and white Israeli flag. Ismael wanted to punch it in its solar plexus, knowing it probably didn't have one. Reading his friend's thoughts, Rayyan put his arm around Ismael's shoulder: "Look, it's one of your favorite breeds!" he laughed awkwardly. "Oh, but it's been scrapping with other poodles," he added, noticing a horizontal scratch across the blue of its chest.

After a pause, the robot retransformed itself back into a drone, and they both sighed with relief to see it fly away. Usually when a robot stopped people like this in the street, someone was either tasered and arrested—or worse. The two men laughed at the day they were having. As they walked in the direction of the Rimal neighborhood, a strange sense of invincibility lightened their steps.

*

Over the following four years, preparations got underway across the city for the vast infrastructure necessary to host such a colossal international event. Ismael's idea of building most of the facilities underground was eventually accepted, and thanks to the unique expertise of Gazan builders in all things subterranean, the work was completed ahead of schedule. Most of the facilities were built within three years. The main challenge was how to build the athletes' village, given there wasn't enough space left aboveground in the republic. The solution came from an expert in the United Kingdom of Saudi (which, since 2036, had assimilated all the other Gulf countries). A Dubai-based architect proposed using the rubble excavated from the tunnels to build a man-made island in the sea, just off the Gaza City shoreline.

Rayyan and Ismael were on the planning committee, chaired by Lamma, their original indiscretion long since forgotten. All members reported directly to the president who was, despite his old age, very keen to follow up on all the details. Mr. Hamoud was also forever receiving delegations from the other Palestinian republics. Indeed, every planning meeting had envoys from the other states in attendance; despite their fury in the early days for not having been consulted—in some cases even threatening war—now they pored over each decision in detail to make sure every shekel allocated by the Olympic Committee could be seen to be benefiting the federation as a whole.

One state had never forgiven Gaza, however. Salah Zourob, the president of Rafah, had been so furious about the application, he severed all diplomatic relations with Hamoud's government and closed down the lift tunnel between the two states. It had been four years since any goods or individuals had traveled between them. In fact, recent noises heard traveling down that particular tunnel had been interpreted by military experts as the sound of troops gathering at the Rafah end.

The party that was most upset by it all was, of course, Israel. Tel Aviv had been trying to host the Olympic Games for decades. The Knesset contested the results and took the International Olympic Committee to court, initially alleging corruption but later changing their stance, claiming the bid had been an elaborate attempt to hoodwink the international community into unwittingly funding a new era of military tunneling: what lobbyists called "the terror from beneath." Unexpectedly these appeals failed to reverse the decision, although Israel, Russia, and the Confederate States of America all declared they would boycott the Games the moment the appeal was overturned. Despite this, the Israeli government still took it upon itself to make sure the preparations for the Games failed, instructing all security agencies to gather more intelligence about the planning and sending in a new swarm of microscopic drones to infiltrate each of the development sites. Aware of this, Mr. Hamoud demanded the utmost secrecy and only discussed plans through encrypted messaging systems. For some reason he tasked Rayyan and Ismael with monitoring security protocols and attempted intelligence breaches by Israel directly. Israel, in turn, encouraged the president of Rafah to attack Gaza, giving President Zourob the intel, weapons, and temporary access to what used to be called Salah Eldein Street—the now overgrown thoroughfare that once ran the entire length of the Strip.

With four years left to go, war loomed, and the dream of hosting the Games "without mishap" grew ever more unlikely. After one particularly long day, the two friends sat down for a shisha vape, in a café in El Rimal Park, near what used to be the Unknown Soldier Statue. The two men never needed much encouragement to reminisce about life at school before the devastation of April 2025, but these days every time they started to, their talk stuttered to a halt, both thinking about the further devastation that awaited them. Their conversations were increasingly given over to these long pauses, so much so that Ismael was relieved when today's silence was broken by the sound of a large drone landing just a few feet away and transforming into a bipedal dog-headed robot. As it conducted its usual retinal scan and screen scroll of their vital information, Ismael noticed a horizontal scratch across its chest.

This time there was something different to the process. Both screens lit up, and a pair of bulky metallic antennas extended from the machine's shoulders, arcing round toward the two men, each holding a pair of self-locking handcuffs. "In accordance with Israeli law," its dog mouth intoned, "I am placing you both under arrest. Any attempt to escape will put your lives in danger." The two friends were wise enough to stretch their hands out willingly as the self-locking handcuffs flew to their wrists, snapping their hands together, before yanking them both to the ground. The dog robot began its transformation back into a drone, ready to airlift Rayyan and Ismael to Ashkelon Prison, where they would no doubt be held indefinitely under "administrative detention" laws.

But as the drone prepared to leave, its muzzle started to flinch oddly and its left leg suddenly jerked upward, kneeing itself in the chest. Orders began to issue from its dog mouth in an array of different languages: English, French, Chinese, and others the men didn't recognize. Its cheek screens scrolled through all kinds of images: schematics of missile launchers, satellite photography, maps of what appeared to be the location of Israeli troops just outside of the city's perimeter fence. One screen froze on this last map, while the other continued scrolling through the names and mug shots of high-ranking Gazans under the title "Assets." Suddenly smoke started rising from the dog robot's head until it stuttered to a complete standstill. The handcuffs sprung open.

Rayyan started running down the street. But his friend couldn't tear his eyes away from the slumped head of the machine in front of him.

"Come on, what are you waiting for?" Rayyan yelled, stopping to turn round. Ismael didn't move.

"Did you see that?"

"See what?" Rayyan shouted, now running back toward him.

"I didn't just jam it," he said holding up a battered-looking handset he'd been clutching all along in his pocket. "It spilled its guts for me."

"As I always say, you're a genius, Ismael, and we need to mass-market those things," Rayyan replied, grabbing Ismael by the upper arm. "But come on."

"Listen. The IDs it just scrolled through—that was its most valuable information. This little device"—Ismael waved the handset again—"gave it a psychic stomach bug, and what it threw up was the most classified information it had access to. Don't you see what this means, bro?"

Rayyan looked lost.

"The AIs have a subconscious! It chose to share this, to confess *this*. It could have shared a million other data sets, but this was the one it was least comfortable with."

"It's a trap," Rayyan said without looking at his friend. "And even if it isn't, what can we do with it? Drones are tracked; if we drag it off somewhere to download all that, the whole Israeli army would be knocking at our door."

Not if we take it underground," Ismael replied, still staring at his keypad. "It will lose its GPS signal. Look, this is a gift; we can't just pass it up. Besides, they know about us already, clearly. They'll just send another drone soon, and then what? Do you want us to keep running forever? Let's just take this one; we have nothing to lose."

Ismael pleaded with his friend, who just stood there trying to think. Rayyan knew that Ismael was right: there was no point in just running; they needed to go into hiding, and they needed any advantage they could get. He didn't relish the prospect of returning to a life on the streets, again, on the run.

"OK, OK," Rayyan conceded, helping his friend to lift the robot's heavy carcass into the back seat of his self-drive, parked across the street from the café. They instructed the car to travel at top speed. Ismael had long since hacked into its limiters, so they watched with some apprehension as the self-drive swerved around kids playing hologram football in the street and pedestrians on motorized skateboards. Five minutes later they were frantically carrying the machine up the steps of the municipality building and bundling it into the nearest lift. After taking a second lift, a few moments later, they felt they were plunging deeper than they had ever gone before. Ismael had been the one choosing the lifts and the destinations. Every few minutes or so he could link his handset to the lift's computer and name a new destination—usually the name of some long-lost village that his grandmother had told him tales about—coupled with the phrase "but don't alight." This, he explained to Rayyan, was his way of making a longer journey, which, combined with his handset's masking hack, would make the journey untraceable in the lift's records.

"All those permit applications they rejected," Rayyan said in awe. "We could have hacked our way out of Gaza all along."

When the doors eventually opened, they came out into a platform marked "Amman Tunnel." They had crossed the entirety of Palestine and now appeared to be in a different country altogether. The tunnel, Rayyan explained to Ismael, was strictly for emergencies and for use by the president and his diplomats only.

"What do we do now?" Rayyan asked, contemplating the lifeless dog robot on the floor of the platform beside them.

"Well, now we reboot it and find out what it was trying to share with us. Believe me, I was born for this hack. Hey, why don't you go get us some food and coffee, and I'll get started." Without even looking at his companion, Ismael started unzipping his backpack, opened his laptop, and patched it into the robot. Meanwhile, Rayyan headed up a flight of old-fashioned stairs to ground level. On their way here, he had shown Ismael the schematic of where the lift would come out, slap-bang in the heart of Amman, opposite the Third Circle, not far from Rainbow Street. They had both heard stories about how crowded Amman was, being the only reliably peaceful country in the whole region. With the exception of the United Kingdom of Saudi, it was also the only country in the region that hadn't been divided into various states. When he returned an hour later, laden with falafel sandwiches and bottles of Coca-Cola, he couldn't stop talking about what he'd seen: billboards advertising gadgets he'd never heard of; Israelis, Jordanians, and Pal-refs laughing and joking with each other in the shops—clearly living side by side. Shops accepting shekels. So full was he with his own news, he barely noticed the beaming grin on his friend's face, the lights pulsing behind the robot's eyes, and the data streaming down the laptop's screen.

"Look at this," Ismael screeched.

"Hey, what did I call you? Oh yes, Balfour! Hey, Balfour, dance for us!" The robot started twirling around, playing Hebrew music and gyrating the way you might expect a bipedal robot with a dog-shaped head to gyrate.

"What the hell?"

"It's mine now—my own little pet. I have overridden all the IDF protocols, and I can make it do whatever I want!"

"This is dangerous," Rayyan muttered.

"More dangerous than what we've done already? Why?"

"Well, we get it to do anything we like? Any crime we want, any retaliation; it will make us invincible."

"Damn right!" Ismael interjected. "The information it's shared alone is game-changing. Man, I have details of President Zourob's imminent attack against us. I have the names of people leading the forces, the names of Israeli officials supporting it. But above all, this damn thing is somehow connected to the central database in Israel, and guess what? I have access to everyone's details, including phone numbers in Palestine, Israel, Jordan, and Egypt. I can send all of them a text message right now if I want to."

"What?" the plastic bag with falafel sandwiches fell from Rayyan's hands. "Wait, we need to take this back to the president. We need to let him know."

Without thinking, Rayyan bundled the three of them back into the lift and hit a button on his handset. Their stomachs grumbled as they tunneled sideways through the Judean mountain crust. Ismael in particular lamented the image of the plastic bag containing his falafel abandoned on the platform. Eventually they arrived at the Gaza City Municipality Building and switched into the lift marked with what Ismael now recognized as the president's seal. Lamma was already in the office, having received their message insisting on her attendance. She couldn't believe her eyes when the two of them walked through the door carrying the robot.

"What the hell?" she said, looking at Rayyan, and immediately called for her personal assistant to come in and apprehend the two visitors. "Are you Israeli agents now?" she asked bluntly. Mr. Hamoud sidestepped toward his desk, with thoughts of the panic button written all over his face.

"No, wait—please don't, Mr. President, we can explain."

Ismael did all the talking. Rayyan simply stood still, at first frozen with fear, but after a moment a little smile flickered across his face.

"This machine came to arrest us this morning, but it malfunctioned, and we managed to hack it. It reports to me now; it does anything I want it to. Watch. Balfour, become a drone!" The machine instantly folded its limbs, extended its antenna, and began hovering toward the ceiling. "Balfour, tell Lamma who your master is and who your enemies are!"

"My name is Balfour, and my master is Mr. Ismael. My enemies are the enemies of the Republic of Gaza City."

Rayyan and Ismael explained everything about the leaked attack plans, the informants' IDs, and most of all the databases.

"Sir, this thing is tracked," Lamma interrupted. "We have to destroy it immediately. It could be relaying this conversation, and our location, to the Israelis right now."

"Don't worry," Ismael smiled. "I've disabled that too. We're safe—well, not Rayyan and me, because we're still on their list—but you are."

"OK, you two need to be taken to a safe house," the president answered firmly. "I need to think about what I am going to do with this. Once more, it seems, you two bozos have brought us another gift without fully understanding it. Lamma, will you get me Senator Shawwa?"

*

Ms. Shawwa was sweating as she reread the final draft of the message that was going to be sent out to all citizens—over three hundred million people—across the entire region.

"Mr. President. It's ready. Would you like to press the send button?"

Mr. Hamoud stared over her shoulder, reading for what felt like the millionth time:

> To all those who believe in justice, to those who still believe in the future, I, Mr. Hamad Hamoud, President of the Republic of Gaza City, appeal to you to stand with us. When we won the privilege of hosting the Olympic Games, we saw it as an opportunity to redress decades of separation and a century of fighting—to come together as humans, no matter what our differences. However, it has recently come to our attention that the Israelis and the president of Rafah are planning to attack us with the express purpose of canceling the Games. I appeal to you to rise tomorrow at midday, come out in the streets, walk with your leaders, and declare your opposition to this. Let us make this a show of solidarity and a rejection of any further wars. Thank you, and may Allah bless you all.

Mr. Hamoud cross-checked the Hebrew translation, and then he pressed the button. For a moment everyone stared at the floor in silence. Lamma eventually broke the spell by walking toward Ismael and Rayyan and patting them heartily on the shoulders. "You two brought so much trouble to this city; why couldn't you be like everyone else and just live your lives?"

"We chose none of this," Rayyan was quick to answer.

Lamma approached the president, who looked tired and anxious. "My fellow Palestinians," he addressed those in the room. "We've done what we can. Let's see what happens. I am tired now. I need a rest. Tomorrow we will either wake up with peace or further trouble. Whichever it is, things will never be the same again. These two idiots may be what we've all been waiting for, for better or worse. Good night, Lamma. I hope you can lead this nation to peace after I'm gone."

*

At 11 a.m. the following morning, the president, Lamma, Rayyan, Ismael, Ms. Asmaa, and the entire municipality building staff stood outside the president's office. A TV crew was recording the scene as Mr. Hamoud declared the start of his March for Peace. Knowing that half of the city now surrounded the building, he spoke directly to the camera, asking the rest of Gaza's citizens, those not yet out in the square, to walk with him, from here up to the northernmost border point, then down to the southernmost, from the gates of Erez to the gates of Nuseirat. "I believe that our fellow Palestinians will join us."

As they started to march from the president's office, whoever remained in their homes or offices came out and joined the throng. As the president's march passed by El Wihda Street, the momentum was visibly gathering. People started closing their shops; others came out of the mosques to join in. By the time they reached El Jalaa Street, the march was already two hundred thousand strong, all chanting and calling for peace.

The march continued through El Saha, then upward onto Omar El Mukhtar Street. By the time they got to Shujaia, the numbers had reached over three hundred thousand. The scene was overwhelming for Rayyan, who chanted louder and more excitedly at every new corner.

Everyone was marching peacefully until they reached the Sheikh Ejleen area by the beach, very close to the border with Nuseirat. An

Israeli drone appeared, transforming into a bipedal robot as it landed, effectively blocking the path of the march. It extended its shoulder antenna and crossed them resolutely, staring at the advancing crowd.

"Mr. Hamoud," it announced in its monotone, "it has been deemed that you are contravening Article 48A of the 2026 Peace Accord; I am hereby placing you under arrest."

The crowd fell silent as hundreds at the front tried their best to casually look away, look up or down, so the robot couldn't scan them. The president, by contrast, walked straight up to the drone and stared directly into its lifeless eyes. He gave it a kick with his foot, and everyone cheered again.

"Security unit under attack: engage now," the robot intoned, then fired a round of bullets directly between the president's eyes.

The president's body fell backward, sending up a small cloud of dust as it hit the ground. The cheering ceased and everyone stared dumbstruck at the pool of dusty blood spreading slowly from the back of their leader's head. People started to scream and run toward the robot, presumably to attack it. Meters before reaching it, they all found themselves fragmenting, midair, as the TV cameras automatically powered down.

More drones appeared in the sky, and before too long, an army of metallic robots had assembled to face the angry protesters, who were undeterred and started running toward them. The robots opened fire across the promenade where the president had been shot, as well as across the beach where many protesters had fled. They continued to scour the area, spraying bullets in all directions, for a further forty-five minutes. When they eventually stopped, the air was thick with dark smoke. Waves lapped the shore with blood.

Thousands more, many of whom were at the rear of the march, managed to run away in all directions. Ismael was on the ground, crouching behind a vape kiosk. He had been shot in the knee, but once the bullets had stopped, he started hobbling back along the promenade to look for Rayyan. There was no sign of him.

His legs gave way and he collapsed—to his knees first, then his hands caught the ground before it slammed into his chest. All was silent; the whole city lay lifeless—only Ismael's heavy breathing and the sound of waves could be heard. After a few moments, he tried crawling on all fours, then, slowly gathering strength, he got up and began limping across a terrain strewn with corpses, dark gouts of blood crusting on the yellow sand. Ismael kept walking until he reached the border. He wanted the robots to come back, to shoot him. Two crows came into view and started cawing loudly as they circled the corpse of a woman. Ismael wondered whose body it was; she looked in her twenties, lying to her side with one hand clutching her stomach where the bullet had hit. He thought of the woman's family and whether they were waiting for her at home or if they too were lying dead somewhere nearby. Ismael shut his eyes.

*

He woke up three days later in Al Ahli Hospital, his leg bandaged and his head spinning from the medication. Through blurred eyes he tried to focus on the TV screen on the other side of the room. One headline declared that the International Criminal Court would conduct an investigation into what had happened. Then another headline ran along the bottom of the screen about an emergency meeting that the IOC was holding in Zurich to determine whether to go ahead with the 39th Games in a new location or, for the first time in the modern era, to let the torch go out.

Fuck Your Lecture on Craft, My People Are Dying
NOOR HINDI

Colonizers write about flowers.
I tell you about children throwing rocks at Israeli tanks
seconds before becoming daisies.
I want to be like those poets who care about the moon.
Palestinians don't see the moon from jail cells and prisons.
It's so beautiful, the moon.
They're so beautiful, the flowers.
I pick flowers for my dead father when I'm sad.
He watches Al Jazeera all day.
I wish Jessica would stop texting me *Happy Ramadan*.
I know I'm American because when I walk into a room something dies.
Metaphors about death are for poets who think ghosts care about sound.
When I die, I promise to haunt you forever.
One day, I'll write about the flowers like we own them.

Samir Harb, *Rafah*, 2024. Screengrab from animation. Courtesy of the artist.

Rafah

SAMIR HARB

Against a soundtrack of real bombs dropping around a tent in Rafah, an already blurred drawing of a yellowed cityscape shakes with smoke and white outbursts as the word *Rafah* flashes in Arabic and English. Samir Harb's eerie sixteen-second animation captures the artist's outrage. He writes on Instagram: "WAKE UP—actually, don't wake up. It is unnecessary. Save your #humanity, and save the last bit of it. Rafah is the last city left, with more than 1.5 [million] people being bombarded!" Harb and @palestinianhustle, which originally posted the bombing sounds, belong to an ecosystem of Palestinian artists and activists on social media who will not be silenced.

Mohammad Sabaaneh, *She Is Mum*, 2023, detail. Brush-pen and ink drawing, 14 x 14 cm. Courtesy of the artist.

They Kill Writers, Don't They?
JORDAN ELGRABLY

Murder is the ultimate form of censorship, yet when a regime kills a writer, a poet, or a journalist, the writer's words live on. Spain's dictator, Francisco Franco, who ruled the country for four decades, pursued a brutal policy of repression against Spanish poets and writers, evidenced by the fascist murder of poet Federico García Lorca. Franco feared the threat that writers posed; little known is the fact that he had been a journalist who wrote ninety-one articles under three pseudonyms for the right-wing rag *Arriba*.

In Iran, Ayatollah Khomeini and Mohammad Khatami and their regime's supporters were responsible for a spate of murders, from 1988 to 1998, that included dozens of writers, poets, translators, and intellectuals, including Dariush Forouhar, Mohammad Mokhtari, Mohammad Jafar Pouyandeh, Majid Sharif, Ali Akbar Saidi Sirjani, and Fereydoun Farrokhzad, the brother of the late poet Forugh Farrokhzad.

Under Joseph Stalin, many writers were imprisoned, sent to Siberian work camps, or driven to suicide (among them Osip Mandelstam, Sergei Yesenin, and Vladimir Mayakovsky). In recounting Stalin's story, the historian Simon Sebag Montefiore wrote, "Literature mattered greatly to Stalin. He may have demanded 'engineers of the human soul' but he was himself far from the oafish philistine which his manners would suggest. He not only admired and appreciated great literature, he discerned the difference between hackery and genius." Nonetheless, one of the writers Stalin silenced was Isaac Babel, who had published stories critical of the Russian army. Babel was accused of "being a member of a terrorist conspiracy" and cut down by a firing squad. Before they took him out into the yard, he denied all the accusations against him, his last words being, "I am asking for only one thing—let me finish my work." Decades later, after the fall of the Soviet Union, the archives of the KGB were opened and Babel was exonerated.

Today, Israel declares itself "the only democracy in the Middle East" and insists it follows international law, yet it offers no explanation or legal justification for having murdered more writers than any other country in the world.

*,

I remember feeling shock and disbelief when I first learned about writers who were killed for their books and ideas, for their poems and short stories. Were their words so dangerous as to merit their execution? Could writing really be a lethal profession? This is especially egregious when it comes to Arab or Muslim writers, whose lives, after all, appear to be worth far less in the eyes of the West. We saw the explicit discrimination and double standards with which Arab casualties are treated in the response to the war in Ukraine, when the public and media were outraged by Russian bombs murdering Ukrainian women and children yet had been indifferent to the same wanton killing of Syrian women and children when Russian munitions assisted Bashar al-Assad in the murder of his own people.[1] We witnessed it again in the universal condemnation of Israel's killing by drone of the seven humanitarian aid workers deployed by World Central Kitchen in Gaza, and yet there was no public outcry in response to the killing of more than two hundred Palestinian humanitarian aid workers in the months prior to Israel's April 1, 2024, attack.[2]

One of the reasons I was determined to launch the *Markaz Review* was that I knew from experience that Western readers could not easily find original writing and work in translation from Arab and other writers from the Middle East and North Africa, who were speaking

---

1   Anna Lekas Miller, "Ukraine War Reminds Refugees Some Are More Equal Than Others," *Markaz Review*, March 7, 2022.
2   Bethan McKernan & Ben Doherty, "Seven Gaza Aid Workers including UK, US and Australian Citizens Killed in Israeli Strike, Charity Says," *Guardian*, April 2, 2024.

in their own voices. I have been endlessly enriched by reading the poets and writers from the region I prefer to call "the center of the world" rather than the greater Middle East. But one wonders, are these Palestinian, Syrian, Iraqi, Egyptian, Lebanese, Moroccan, Libyan, Sudanese, Algerian, Tunisian, Turkish, Kurdish, Afghan, and Iranian writers, among others, receiving their due recognition, taking their place on the shelves of their Western peers? Or do they remain mostly marginal, rarely to be recognized in the canon of world literature?

*

Ghassan Kanafani would be among the first writers to be killed by Israel. It is the brevity of his life and the manner his death that strikes me as not only harrowing but ironic, for despite his assassination, the writer has remained omnipresent with us over the years—almost as if his killers had never fulfilled their nefarious mission.

Kanafani was born in Akka, Palestine in 1936. He was twelve years old during the exodus from the war that would set the stage for the Israeli–Palestinian conflict that endures to this day. In 1948, as a result of the Nakba, his lawyer father fled with the family, first to Beirut and then to Damascus, where Kanafani attended university to become a writer, and along with Samira Azzam,[3] a forerunner of contemporary Palestinian fiction.

Over four collections of short stories, Kanafani captured the desolation of statelessness, of Palestinians without passports, of refugees who carried with them on their exodus the deeds and keys to their homes, to which Israel would never allow them to return.

On July 8, 1972, Kanafani was killed when his car blew up in downtown Beirut. With him was his sister's seventeen-year-old daughter, Lamees, who was visiting Beirut for the first time from Damascus, eager to see the sights.

Kanafani was a member of the Popular Front for the Liberation

---

3   See Samira Azzam's story collection *Out of Time*, trans. Ranya Abdelrahman (ArabLit Books, 2022).

of Palestine (PFLP), a secular revolutionary socialist organization founded in 1967 by his friend George Habash; Kanafani was the founder and editor of the PFLP's much-read and widely quoted weekly newspaper, *Al-Hadaf*.[4]

Kanafani never so much as touched a weapon but wielded his pen prolifically. He was above all a Palestinian writer who wrote as a form of resistance, wanting to free Palestinians from their shackles. At the time of his death he had published three novellas: the most famous of them being *Men in the Sun*, but also *All That's Left to You* and *Return to Haifa*.

He insisted that he'd become a novelist because of his political devotion to the Palestinian cause, which he believed did not concern Palestinians only but was a cause for all freedom fighters. Unfortunately for his readers, when the Mossad blew up his car in downtown Beirut, they obliterated Kanafani's chance to complete three novels left unfinished, *Al-Ashiq* (*The Lover*), *Al-Ama wa Al-Atrash* (*The Blind and the Deaf*), and *Barquq Nisan* (*April Anemones*).[5]

The next writer on Israel's hit list was Wael Zwaiter (1934–1972), a Palestinian in Rome who had studied literature and philosophy and whose great life project was to translate *One Thousand and One Nights* into Italian. His father, Adel Zwaiter, had been a lawyer and a scholar who translated Voltaire and Rousseau into Arabic. Fluent in Arabic as well as French, Italian, and English, Zwaiter was a bon vivant who had befriended the great Italian novelist Alberto Moravia and lived for the power and beauty of words. Two Mossad agents riddled him with eleven bullets in the lobby of his apartment building in Rome on October 16, 1972, just three months after the agency had killed Kanafani.[6]

Next they tracked down exiled Palestinian intellectual Mahmoud Hamshari (1939–1973). A writer with a PhD in history from Jussieu, he was the Paris representative of the Palestine Liberation Organization, but the Israelis accused him, erroneously as it turns out, of being a

---

4   Elias Khoury, "Remembering Ghassan Kanafani, or How a Nation Was Born of Storytelling," *Journal of Palestine Studies* 42, no. 3 (Spring 2013).

5   See introduction to *All That's Left to You*, trans. May Jayyusi and Jeremy Reed (University of Austin Press, 1990).

6   *My Great Arab Melancholy*, Lamia Ziadé (London: Pluto Press, 2024), 256–258.

leader of the Black September Organization, which had been blamed for the deaths of Israeli athletes in Munich in September 1972.[7] The Mossad booby-trapped his home phone, which blew up in his hand on December 8, 1972, and he died in the hospital a few days later.

The Israelis considered these three men "terrorists," while we might think of them as freedom fighters—although none of them was a trained militant.

Decades later, not satisfied with silencing short story writers, novelists, and translators, an unknown Israeli politician or military commander would order the extrajudicial killing of Palestinian American journalist Shireen Abu Akleh (1971–2022). She was reporting for Al Jazeera from Jenin, in the occupied West Bank, when she was shot in the head by a sniper on May 11, 2022. A television journalist wearing blue body armor marked PRESS, visible from a great distance, Abu Akleh had been an intrepid reporter covering Israel/Palestine and the Arab world for more than two decades. Her death caused a great commotion among all Palestinians and members of the press, who feared that if Israel could shoot a journalist—an American citizen, no less—point-blank, in broad daylight, and get away with it, then more than ever before, our lives as journalists would be greatly endangered around the world.

That summer, the US Department of Justice issued statements leading those concerned to believe that the US would search for her killers, while both the *New York Times* and the *Washington Post* ordered their own investigations. But on July 4, 2022, US State Department spokesperson Ned Price declared that while "gunfire from IDF positions was likely responsible for the death of Shireen Abu Akleh," there was no reason to believe "that this was intentional but rather the result of tragic circumstances during an IDF-led military operation against factions of Palestinian Islamic Jihad on May 11, 2022, in Jenin, which followed a series of terrorist attacks in Israel."[8]

---

7   Most of the Israeli athletes were killed when West German police fired upon them at the Munich airport, where Black September militants were holding them hostage. *Brittanica*, s.v. "Munich Massacre."

8   Ned Price, "On the Killing of Shireen Abu Akleh," US State Department, July 4, 2022.

An Israeli military press officer could not have done a better job of composing what sounds suspiciously like *hasbara*, standard Israeli propaganda that whitewashes the violence of the occupation. Still today, the identity of the Israeli shooter who killed Abu Akleh remains unknown. However, in an extensive report, Forensic Architecture, which was recognized for its work in the field of journalism with a Peabody Award for Digital and Interactive Storytelling, in 2021, found that "the Israeli army marksman deliberately and repeatedly targeted Shireen and her fellow journalists with the intention to kill."[9]

As former PLO negotiator and Haifa-based lawyer Diana Buttu noted, Abu Akleh's assassination followed an Israeli pattern of targeting the media. In 2021 they "bombed the offices of the Associated Press and Al Jazeera in Gaza City, destroying a twelve-story building in a densely populated urban area. The military claimed that it was targeting Hamas military intelligence. But press-freedom groups accused Israel of trying to obstruct journalists, and AP's president and CEO at the time said there was no indication of any Hamas activity in the building."

Buttu went on: "A complaint filed at the International Criminal Court by the International Federation of Journalists and two Palestinian organizations two weeks before Shireen was killed accused Israel of systematically targeting Palestinian journalists working in the occupied territories. The Committee to Protect Journalists has confirmed the killing of 19 journalists in the occupied territories since 1992, 15 of whom were Palestinians."[10]

October 7, 2023

Many more poets, writers, and journalists were killed by Israel in the war that began on October 7, 2023. On that Saturday, Hamas pulled off a surprise military raid in southern Israel, in which thousands of

9 "Shireen Abu Akleh: The Extrajudicial Killing of a Journalist Extended Report," Forensic Architecture & Al-Haq, November 4, 2022.
10 Diana Buttu, "Journalist Shireen Abu Akleh Was Killed in Jenin. Who Will Be Next?" *New York Times*, May 25, 2022.

militants broke out of Gaza and killed nearly 1,200 Israeli soldiers, police, and civilians, including women and children, taking more than 250 hostages. Israel framed the raid as Israel's 9/11, defining it as the worst attack on the Jews since the Holocaust.

In reprisal, among the thousands of Palestinians who would die beneath the bombs in the ensuing months was one of Gaza's most beloved poets and storytellers, Refaat Alareer (1979–2023). A professor of English literature at the Islamic University of Gaza, where he taught Shakespeare and the poetry of T. S. Eliot, among other subjects, Alareer had cofounded the We Are Not Numbers initiative and intentionally wrote in English to share Palestinian stories with the world.[11] But the university was bombed, its buildings destroyed on the night of October 10, 2023, and Alareer was killed on December 8, 2023, after he had received a menacing phone call from Israeli military intelligence.[12]

In November he shared one of his poems, which would be recited by celebrity actors and others and reposted by thousands on social media. The poem concluded, "If I must die / let it bring hope / let it be a tale."

Early in the war, the Palestinian legal and human rights NGO Al-Haq, along with Law in the Service of Man, Al Mezan Center for Human Rights, and the Palestinian Centre for Human Rights appealed to the UN to intervene with Israel to protect journalists, who were being killed, arrested, or disappeared.[13]

Human Rights Watch determined that the Israeli strikes in southern Lebanon on October 13, 2023, which "killed Reuters journalist Issam Abdallah and injured six other journalists was an apparently deliberate attack on civilians and thus a war crime."[14]

Closely monitoring the conflict, the Committee to Project Journalists

---

11 See *Gaza Writes Back: Short Stories from Young Writers in Gaza*, ed. Refaat Alareer (Charlottesville, VA: Just World Books, 2014).

12 As related by his poet friend, Mosab Abu Toha, in a Twitter (X) post shortly before Alareer was killed.

13 "Joint Urgent Appeal to UN Special Procedures on Journalists Killed While Reporting in Gaza, Highlights Israel in Breach of International Law," Al-Haq, October 13, 2023.

14 "Israel: Strikes on Journalists in Lebanon Apparently Deliberate," Human Rights Watch, December 7, 2023.

claimed there was a "pattern of journalists in Gaza reporting receiving threats, and subsequently, their family members being killed." According to the CPJ, Al Jazeera journalist Anas Al-Sharif told his employers "that he had received multiple phone calls from officers in the Israeli army instructing him to cease coverage and leave northern Gaza. Additionally, he received voice notes on WhatsApp disclosing his location."[15]

On the long list of those killed in Gaza are Asem Al-Barsh, journalist for Al Najah radio, taken out by sniper fire; Bilal Jadallah of the Palestinian Press House, victim of a direct missile strike on his car as he was leaving his place of work; Montaser Al-Sawaf, whose house was twice targeted by missile fire; Rushdi Al Siraj, victim of a direct hit on his home; Hassouna Salim of the Quds News agency, killed by a missile after receiving death threats; Sari Mansour, photojournalist for Quds News, killed in the same attack; Samer Abu Daqqa, Al Jazeera correspondent who appears to have been killed by precision drone fire, an attack in which Al Jazeera bureau chief Wael Dahdouh was wounded.[16] Early in January 2024, Israel killed Dahdouh's son Hamza Dahdouh, also a journalist with Al Jazeera, along with journalist Mustafa Thuraya, when both were traveling in Khan Younis in a car that was hit by a missile.[17] As of this writing Wael Dahdouh is still alive, but Israel has killed most of his family members.

On December 29, 2023, the Republic of South Africa initiated proceedings in the International Court of Justice against the State of Israel, alleging breaches of the 1948 Convention on the Prevention and Punishment of the Crime of Genocide. After more than one hundred days of war and over eighty-five journalists dead, Reporters Without Borders had filed two complaints against Israel in the International Criminal Court in the Hague. On January 5, 2024, ICC prosecutor Karim

---

15   Chris McGreal, "Israeli military accused of targeting journalists and their families in Gaza," *Guardian*, December 21, 2023.
16   "Israel-Gaza War Takes Toll on Journalists," Committee to Protect Journalists, December 21, 2023.
17   "Hamza, Son of Al Jazeera's Wael Dahdouh, Killed in Israeli Attack in Gaza," Al Jazeera, January 7, 2024.

Khan's office stated for the first time that crimes against journalists were included in its investigation of possible war crimes committed by Israel.

According to the Gaza's Government Media office, between October 7, 2023, and January 11, 2024, Israel killed 117 journalists and media workers in the Gaza Strip, including at least 14 female journalists, and destroyed over 80 media institutions. On January 11, 2024, Al-Haq et alia issued a call for an investigation, stating, "We, the Palestinian Centre for Human Rights (PCHR), Al Mezan, and Al-Haq, maintain that the Israeli authorities have continuously and intentionally targeted journalists since the start of the military campaign against Gaza. These widespread attacks are aimed at normalizing the targeting of journalists and their institutions and turning them into legitimate and permissible targets. We believe that this is part of a systematic policy aimed at intimidating journalists and silencing their voices in order to obscure and hide the crimes and atrocities committed in Gaza, including the ongoing crime of genocide."[18]

According to UN special rapporteur Francesca Albanese's March 24, 2024, report on Israel in the occupied Palestinian territory, "Anatomy of a Genocide," the more than 30,000 Palestinian victims in Israel's assault on Gaza included 125 journalists.[19]

Dr. Atef Abu Saif, author of *Don't Look Left: Diary of a Genocide* (Comma Press, 2024), noted in a December 2023 report from Gaza's Ministry of Culture: "The war on culture has always been at the heart of the aggressors' war on our people, as the real war is a war on the narrative to steal the land and its rich treasures of knowledge, history, and civilization, along with the stories it holds."[20]

---

18 "Israel's Continued, Deliberate Targeting of Journalists in Gaza Warrants Investigation as Crime Against Humanity of Persecution," Al-Haq, January 11, 2024.
19 Download a PDF of the report at https://www.un.org/unispal/document/anatomy-of-a-genocide-report-of-the-special-rapporteur-on-the-situation-of-human-rights-in-the-palestinian-territory-occupied-since-1967-to-human-rights-council-advance-unedited-version-a-hrc-55/
20 "The Second Preliminary Report on the Cultural Sector Damage," ArabLit pdf, December 2023.

A nonexhaustive account of the poets and writers killed in Gaza[21] in 2023 must include, as LitHub noted:

* Thirty-two-year-old novelist, poet, and educator Hiba Abu Nada was respected in the Palestinian literary community. She was the author of the novel *Oxygen Is Not for the Dead* and was killed alongside her son by an Israeli air strike in Khan Yunis on October 20, 2023. She shared her last poem on X just days before she was killed: *"Gaza's night is dark apart from the glow of rockets, quiet apart from the sound of the bombs, terrifying apart from the comfort of prayer, black apart from the light of the martyrs. Goodnight, Gaza."*

* The poet, novelist, and community activist Omar Faris Abu Shaweesh was killed on October 7 during the shelling of the Nuseirat refugee camp in Gaza.

* The writer and Palestinian heritage advocate Abdul Karim Al-Hashash, along with many of his family members, was killed on October 23 in the city of Rafah.

* Inas al-Saqa, a celebrated playwright, actor, and educator who worked extensively in children's theater, was killed along with her three children, Sara, Leen, and Ibrahim, by an Israeli air strike in late October.

* Dr. Jihad Suleiman Al-Masri died on October 17, succumbing to injuries sustained in the Israeli shelling of Khan Yunis. He had been on his way to join his wife and daughter at the time of the attack. Al-Masri was a historian and university professor whose contributions spanned generations.

* Writer, journalist, and photographer Yousef Dawas was killed by an Israeli air strike on his family home in northern Gaza on October 14.

* Poet and educational researcher Shahdah Al-Buhbahan was killed,

---

21 Dan Sheehan, "These are the Poets and Writers who have been Killed in Gaza," *LitHub*, December 21, 2023.

alongside his granddaughter, by an Israeli air strike in Gaza on November 6.

* Poet and writer Nour al-Din Hajjaj was killed by an Israeli air strike on his home in Al-Shujaiyya on December 2.

* Writer and journalist Mustafa Hassan Mahmoud Al-Sawwaf was killed, alongside several members of his family, when an Israeli shell struck his home on November 18.

* On October 16, writer Abdullah Al-Aqad was killed, alongside his wife and children, when an Israeli shell struck his house in Khan Younis.

* Writer Dr. Said Talal Al-Dahshan and his family were killed by an Israeli air strike on October 11.

* Saleem Al-Naffar was a renowned poet who advocated for peaceful resistance and whose poetry expressed the struggle of Palestinians to survive and to be remembered in history. On December 7, Al-Naffar and his family were killed in an Israeli air strike on their home in Gaza City.

Cultural Annihilation

Israel's attacks on Palestinians have not been limited to writers, poets, and journalists. It appears to be pursuing a policy of cultural annihilation. One of hundreds of examples over time includes the Israeli army's assault on the Sakakini Cultural Center, in Ramallah, in 2002. "They broke in and trashed the place," said cofounder Adila Laidi. Reporting for the *Guardian*, author William Dalrymple added:

> The previous day, on a visit to Bethlehem, I had seen a
> similar arts centre run by the Lutheran Church. The
> pastor had taken me around, showing how Israeli troops
> had completely smashed up the new $2 million Lutheran
> centre, blowing up workshops, smashing windows and fax
> machines, shooting up photocopiers, and bringing down
> ceilings with explosive charges in an oddly pointless bout of
> thuggery that caused over half a million dollars' worth of

damage. Compared to that, the Sakakini got off lightly, with permanent damage only to doors and computers.[22]

There was also the air strike on Gaza's Said al-Mishal Cultural Center, a large venue for theatrical and music performances and a major symbol of Palestinian culture and identity. This did not take place during one of the four major Israeli onslaughts—2008 to 2009, 2014, 2021, or 2023 to 2024—but on August 9, 2018, during a twenty-four-hour skirmish between Hamas and the IDF. Ahead of its destruction, nearby Gazan residents received word from the Israeli military that the building would be hit, but why raze this cultural landmark, which contained a library and the offices of arts associations? Mohammed Obain, who helped run a *dabke* dance company, said afterward, "Our memories have vanished now. I don't know if we can create new ones. We will try again, but I am not sure if I can convince my colleagues to continue."[23]

On November 27, 2023, the main public library of Gaza was destroyed. For what purpose? The Israeli military provided no explanation. According to a story reported in *LitHub*, "Municipal authorities in Gaza have accused the Israeli army of deliberately destroying thousands of books and historical documents. They have also called for the intervention of the United Nations Educational, Scientific and Cultural Organization (UNESCO) to 'intervene and protect cultural centers and condemn the occupation's targeting of these humanitarian facilities protected under international humanitarian law.' "[24] At the time, a writer for the *Los Angeles Times* asserted, "Libraries are cultural repositories. They hold collective memory, preserve cultural heritage, showcase societal development, and afford individuals the opportunity for learning and growth."[25]

Often when libraries and other cultural repositories, such as museums and universities, are bombed, irreplaceable books, archives, and

---

22 William Dalrymple, "A Culture Under Fire," *Guardian*, October 2, 2002.

23 Hazem Balousha and Oliver Holmes, "'Our Memories Have Vanished': the Palestinian Theatre Destroyed in a Bomb Strike," *Guardian*, August 22, 2018.

24 Dan Sheehan, "Gaza's Main Public Library Has Been Destroyed by Israeli Bombing," *LitHub*, November 27, 2023.

25 Laila Hussein Moustafa, "When Libraries Like Gaza's Are Destroyed, What's Lost Is Far More Than Books," *Los Angeles Times*, December 12, 2023.

artifacts are forever deleted from human history. The potential losses to our collective memory are staggering.

As of February 15, 2024, nearly all of Gaza's libraries, universities and cultural centers had been partially or completely decimated.[26]

✳

PEN International defends the rights of writers, and the International Federation of Journalists and the Committee to Protect Journalists both champion freedom of the press. In fact, the CPJ maintains an annual Global Impunity Index. It has found that in eight out of ten cases the murderers of journalists go free. "The murder of a journalist is the ultimate form of censorship, yet the perpetrators of such crimes are seldom held to account."[27]

The CPJ's 2023 Global Impunity Index lists the top twelve countries where the murderers of journalists go free. Israel heads the list, having killed more media workers between October 7 and December 31, 2023, than all the reporters killed during World War II. For Israel, to be a Palestinian writer, it seems, is to be an enemy of the state. There is no question that the voice of Ghassan Kanafani alarmed the Israelis to the point that they ordered his extrajudicial killing, but while Isaac Babel was exonerated long after his death, who will exonerate Kanafani for the crime of having been born in Akka, Palestine? Who will punish his murderers, among them Ehud Barak, who once boasted that he was part of the hit team that assassinated Kanafani and his niece in Beirut?[28]

And yet Israel is not Saudi Arabia or Iran—countries that do not pretend to be democracies. I contacted a number of Israeli officials for comment, asking:

---

26 "Israeli Damage to Archives, Libraries, and Museums in Gaza, October 2023–January 2024: A Preliminary Report from Librarians and Archivists with Palestine," Librarians with Palestine, February 2024.

27 Committee to Protect Journalists, Campaign Against Impunity.

28 When Kanafani turned on the ignition of his Austin 1100, a grenade connected to the ignition switch detonated and in turn detonated a three-kilo plastic bomb planted behind the bumper bar, according to Ami Pedahzur in *The Israeli Secret Services and the Struggle Against Terrorism* (New York: Columbia, 2009).

1. Why did you resolutely decide not to allow any foreign journalism coverage of your campaign in Gaza? (Even during World War II, foreign journalists were able to cover the fighting, just as foreign journalists are now covering the conflict in Ukraine with Russian forces.) Don't you want the world to hear your side of the story from independent, objective reporters?

2. Palestinian journalists and educators in Gaza have reported receiving phone calls from Israeli military units, threatening them with death before they were in fact targeted, either by missile, mortar, or sniper fire. How do you respond to the suggestion that Israel is deliberately targeting and killing journalists in Gaza?

3. Almost all of Gaza's universities and libraries are now partially or completely destroyed. Is there a policy of dismantling or destroying Palestinian educational facilities in Gaza, and if so, can you explain your reasoning?

Urgently seeking any kind of intelligent response, I reached out on multiple occasions to the offices of Israel's prime minister, minister of justice, minister of defense, and minister of education. No one within the government ever responded. Nor could I find any instance of Israel's media deploring the deaths of their Palestinian colleagues.[29] I asked law professor Neve Gordon, who formerly lived in Israel and is now based in the UK, for his thoughts on how Israel could possibly be justifying such a blatant violation of international law by killing Palestinian journalists, poets, and writers. In an email on April 8, 2024, Gordon wrote, "Ultimately, in my view it is all about restricting the flow and circulation of knowledge, trying to hide the atrocities Israel is carrying out in Gaza. In my mind, it is connected to

---

29 I don't include in this casual survey journalists such as Amira Hass and Gideon Levy, whose independent and often critical voices do not represent the publications they write for. However, see Ben Samuels, "Number of Journalists Killed in Israel-Gaza War Unparalleled, According to Committee to Protect Journalists Report," *Haaretz*, December 21, 2023.

the clamp down on human rights organizations, and the designation of six Palestinian organizations as supporting terrorism. Israel would like to carry out its crimes in the dark. Also important in this regard, is that since October 7, apart from *+972*, *Local Call* [*Sikha Mekomit* in Hebrew] and to a certain extent *Ha'aretz*, Israeli media outlets have been acting as amplifiers of the government's messages and not as watchdogs, which is their role in any open society."

Toward the end of 2023, Moustafa Bayoumi, author of *How Does It Feel to Be a Problem? Being Young and Arab in America* and *This Muslim American Life*, commented on the reality for Palestinian writers. "We know that in the history of the Palestinian struggle," he said, "Israel has actually assassinated many intellectuals—people who have never even picked up a gun but just picked up a pen. And that illustrates the power of culture, the power of thought, the power of precisely what is most menacing and dangerous to the oppressive."[30]

As long as Palestine writes, Israel will be reminded of its vain attempts made in 1948, 1972, 2023 to 2024, and all the years in between to stamp out and silence Palestinian culture. By reading Palestinians, we can refuse to allow Israel's assassinations of writers, poets, journalists, educators, and others who are part of the cultural narrative to succeed at erasing their memories. For they can kill writers, but they can never kill their words.

April 9, 2024

---

30   Radio Tabbouli, "Public Intellectuals," conversation with writers Lina Mounzer, Hisham Bustani, and Moustafa Bayoumi for the *Markaz Review*, November 1, 2023.

Jaime Scholnick, *Gaza: Mowing the Lawn*, 42, 2014, detail. Mixed media on panel, 7.5 x 11 in. Artwork appears courtesy of the artist.

Edward Said
Writing in the Service of Life
LAYLA ALAMMAR

In her 1919 biography of Egyptian feminist Malak Hifni Nasif, the *littérateur* May Ziadeh writes, "Life has a way of producing those who will be in her service." She goes on to explain how there are men and women who are born into a particular set of circumstances, who possess innate gifts, who are confronted by pressing conditions or an unbearable status quo, all of which compel them to say what has never been said before. They forge new trails, formulating groundbreaking knowledge or innovative modes of cultural and sociopolitical resistance. They emerge in a nexus of word, action, and passion to present life with what she finds herself in need of. The Palestinian American academic, critic, and political activist Edward W. Said (1935-2003) was one such soul—a man whose background, life trajectory, intellectual capacity, and talents coalesced to make him one of the great thinkers of our time.

September 2023 marked twenty years since Said's passing, leaving behind a legacy that has cast a long shadow across the Arab world and, in particular, the role of the intellectual in public life. Said authored dozens of books, essays, and lectures on topics such as the responsibility of the critic, the poetics of decolonization, classical music, the relationship between culture and imperialism, the agonies of exile, and the Palestinian cause. His landmark work *Orientalism* (1978) became a foundational text of postcolonial studies, influencing generations of scholars, writers, and artists. The book fundamentally reshaped our understanding of the networks linking power, knowledge, narrative, and perception. More importantly, it showed us how these networks operate on the flesh-and-blood landscape of history and, by extension, present-day realities.

As Said's popularity grew, so did his commitment to his burgeoning role as a public intellectual. He wrote newspaper articles and appeared in television interviews to speak on matters of representation, Arab and Muslim stereotypes in the media, and America's imperial ambitions in the Middle East. In packed lecture halls he debunked popular myths, such as Samuel Huntington's warmongering cry of a "clash of civilizations," and skewered orientalists for their lazy claims and shoddy scholarship (the shade he routinely threw at Bernard Lewis is, for me, a particular source of delight). Concurrently, his sense of duty toward the Palestinian struggle increased, and he served for fifteen years as an active member of the Palestinian National Council before parting ways with the leadership in 1993, over what he rightly saw as the surrendering of Palestine with the signing of the Oslo Accords.

I'll not go into detail about Said's life and work, for these have been covered across a range of books and articles. Instead, I'd like to focus on what Said has meant to me—as a writer, an academic, an Arab, and someone with a keen interest in the dialectic of power and representation. If you are lucky enough to ever be gripped by the workings of an exceptional mind, you'll find that the impact happens on multiple levels—intellectual, emotional, ontological—and the intimacy with which you begin to comprehend them washes over you in waves. When you find yourself in love with someone's mind, what you desire is complete immersion.

Like many others, my first exposure to Said came with *Orientalism*. I read that book at the vulnerable age of nineteen, and it resonated with me at a very visceral level, by which I mean that certain passages rang true even if I didn't completely understand what I was reading (for as much as I adore his prose, *Orientalism* is quite dense in parts). I read the book at an age when you begin to interrogate things you presumed were a given. I was questioning who I was and who I thought I might want to be; I was wrestling with my faith and what it was I truly believed in; I was reading more widely and deeply than ever before, leading me to the realization we all have (or *should* have around that age), which is that we really don't know very much at all. I'd been writing fiction for as long as I could remember, but this was also the time when the ambition for more began stirring in my breast. It was when I started entertaining the idea that a day might come when I would walk through a bookstore and find my own novels on the shelf.

I wondered what those novels would look like. What would they be about? Would they be set in my home country of Kuwait? Would they deal with the frustrations my friends and I felt in a society struggling with what it means to be modern? I wondered how a soccer mom in Dallas picking up my novel at her local Barnes & Noble might receive it. In *Orientalism*, Said writes, "It is a fallacy to assume that the swarming, unpredictable, and problematic mess in which human beings live can be understood on the basis of what books say; to apply what one learns out of a book literally to reality is to risk folly or ruin." And yet I knew, instinctively, that that was exactly what would happen. My novel would be understood as representing Kuwait in its totality. As *the* truth rather than *a* truth. Based on the book, assumptions would be made about an entire country, with its complexities and vastly differing sensibilities, and certain misconceptions might be confirmed and confidently tucked away. From Said's book I understood, for the first time and with enormous depth, that there was an image of Kuwait already constructed in and *by* what we might simplistically call the "Western world" and that it exerted tremendous power over any portrayal of *my* world that I might construct. In the introduction to *Orientalism* he calls this "the nexus of knowledge and power [that creates] 'the Oriental' and in a sense obliterat[es] him as a human being."

Nineteen-year-old me drew a severe red box around the last part of that sentence.

In my naiveté I had believed in the empathic power of literature, in its ability to create solidarities and foster human connections. I thought everyone read novels the way I did—as partial representations rather than as some total and objective truth. It took me a long time to realize that where I had almost infinite images of, say, America or England, readers there had very few, if any, images of Kuwait. Where any college-educated Kuwaiti would be able to rattle off a list of American novels or English writers, what would the average American be able to say about us? . . . apart from how their army cousin had been stationed in the country at some point. I began to see that it's only through a multiplicity of representations (what Deleuze and Guattari, in *Kafka: Towards a Minor Literature*, call an "assemblage of enunciation") that any semblance of "truth" might be approached. Said, for his part, was dubious about the entire enterprise, asserting that "representation is *eo ipso* implicated, intertwined, embedded, interwoven with a great many other things besides the 'truth,' which is itself a representation."

It takes time for an idea like that to truly sink in, to think of truth itself as a representation that is constructed and circulated, received and consumed, or to conceive of it as something that travels far beyond its origins, that outlives the context that produced it. Consider the "great many other things" that are interwoven with representations: language, culture, history, political and religious leanings, all the known and unknown idiosyncrasies of the representer. These constructions don't emerge from a vacuum, nor do they subsequently float in empty space. Rather, they inhabit what *Orientalism* determines to be "a common field of play [that has been] defined for them." In his more charitable moments, Said conceives of representations (such as novels) as belonging to a family, existing in a kind of ecosystem of references and linkages. His thoughts on the nature of representation are some of his most insightful and had a profound effect on how I would conceive of my writings, both creative and scholarly, from that point on.

So gripped was I by *Orientalism* that I went on to read (and reread) nearly everything Said wrote—from *Culture and Imperialism* to *Freud and the Non-European* to *Beginnings* to his brilliant essay collection, *Reflections on Exile*. Immersing myself in his corpus showed me a few things, perhaps the most significant of which was that you cannot be content with an intellectual's first utterance on a topic. Too often, it seems to me, references to some grand theory or statement begin and end with the first iteration of it—whether it's Said's *Orientalism*, Freud's theories of mourning and melancholia, or Adorno's claim regarding the writing of poetry after Auschwitz. These are but initial forays into extraordinarily complex spheres of interest and are in no way etched in stone. It's not enough to stop there. It's incumbent upon us to appreciate the totality of a great mind, to trace the genealogy of their thinking, the evolution of their statements on a given topic. It's bad enough that in many quarters Said has been reduced to a single idea; what's worse is that he's been confined to the very first shape that idea took when, in fact, he returns to it multiple times over the course of his career—in interviews, in other books, in prefaces to subsequent editions of *Orientalism* and in standalone essays.

My immersion in his writings also hammered home for me the value of rereading texts. An intellectual's work will always reward multiple encounters. The truth is that when we read, we never read with total concentration. There are always passages that our eyes will merely take in while the mind wanders off. More than that, we are not the same person with each reading. We will have grown, read other books, discovered other concepts, had experiences and met new people who enrich our lives. All of this will influence how we take in a text, what we get from it, what resonates most strongly at any given moment in time. My copies of Said's books register a topography of affect. In different colored highlighter pens, stars and exclamation points, lols and notations in the margins, I can trace the impact his words have had on me through the years. I can see clearly those illuminations that I found useful for a novel or my scholarly work or paragraphs that simply blew my mind.

I realize that at this point I run the risk of sliding into saccharine fawning, so let me acknowledge that Said's work is not without its limitations and blind spots. *Orientalism* has had its fair share of criticism—some legitimate, some utter nonsense. His views on Arab literature are restricted to mostly canonical work, such as that of Naguib Mahfouz, Ghassan Kanafani, and Tayeb Salih, and he displays shockingly little knowledge of women writers and intellectuals, whether Arab or not. In fact, in his 1993 Reith lectures, *Representations of the Intellectual*, only Virginia Woolf is mentioned. These weaknesses don't warrant dismissal of Said, of course, but they do tell us we need to proceed with caution when applying his thought to the sprawling mess that is the contemporary Arab world, as well as in thinking about our place and sense of being (as writers, academics, artists, etc.) within it.

By his own admission, Said found no topic so tedious to discuss as identity, which is ironic since, next to representations, his writing on the subject played such a large role in my conceptualization of identity, whether in my scholarly work, in my novels, or for my own sense of self. My first encounter with these ideas came toward the end of *Culture and Imperialism*. He talks about the push and pull between centers and peripherals, between hegemonic powers and those they impinge on. These forces are pivotal in shaping who we are and who we become. He says flashes of brilliance result from such "contrapuntal" living, from our awareness of and resistance (in literature, in art and film, in politics) to "the imperialist power that would otherwise compel you to disappear or to accept some miniature version of yourself as a doctrine to be passed out on a course syllabus."

Loathing the notion of labels or fixed parameters, identity for Said was dynamic, elastic, in constant flux and motion. He quotes Iranian intellectual Ali Shariati, who sees our identity as "a struggle, a constant becoming," that we are all "migrant[s] within [our] own soul[s]." Mahmoud Darwish, in his elegy to Said, expresses a similar sentiment, claiming that, like the wind, identity "has no ceiling. It has no abode. . . . He says: I am from there. I am from here. But neither am I there, nor here." Further ventriloquizing Said, he echoes the truth that we are all ultimately responsible for who we become, for identity, he says, is "the innovation of the individual to whom it belongs." It's an unending process of discovery, a tapestry we never complete and perhaps are not meant to.

I opened this piece saying that Said is someone who wrote in the service of life. His formulations had a profound impact, both subtle and explicit, on a wide range of fields and interests. It's not too much to say that his body of work has irrevocably altered the way we think about the power of narrative and representation as well as the relationship between knowledge, culture, and colonial force. More than that, he offered strategies for counteracting these forces (contrapuntal reading, worldliness) and urged us to go beyond trifling assertions of identity, to not be content with merely having a seat at the table, but to do something with it. As a public intellectual he modeled how one ought to hold fast to their principles, even when it complicated matters; indeed, the vocation of the intellectual, he writes, "involves both commitment and risk, boldness and vulnerability." Said recognized that, in every sense of the word, "intellectuals are *of* their time, herded along by the mass politics of representations embodied by the information or media industry, capable of resisting those only by disputing the images, official narratives, justifications of power circulated by an increasingly powerful media—and not only media, but whole trends of thought that maintain the status quo, keep things within an acceptable and sanctioned perspective on actuality." Time and again, Said would embody this ethos in his writings and public utterances.

But where does this leave us? All our atomized Arab souls, crushed over and over by unrelenting, gargantuan forces. We were never short on intellectuals in the past—men and women who were able to harness the seething political, social, and psychical energies around them, to capture the screaming consciousness and transmutate it into language, image, and form. I'm thinking of Rifa'a Rafi' at-Tahtawi and Abbas al-Aqqad, Georges Tarabichi and Mohammed Abed al-Jabri, Ghada Samman and Nawal el-Saadawi, Elias Khoury and Ghassan Kanafani. Across their work not only can we trace the failures of Arab modernity but we can catalog resistance to totalitarianism, neopatriarchy, imperialism, sectarianism, and all the myriad factors that have derailed our progress over the decades. We are a people given to looking behind, more comfortable in the past. In other cases, we are too mired in the unbearable present to be able to see ahead into an increasingly hazy future.

Who are our public intellectuals of today? A friend asked me that question a few months back and I struggled to find an answer. What would an Arab public intellectual look like in today's world? This world of knee-jerk reactions and lazy cynicism, a world that's grown suspicious of—if not outright hostile to—intellect and impatient with nuance, a world so quick not only to point out a flaw in someone's argument but to allow that flaw to eclipse the entirety of their intellectual output. It is a world of hyperpresentism, of now, of surface readings, of quick and concrete conclusions. It's a world tailor made for the pseudointellectual and grossly inhospitable to the true one.

This is no longer the world of Edward Said nor is it the world of Arab intellectuals of the past. It's a world grown exponentially more complex by virtue of overwhelming digital connectedness, hypercapitalism, technological advances too rapid for moral reasoning, and all the excesses of neoliberal policies. In a postideological, posttruth world, who has life produced to be in her service? A few names come to mind: Alaa Abd El-Fattah, Mohammed El-Kurd, Samar Yazbek. They are souls who have put their lives on the line to say what must be said. Their work and writing are fused with and, in Said's words, "remain an organic part of an ongoing experience in society: of the poor, the disadvantaged, the voiceless, the unrepresented, the powerless."[1] Comprehending the seen and unseen forces that press down on us from all sides, the intellectual feels compelled to represent them in a way that speaks to their constituency first, followed by an ever-expanding audience. The intellectual bridges the gap between theory and praxis, a melding of word and action. In Gramsci's words, it's to tread the line between "the pessimism of the intellect," which might otherwise cast you into melancholic despair, and "the optimism of the will," which compels you to stand up and try again.

That is the life the public intellectual models for us. And in the end, that is the legacy they leave behind.

October 9, 2023

---

1   *Culture and Imperialism*, Edward Said (New York: Vintage Books, 1994), 84.

Fady Joudah's [. . .] Dares Us to Listen to Palestinian Words—and Silences

EMAN QUOTAH

[. . .], by Fady Joudah (Milkweed Editions, 2024)

What future will we look back from, onto the current moment? An unprecedented catastrophe, when Israel's military has killed and buried tens of thousands of Palestinians alive in a matter of months. This moment (meaning "period in time") when every moment (meaning "fraction of an hour"), the Israeli state kills even more Palestinians in Gaza, by bullet, bomb, or starvation. This moment when the words we wrote one week after Hamas's invasion and killing of 1,200 Israeli Jews and others, one week after the beginning of Israel's bombardment and ground invasion that has, as of now, killed more than 30,000 Palestinians, including so, so many children—when what we wrote then about the scope of the horror Gazans faced seems no different than the words we could write today. And yet every day the horror intensifies. Words are never adequate and often racist; grammar fails; adjectives steep in bias. And time keeps accumulating.

Words, language, are never adequate, but whatever future we look back from, we will have a large body of poems and other writings composed by Palestinians, both inside and outside of Gaza, during this time of genocide and attempted erasure.

Palestinian American poet, translator, and physician Fady Joudah's [. . .], his sixth collection of poetry, takes on the inadequacy and necessity of language to convey the pain and hope of Palestinians right now.

Joudah has lost many family members in Israel's bombardment of Gaza. Written mostly from October to December 2023, his new volume's nontitle repeats as the nontitle of more than half its poems. In resisting titling and the way titles make and direct meaning—not

143

just by leaving his work untitled but by drawing attention to his erasure of titles—Joudah makes a bold craft choice. On the *PalCast—One World, One Struggle* podcast, on March 5, 2024, the poet explained, "I couldn't imagine words as the title" of the collection.

Instead he wanted to indicate silence—the silencing of Palestinians in what he refers to as "English"—by which he says he means the "language of hegemony," whether English, French, or German. To acknowledge the world's tendency to yank away from Palestinians their ability to *be* silent, a silence they sometimes need, whether out of grief or in search of healing or because words cannot express the magnitude of their losses and grievances.

And also the silencing that is death.

"It is a book that asks people to really consider what kind of listening have they not been offering to the Palestinians," Joudah said on the podcast. "What kind of listening they think they have been offering to the Palestinians but have not, especially in English."

In other words, a book that tells us to shut up and listen.

The recent kerfuffle at *Guernica* magazine underscores Joudah's point. In early March 2024, the magazine retracted "From the Edges of a Broken World," an essay by British Israeli writer and translator Joanna Chen, following the resignation of dozens of volunteer editors and slush readers over the essay's publication and a months-long internal disagreement about the magazine's stance on Boycott, Divestment, and Sanctions. The retraction has been criticized widely. But predictably, none of the half dozen or so news or opinion articles about the controversy traces the series of events back to the Palestinian writers whose criticism of the essay, on X, triggered the resignations. And none truly engages with their critique of the article as colonialist and unwilling to truthfully grapple with Israel's apartheid realities. Those writers included Joudah, who pulled from forthcoming publication at *Guernica* a Q&A that was published elsewhere.

*

Much can be made of the symbol [. . .], but how does it [re]direct our reading of the poems? It is a convention in poetry to refer to an untitled poem by using the first line or a portion of it in brackets or parentheses. So Shakespeare's Sonnet 18 is "[Shall I compare thee to a summer's day]," and the first sonnet of Diane Seuss's *Frank: Sonnets* is "[I drove all the way to Cape Disappointment]."

With that logic, Joudah's poem "[. . .]" that begins, "Daily you wake up to the killing of your people, their tongue accented / in your mother's milk," is denied a bracketed title, and is therefore also, perhaps, missing a first line. The line isn't there because we weren't listening. Because the narrator has not wished us to hear it. Because the narrator began with a line of silence. Because the line was erased or removed, by the narrator or a censor. Because [. . .].

Similarly, the poem "[. . .]" that begins:

> You have entered the tunnel.
> There is a light in the endless tunnel.
> Every word you think of
> has already been written
> by you or others who skim
> the spume of their seas.
> They love to travel.
> They love you more when you're dead.
> You're more alive to them dead.

How do we read and understand these lines when we perceive them to have been preceded by a blank space? A line we cannot make meaning of because of its absence? Does the missing line suggest the tens of thousands of missing Palestinians in Gaza, buried under rubble or buried anonymously? Or the thousands of Palestinians Israel has detained, the thousands missing from their homes and families and communities? Does it suggest endless displacement?

Does the silence force you to listen?

Now read the first lines of this next one and imagine a long pause, a deep breath taken before speaking, or a silence lasting a moment or more—a moment of silence, if you will—at the beginning:

[. . .]

They did not mean to kill the children.
They meant to.
Too many kids got in the way
of precisely imprecise
one-ton bombs
dropped a thousand and one times
over the children's nights.

Joudah is not alone among Anglophone (or, more accurately, bilingual) Palestinian poets in rendering absences visible. For example, Palestinian American poet, novelist, and psychotherapist Hala Alyan's "Revision," published in November 2023, makes itself illegible at times:

I had a grandmother once.
She had a memory once.
It spoiled like milk.
On the phone, she'd ask me about my son, if he was fussy,
if he was eating solids yet.
She'd ask if he was living up to his name.
I said yes. I always said yes. I asked for his name and it was
[   ].
I dreamt of her saying:
[   ]
[   ]
[   ].

And lines later, Alyan writes:

If you say Gaza you must say [   ].
If you say [   ] you must say [   ].

I've heard Alyan read this poem, and when she reads the bracketed blanks, she says "redacted." It's chilling. It evokes censoring by others, self-censorship, and false listening, as when politicians say they are concerned about civilian deaths, but we can imagine them plugging their ears with their fingers and saying, "Lalalalala" (which in Arabic we hear as "Nonononono"). When you or I read or listen to Alyan's or

Joudah's poems, we should think of what Palestinian American writer and performance artist Fargo Nissim Tbakhi says about catharsis in his essay "Notes on Craft: Writing in the Hour of Genocide":

> Nobody should get out of our work feeling purged, clean.
> Nobody should live happily during the war. Our readers
> can feel that way when liberation is the precondition for our
> work, and not the dream. When it is the place we stand, and
> not the place we shake ourselves towards.

In his collection, Joudah pushes against a challenge Palestinian poetry faces, perhaps especially poetry written in English, where poets, as much as they resist doing so, are expected to explain the Palestinian condition. The problem, of course, is not the poetry itself or the Palestinian-ness of the poet, but rather the ongoing, relentless occupation and Nakba. The feeling of being stuck in a time loop, so that a poem written in 2021 or 2014 or 2011—or 1982—about the state of occupation and apartheid, bombardment, and impending Palestinian death, reads like it could have been written today and vice versa. Take Palestinian poet and professor Refaat Alareer's now-famous "If I Must Die," in which the narrator contemplates his own death and asks the reader to remember him: "If I must die / you must live / to tell my story." Alareer posted the poem on X, formerly Twitter, a month before the Israeli military murdered him and members of his family in Gaza in a targeted strike on December 6, 2023; many people on social media who read the poem then thought it had been freshly written. In fact, Alareer wrote "If I Must Die" in 2011.

Alareer was not clairvoyant. He couldn't see the future. He was simply living under the conditions of an endlessly repeating cycle of life-threatening terror.

Joudah pays homage to Alareer's poem—which has, since Alareer's death, been translated into some forty languages—and to the poet himself in a poem [un]titled "[. . .]" that begins with the lines, "Suddenly I / 'in a blaze' died." It is given pride of place on the back cover of [. . .], where blurbs and a book description would normally go. Unlike Alareer's lyrical, hopeful verse, with its image of a white kite in the sky that a child believes is an angel looking down, Joudah's poem is fitful and frantic, unwilling to pass to the reader the cathartic role of storyteller and torchbearer. And yet it ends powerfully with "I" (repeating its first line), as though the martyr is reborn, repeatedly, despite the occupier's every attempt to snuff him out. Read together, Alareer and Joudah's poems deliver and defy sentimentality; they soar and crash into the ground; they accept the so-called inevitable and resist it; they embrace beauty and lyricism and reject it.

The power of "I" reveals itself even more when one turns to the book's final poem, "Sunbird." The narrator moves from *I* to *we* and back again, beginning with the lines, "I flit / from gleaming river / to glistening sea. // From all that we / to all that me." Soaring with the sunbird (also known as the Palestine sunbird, a symbol of Palestinian freedom, resistance, and hope), the poem moves across all directions of the land, "Fresh east to salty west, / southern sweet // and northern free." Finally, it swoops, "From womb / to breath, / and one with oneness // I be: / from the river / to the sea."

In that spirit of oneness, Joudah's collection is best read in conversation with other Palestinian poets writing in this moment. Alyan, as well as Zeina Azzam, whose "Write My Name" was written and published last fall in response to reports that Palestinian parents were writing their children's names on their limbs to help identify them if parent or child died. Mosab Abu Toha's every tweet and Instagram post has become something like a poetry of resistance and witness over the past five months. Haya Abu Nasser, currently in Gaza. Rasha Abdulhadi, who turns even her bio into a document of protest. And many others. As well as the work of other Arab writers, like Omar Sakr's ". . . in the Genocide" series of poems.

Most importantly, Joudah's poems and the work of these other poets cannot simply be words we read. To read the work of Palestinians now and not also speak out or take action to end the genocide, to return all Israeli and Palestinian hostages home and help strive for freedom and liberation for all, is a betrayal of epic proportions. We can't allow ourselves to feel catharsis. We must really listen so the future we look back from is the future we want and need.

March 25, 2024

38 Days of Re-Collection
STEVE SABELLA

For thirty-eight days, Steve Sabella lived in and photographed a Palestinian home that had been abandoned in 1948. It belonged to a family in the village of Ein Karem, who fled after hearing of the massacre in nearby Deir Yassin. Some of the stone and plaster fragments on which the images were printed come from the Old City of Jerusalem—including the home of the photographer's parents. The artworks glimpse a lost, unresolved past.

Steve Sabella, *38 Days of Re-Collection*, 2014. UNIQUE. 47.8 x 27.4 cm. Black-and-white photo emulsion on paint fragments. Collected from Jerusalem's Old City house walls. Courtesy of the artist. In the collection of Margherita Berloni.

Steve Sabella, *38 Days of Re-Collection*, 2014. UNIQUE. Black-and-white photo emulsion on paint fragments, 27.5 x 29.6 cm. Collected from Jerusalem's Old City house walls. Courtesy of the artist. In the collection of Zaki Nusseibeh.

My House
MAYA ABU AL-HAYYAT

None of the many houses I lived in
concern me. After the third house
I lost interest, but lately my organs and body parts
have been complaining of unexplainable ailments.
My arms extend higher than a tree.
My acromegaly. And when I run
it's at inconsistent speeds.
The important thing is to pass those walking
closest to me, leave them behind
before they leave me.
A Tunisian doctor
told my dad "It's a psychiatric condition."
I had liked her and considered her a house
before she spoke that sentence
which caused a lot of bruises
and brought down the house.
I read several texts I took for houses
and stayed in them a while: "Liquid Mirrors"
was a crazy abode in which I forgot
my first love. There were magazines, too:
Al-Karmal, *Poets*, and *Aqwass*,
then I studied engineering,
specialized in earthquakes
to build houses whose foundations
resist climates and the unpredicted.
My children dug up a trench for me
and said, "Here, rest a bit, Mom."
But trenches leave marks on skin
as if on a field, and the birds

gathered and pecked my seeds
after the field had drowned in stagnant water.
In a text, I can build a house
with windows and balconies
that overlook galaxies and stars,
paint it with the writings of Amjad Nasser
who said that for the sake of a solid house
one should distinguish
between imagination and knowledge
even if the house is built on illusion.
I will raise my house on the backs of horses
that will carry it to the fields,
there my legs will pause.

Translated from the Arabic by **FADY JOUDAH**

Childhood

AHED TAMIMI AND DENA TAKRURI

The main rule was that our grassroots resistance movement had to be unarmed. The aim was to struggle and resist without hurting or killing anyone. Detractors have pointed to our youth throwing stones as a contradiction of this principle, accusing us of being violent.[1] Our response has always been that a stone is not a weapon. It has long been a symbol of defense in Palestinian consciousness and mythology. If a Palestinian walking around his land encounters a wild boar or a snake, he instinctually reaches for a stone to defend himself against the creature, but not to preemptively attack it.

The other point to consider is the armed and violent nature of the Israeli soldier who is intruding upon our land. Given the bulletproof uniform he's wearing and the armored vehicle he's riding in, a stone is highly unlikely to cause him any serious bodily harm. A stone, for us, is a symbol. It represents our rejection of the enemy who has come to attack *us*. To practice nonviolence doesn't mean we'll lie down and surrender to our fate submissively. We still have an active role to play in defending our land. Stones help us act as if we're not victims but freedom fighters. This mindset helps motivate us in the fight to reclaim our rights, dignity, and land.

And so, with those principles and ground rules, Nabi Saleh's grass-roots resistance movement took off. My father hoped that we could model a form of resistance that would spread to other West Bank

---

1 "Any kid you see with a stone, you can shoot," according to former Israeli soldiers, following orders of their brigade commander, quoted in *Our Harsh Logic, Israeli Soldiers' Testimonies from the Occupied Territories, 2000–2010*, compiled by Breaking the Silence (New York: Metropolitan Books, 2012).

villages and towns. And if there was to be a Third Intifada, the West Bank village of Nabi Saleh would be its birthplace.

That said, I hated Fridays. All week, I dreaded the day's approaching, and once it finally arrived, my anxiety would be in full force. Friday was the day everyone I loved went out to march, risking their safety, while I stayed home. As a terrified eight-year-old, I strategically sought refuge in the room in the house with the fewest windows and spent all day crouched in its farthest corner. I figured this was the safest place to protect myself from getting struck by anything the Israeli soldiers might fire through the window. I usually hid there until the early evening, when everyone returned home.

Family members, with their adrenaline still rushing, would brief me on the battle that had raged right outside our house: who got shot, who was arrested, how the settlers had attacked them, and how the soldiers had cracked down. With each passing week, I began to better grasp the scope of the struggle and what was at stake. I understood the asymmetry of it all; despite the fact that our flags, chants, and stones were no match for their rubber-coated steel bullets, tear gas, and sound grenades, the Israeli forces had no moral qualms about unleashing brute violence upon us.

This realization filled me with even more fear, because I knew I could lose someone I loved at any moment. But I also knew that our cause was righteous. Even as a child, the moral stakes were obvious to me. Daring to defend what was ours was not a crime. If anything, it was a duty. After three months of hiding indoors, I finally mustered the courage to say, "OK. I'm ready to join." And of course I took my best friend, Marah, with me.

In the beginning, even as we joined the marches, Marah and I stood as far as possible from all the action, watching it unfold from a safe distance. We flinched each time we heard the booms and pops of the sound grenades and the rubber-coated steel bullets being fired. As soon as we saw the streaks of tear-gas smoke line the sky, we ran as far as we could to avoid inhaling it. We didn't dare get close to the main street or the spring, for fear of being attacked by soldiers or settlers.

Instead, we became merely apprehensive spectators, often having to jump into action to help one of our parents or siblings or cousins when they came hobbling up the hill bruised or bleeding because they had just been shot. It didn't take long for violence to become a completely normalized aspect of our lives.

Some of the hardest moments for me during those early days of our demonstrations were when my mother got arrested—something that would happen six times during the course of our resistance movement. Over time, the shootings and arrests of my loved ones became routine. The smell of tear gas grew familiar, and the loud bangs fired from the soldiers' weapons were no longer as startling . . .

The popularity of our movement meant that more people from outside Nabi Saleh—including foreign activists, Palestinians from other towns, and even Israelis—would increasingly join us in solidarity. Every Friday afternoon, in an attempt to suppress us and stop our demonstrations from even happening, the Israeli army would declare our village and the area by the spring a closed military zone. This meant they effectively laid siege to the entire village, shutting down the road, sealing off all entrances, and forbidding anyone from outside to enter Nabi Saleh. To subvert this, dozens of determined activists would arrive early on Friday morning, before the army closed the village, and join us for breakfast to fuel up for the day. Then we'd all wait for the march to begin.

Like most other Palestinians who had grown up under occupation, I had little experience with Israelis other than the armed, uniformed soldiers who raided our villages and stopped us at checkpoints and the illegal settlers who stole our land and then attacked us for trying to defend it. I knew that, historically, Jews, Muslims, and Christians coexisted prior to Israel's establishment, living side by side as neighbors and friends. But today's apartheid system has all but ensured that we have no civil interaction with Jews. And so it blew my mind to be meeting, for the first time ever, Jewish Israelis who had traveled to our village, in defiance of their own government's policies, to stand in solidarity with us. They condemned the occupation with their words and their actions, and they fervently advocated in support of Palestinian rights.

Through them, I learned that our problem was not with the Jewish people but rather with Zionism. It's not a religious problem but a political one. Zionism is the ideology that says that historic Palestine must be a country for Jews only. Zionism is what led to the dispossession of our land, which continues to be seized and occupied. But more dangerous than that is how Zionism has occupied the minds and the humanity of far too many Israelis. *That* occupation is truly more frightening and intractable.

I see that occupation in the thirteen-year-old armed settler who carries a rifle slung over his shoulder everywhere he goes. I see it in the twenty-year-old Israeli soldier who aims his weapon right at us and shoots, undeterred by the presence of children or by basic morality. But our Israeli activist friends showed me that there are good people on the other side—people with whom we can build together. They showed me that there's hope.

*

The Israeli army brought in a new method of crowd control: skunk water. It's hard to describe the putrid stench of skunk water in words—because it's unlike anything I've smelled before or since. But I'll try anyway. Imagine the odor of a pair of socks pulled from the feet of a rotting corpse and drenched in sewage for days. That's skunk water.

No one had any idea what it was when it made its debut in the village. We were marching that day when I noticed everyone staring in awe at the sight of an armored tanker truck equipped with a revolving cannon. It was spewing powerful jets of water all around the village. One of the many horrible consequences of the Oslo Accords is that it gave Israel full control of the water supply in the West Bank. At best, we get only about twelve hours of running water a week, compared to the twenty-four-hours-a-day supply of water (plus swimming pools) enjoyed by the settlers of Halamish, across the road. It's one of the reasons the loss of our spring was so devastating for us.

The sadistic nature of skunk water is that its stench lingers for days, not just on your body and hair, but also in the street—a stench that seemed to be activated further by the morning dew. It was invented by an Israeli company called Odortec, which hails itself as a "green" company and calls its product "100 percent safe for people, animals and plants" in addition to being "the most effective, cost-efficient and safest riot control solution available." The Israeli military has praised skunk water's efficacy as a nonlethal riot-dispersal method, and the Israeli police have called it a "humane option." But there's nothing humane about how the military deliberately targets our homes with the skunk truck, shattering windows and punishing even those who seek refuge indoors, nor how it can injure anyone in its path.

One time my mother was participating in a march when the skunk truck accelerated in her direction and began spraying skunk water right at her. She lowered herself to the ground and sat on her knees with her back turned to the truck. The water sprayed her from behind with such great force, it propelled her forward onto the cement. When she came home, her knees and shins were cut up and bloody, and she reeked. Even after showering, the odor was so offensive that my dad joked that he was on the brink of divorcing her.

Most of the time though, it was hard to find humor in the hell we suffered at the hands of the Israeli military. And the hell only got worse as the protest marches increased in size and notoriety. The nighttime military raids were a particularly cruel and terrifying method of punishing us, and they took place hundreds of times. It would typically be past 1:00 a.m., with everyone fast asleep, when a unit of fully armed and sometimes masked soldiers banged on our doors and barged in without a warrant. They'd rummage through all our belongings as if they owned the place, turning the house upside down and breaking things in the process. Sometimes they even brought dogs with them.

It was scary enough to be children witnessing everything we did in the daylight hours. But to then have our slumber interrupted by an invading army pointing their weapons at us while we were still half asleep was beyond traumatizing. One night I woke up to a couple of soldiers standing right above me. My brother Abu Yazan had fallen asleep in my room, and the soldiers had come to arrest him for his participation in a march. On another summer night, I was fast asleep alone in my room when I heard a noise nearby. I turned on my bedside lamp only to see a rifle aimed a few inches away from my face as I lay in bed. A soldier had poked it through my bedroom window, which I had kept open to try to circulate some air in the sweltering summer heat. I stared at him blankly, too paralyzed even to scream. As soon as he pulled his rifle back, I ran to my parents' bedroom to tell them what I'd seen, but by the time I got there, the soldier was already banging on our front door.

Despite the fact that they occurred in the middle of the night, the raids were never peaceful or quiet. The invading soldiers often demanded to see our identification cards, an outrageous display of brazenness, considering we were in our own homes. They frequently filmed the raids as part of their continuous effort to collect data on us and map out all the households and relationships in the village. Such intelligence came in handy for the Israelis as they plotted whom to arrest or how to question those who had already been arrested and were undergoing interrogation.

But we filmed the night raids, too. It was important to document them to show the world the gross violations and overwhelming aggression we routinely faced. I recall one raid when the army invaded our house to arrest my dad—a punishment for his role in organizing the grassroots resistance movement. My mother was filming the raid in the kitchen when a few male soldiers started pushing her around and hitting her, ordering her to stop filming. My grandmother Tata Farha tried to jump to her rescue, but a soldier aimed a rifle at her, forcing her to freeze in her tracks. So my mom turned to where I was standing, several feet away, and tossed the camera over to me.

"Here, take this and keep filming," she instructed.

There was no way she was going to let them confiscate the camera along with everything stored on its memory card. I managed to catch the camera and took advantage of my notably short height to weave myself through the crowd of soldiers, eventually making my way to the entrance of the house, where I had a better vantage point to film the whole scene. I tried my best to capture the soldiers hitting my mom and grandma and arresting my dad, but the sight of it all left me trembling in fear, and my hands couldn't manage to get a steady shot. The second I saw another of my three brothers, Waed, standing on the other side of the room, I sprinted over to him to hand him the camera and told him to keep filming. Then I ran over to my mom to try to save her from the soldiers' abuse. While I was clutching onto her, a soldier slammed my shoulder with the butt of his rifle, nearly knocking me to the ground.

We chased after the soldiers as they abducted my father and took him to prison yet again. My brothers and I hurled rocks at their jeeps as they drove off with him. Later, Amnesty International would declare my father a "prisoner of conscience" because he was once again being held for "peacefully exercising his rights to freedom of expression and assembly." But such labels didn't mean much to us at the time. We wanted nothing more in the world than to have our dad at home with us.

On other occasions, when they weren't raiding our house to arrest a member of our family, they confiscated our belongings. One such raid took place when my father was in prison. The Israeli soldiers took a laptop from one bedroom and a computer tower from the room of Abu Yazan and my youngest brother, Salam, as they lay in their beds, petrified, peeking their heads out from under the covers occasionally to see what was happening.

Tata Farha implored the soldiers to leave, reminding them that there were young children in the house. "Have mercy on us!" she begged. "The children are sleeping!" The soldiers then made their way to my bedroom and went through all my papers: homework assignments, report cards, and artwork I had drawn.

*

The march on Friday, December 9, 2011, began like any other. By then, our resistance movement was exactly two years old. Journalists from around the West Bank and even around the world regularly flocked to Nabi Saleh to document the increasingly popular story of the heroic little Palestinian village whose residents dared to stand up to the powerful military ruling over them and protecting the illegal settlement built on their land. I was almost eleven years old and had been reluctantly joining the demonstrations for some time, always striving to strike a balance between being close enough to feel like I was participating and being far enough away to avoid any danger. It was easier said than done.

What started out as an ordinary march that day, though, ended in a tragedy that none of us was prepared to handle. Mustafa Tamimi, my distant cousin, who was twenty-eight at the time, was shot in the face with a tear-gas canister by a soldier who was no more than ten feet away from him. I was standing farther back on the same street when it happened. I had begun retreating to avoid inhaling tear gas when I heard people shouting that someone had gotten shot and to call an ambulance. From a distance, I could see Mustafa lying on his back in the middle of the street in his crisp white shirt and jeans, his face completely covered in blood. A friend of his rushed over to him to try to stop the flow by pressing a checkered black-and-white keffiyeh scarf, a symbol of Palestinian identity and resistance, to his face. Photojournalists snapped pictures of the nightmare from all angles. Mustafa's sister screamed his name hysterically.

Within seconds, a taxi pulled up to where Mustafa lay bleeding, and a medic joined a few guys from the village to carry Mustafa's lifeless body and place it inside the vehicle. That's when I summoned the courage to get closer to see what had happened. Nervously, I took a few steps forward and peered into the car. The gory details of Mustafa's bleeding face are forever seared in my memory. His right eyeball was completely removed from its socket, and the right side of his face looked like it was ripped open. The second I caught a glimpse of him, I backed away, horrified.

As Mustafa was taken to the hospital, the eyewitnesses to his murder—corroborated by photographs from the journalists who captured the moment—revealed what exactly had happened. Mustafa and his friend had been following a couple of armored jeeps, demanding that they leave the village. He was poised to hurl a rock at the jeep right in front of him when a soldier inside it opened its rear door; aimed his high-force, long-range tear gas canister gun directly at Mustafa; and shot him point-blank in the face. The soldier then closed the door, and the jeep drove off as Mustafa fell to the ground.

The Israeli army's own regulations forbid soldiers from firing tear gas directly at people. It must be fired from a distance of roughly one hundred feet and pointed upward, so that the canister lands at the feet of demonstrators. Such rules never stopped the army from aiming directly at people, though, as many demonstrators in Nabi Saleh got hit in the legs. But the head? This was an egregious first.

Mustafa's wounds were so severe that he died in the hospital the next morning. Initially I couldn't absorb the fact that I had seen someone killed before my very eyes. Everyone knew Mustafa. He was a member of our family. And he had been part of the protest movement from the start.

Our grassroots resistance movement had officially gained its first martyr, a price that no one had been prepared to pay. We knew our freedom wouldn't come cheaply, but that knowledge didn't make the pain any easier to handle.

Excerpted from *They Called Me a Lioness: A Palestinian Girl's Fight for Freedom*, memoir/biography by Ahed Tamimi and Dena Takruri (London: Oneworld Publications, 2023).

She Is Mum
MOHAMMAD SABAANEH

Like millions of others, editorial cartoonist Mohammad Sabaaneh was touched by the video of a little Gazan girl that went viral in the first weeks of the war on Gaza. Still bereft from the death of other family members, she finally lost her mother in an Israeli air strike. The Arabic text in the drawing reads: "This is my mum. I know her from her hair."

Mohammad Sabaaneh, *She Is Mum*, 2023. Brush-pen and ink drawing, 14 x 14 cm. Courtesy of the artist.

Write My Name
ZEINA AZZAM

Write my name on my leg, Mama
Use the black permanent marker
with the ink that doesn't bleed
if it gets wet, the one that doesn't melt
if it's exposed to heat

Write my name on my leg, Mama
Make the lines thick and clear
and add your special flourishes
so I can take comfort in seeing
my mama's handwriting when I go to sleep

Write my name on my leg, Mama
and on the legs of my sisters and brothers
This way we will belong together
This way we will be known
as your children

Write my name on my leg, Mama
and please write your name
and Baba's name on your legs, too
so we will be remembered
as a family

Write my name on my leg, Mama
Don't add any numbers
like when I was born or the address of our home
I don't want the world to list me as a number
I have a name and I am not a number

Write my name on my leg, Mama
When the bomb hits our house
When the walls crush our skulls and bones
our legs will tell our story, how
there was nowhere for us to run

In Retrospect
An American Educator in Gaza
DIANE SHAMMAS

A native of Southern California, I have always supported Palestinians' right to self-determination, and thus when the opportunity arose, I fulfilled a dream by traveling each year for five years to Gaza. I am of Lebanese ancestry on my father's side of the family, and, like many youths in what our elders called the Greater Syrian community, I grew up hearing about the history of Palestinian dispossession, which they call the Nakba, or "catastrophe." I would devour each feature on Palestine in the monthly issues of the American Near East Refugee Agency that my father would thoughtfully put at the foot of my bed after he received each mailed publication.

My first visit to Gaza was with the CODEPINK: Women for Peace delegation in May 2009, five months after Operation Cast Lead. For those who are not familiar with Gaza, it is a coastal strip measuring about twenty-five miles long by five miles wide. Israel and Egypt control its borders. In January 2006, the Change and Reform Party (Hamas) won 74 out of 132 seats and Fatah only 45 seats, in a parliamentary election closely monitored by former president Jimmy Carter. Shortly after Hamas's victory and takeover of the Palestinian Authority, tensions percolated within the PA, which eventually led to a civil war between the two main political factions, Hamas and Fatah. In May 2007 Hamas won the Battle of Gaza, which set up its power over Fatah in Gaza. In return, Fatah formed a new coalition government that the West backed and recognizes as the legitimate Palestinian Authority. The resulting split into two Palestinian governments prompted Israel and Egypt to impose a siege on Gaza.

The siege is often popularized by those who read about or experience Gaza directly as being the world's largest open-air prison. Entering the fourteenth year of the siege, Israeli Defense Forces still occupy the Gaza airspace 24/7. The Yasser Arafat International Airport ceased operation in late 2000, before the siege. The Israeli navy limits Gazan fishing to three miles out, and from time to time extends the perimeter to six miles if pressured by the international community (following UNCLOS, the US Convention on the Law of the Sea, the international average is twelve nautical miles from the baseline of the territory). The siege enforces on Palestinians crippling restrictions on freedom of movement and travel, a quota on foodstuffs, a ban on construction materials, and restrictions on exports. In addition to the siege, it is noteworthy that since 1967, when Israel gained control of Gaza, the state has been engaged in an economic de-development plan of the Strip, as Sara Roy has noted in "The Gaza Strip: A case of Economic De-development."[1] In 2021, a Human Rights Watch report officially declared Israel's policies against the Palestinian people as constituting crimes of apartheid, which both the Israeli state and the US government severely censured.[2]

Having a flat topography with restricted access to the world imperils Gaza and makes it particularly vulnerable to Israel's routine air strikes, which evokes a generalized anxiety of never being safe. During one of my extended stays in Gaza, Israel launched a month-long aerial bombardment at Hamas's military bases. These onslaughts inevitably kill or wound any civilian in its path.

Huddling in your flat amidst the somnolent hum of encircling drones and the roar of Black Hawk helicopters or F-16s overhead, poised to release bombs on command, the scrambled images on your TV set were a constant reminder of Israel's surveillance drones, or, as Gazans dub them, *zenana*, and that you might be the victim of an

---

1   Sara Roy, "The Gaza Strip: A Case of Economic De-development," *Journal of Palestine Studies* 17, no. 1 (2021), 56–88.
2   Omar Shakir, "A Threshold Crossed: Israeli Authorities and the Crimes of Apartheid and Persecution," Human Rights Watch, April 27, 2021.

attack at any moment. When anxious thoughts of imminent death would stream through my mind, I would cope by blocking out that I was living in a war zone.

The owner of the neighborhood corner store, a tough, rough-around-the-edges chain-smoker, would tip me off to what might be an evening of intensifying air strikes. If I said, "Hey, we are going to have a hot night tonight?" or naively asked, "How would I know if I would survive?" he would reply dispassionately, "If you hear the descending whistle of a falling bomb, you are still alive."

People often asked me, *Weren't you frightened, living months at a time in the Gaza Strip?* I responded that living there is much different than visiting. You wake up and walk outside as you would in your home in the States. You first greet your landlord, then your neighbors while walking down the street; you pop into your local retailers where you buy your dry goods, vegetables, meat, poultry, and fish. The merchants all get to know you, welcoming you with *"Ahlan wa sahlan"* and, as you exit, *"mas-alaameh."* Two blocks from my apartment was my favorite poultry stand where once every two weeks there would be an outdoor caged display of a Middle Eastern delicacy, live domestic rabbits (*al aranab*). Missing my own pet rabbits at home, I would ask to cuddle individual ones, realizing that they would meet a hastened death by the end of the day. I often would engage in reverie about rescuing the rabbit and bringing it home to my apartment without my landlord noticing, but would soon ditch the idea, as how could I ever convince the government officials at the crossing to exit with four large suitcases and a bunny in tow?

My most rewarding experiences occurred during three-month stays in Gaza between 2010 and 2012, when I taught at Al-Azhar University in Gaza City. My friend, the dean of the English department and director of the American Corner, invited me to teach courses in American cultural studies. One of the main aims of the course was to boost students' oral and written skills in English through content-based material. In the spring of 2012, I patterned my course after a similar course that I taught at the University of Southern California, in the department of American ethnic studies. The course examined how the social construction of race in the US curtailed the citizenship rights of African Americans, Latinxs, Asians, Indigenous groups, Arab Americans, and Muslim Americans.

After the course I conducted a survey that revealed striking findings on how Palestinian students viewed racial, economic, and gender disparity in the US vis-à-vis their own. Many students' beliefs stemmed from how the crippling siege has prevented students from meeting up with Americans. Prior to taking the course, a sizable number of the students were aware of the racial problems in the US, but less aware of the deepening chasm between rich and poor in our country, to the extent that over half of the students reported that there were no American children living under the poverty line. After the course, students responded that culturally they most identified with Arab and Muslim Americans. They also expressed solidarity with the dispossession of Native Americans and engaged in the historical tradition of boycott among African Americans.

Students' journal entries and creative-writing pieces illuminated a critical pedagogical outcome of the course, in that they served as a cathartic outlet to unleash students' anguish under siege and occupation and to relate their life histories to what they learned about settler colonialism, racism, and classism in the US.

The class discourse centered on the concept of whiteness, which is based on how the dominant culture perceives one's phenotype and racial group associations. As the family is the focal point of Palestinians' lives, Langston Hughes's short story *"Passing"* affectively drew students to the Black character who assumes a white identity and laments that he felt compelled to pass his mother on the streets without acknowledging her.

Although within Gazan society a small percentage of citizens are descendants of Africa, the Philippines, and the former Soviet Union, diversity is seen more in terms of differences in religion and political affiliation or being a refugee versus a native from Gaza. Viewed as potentially explosive and divisive topics, vocal participants in the class divulged that prejudice against Palestinian Christians existed in

Gaza, but one student interjected that Palestinian refugees and Gazan natives also harbor biases against each other to the extent that both are more likely to practice endogamy.

One female student, Manar (with the exception of Ismail, pseudonyms here after are given for the university students to safeguard their identity), pointed to the shared history of Native Americans and Palestinians, from ethnic cleansing to flouted peace treaties and accords that served as mere pretexts for further colonization and land expansion. In her journal entry she wrote: "Indians and Palestinians were always deprived from their simplest rights as medical treatment, healthy lifestyle, educational system, and even from their spirituality." She added, "Common struggle, persecution, intentional destruction of their culture, identity by Israel and US, united Indians and Palestinians . . . they experienced the genocide and assassination of their identity. Yet they can't achieve these things [alluding to self-determination, integrity, and identity] without resistance, consciousness, and unity. Although many treaties were signed, they were dead letters." One telling similarity between Native Americans and Palestinians is that both taught their colonizers how to harvest their crops, as Ilan Pappé noted in a keynote address he gave at the Palestine Children's Relief Fund's Healing Hands Conference in Anaheim in 2010.

Acquiring new knowledge from the course, such as America's legacy of the civil rights movement, changed students' perceptions about the US and, as predicted, prompted some students to compare the organized transportation boycotts of the Jim Crow era with their own Palestinian civil-society campaign for BDS: Boycott, Divestment, and Sanctions against Israel. As one class member reflected in his journal, "It added to my knowledge of information that I didn't know about the US's history, and movements that struggled for freedom. The history of racial groups and our history as Palestinians are similar and boycott against Israel and boycott in the US."

Unknown to most Americans, Palestinians have their own legacy of nonviolent popular resistance, dating back to the early 1930s, that rarely receives coverage in the mainstream news.[3]

---

3 Cf. Mazin B. Qumsiyeh, *Popular Resistance in Palestine* (London: Pluto Press, 2011).

Two years after teaching this course, something curious and beautiful occurred, when a coalition of African Americans and Palestinians sprung up in solidarity. In the fall of 2014, after Israel's genocidal assault on Gaza and the police killing of Michael Brown in Ferguson, Missouri, Palestinian activists inside and outside Palestine tweeted messages of solidarity with Michael Brown's family and Ferguson protesters.

Similarly, in 2015, a coterie of US activists from Black Lives Matter and other racial-justice groups formed the Palestinian American–led Dream Defenders' delegation and embarked on a ten-day visit to the West Bank, East Jerusalem, and Israel in order to build alliances.

*

You might wonder what has become of the students that I taught. I followed the progress of three of the students amid their struggle to rebound from Israel's devastating war on Gaza, in the summer of 2014. Emani, one of the most introspective of the class, has managed to complete her master's degree in business administration while carving out a few hours a day to take up dressage at Gaza's only equestrian club—not always viewed as a befitting pastime for a woman living in a traditionally patriarchal, albeit gender-transitioning, society. On her Facebook page, Emani posts daily videos of her Arabian mare, which she arranged for delivery through the Erez crossing. In these captioned videos, we see and feel Emani anthropomorphizing the young mare, Praemia, by gingerly wiping off a tear trickling from her eye, and the bonding of a human and an animal as Emani and Praemia engage in a preliminary lunge-training session.

Recently, Emani and Praemia were mourning a shortage of hay, since where hay comes from for Gaza—the Kerem Shalom kibbutz in southern Israel—had shut down its facility for two weeks. Hay is a staple food for horses and farm animals, and many of the horses at the stable are becoming malnourished due to the scarcity. I asked,

"Should I arrange for someone to bring seeds into Gaza to plant hay?" Alas, she said that there was not enough empty space to grow rows of hay, so they are forced to buy it off the shelf from the occupying force. Whether they supply Gaza or not, Israel profits from the occupation.

Ismail, my "little poet" in the class, is still writing, but it seems as if he has switched his genre from poetry to a social-realism prose. He recently contributed a feature story, "Scarcity No Match for Creativity" for the We Are Not Numbers website. Ismail relates the story of a resourceful female artist who substitutes lipstick, eyeliner, eye shadow, foundation, and spices for charcoal pencils and chalk—art supplies that are not only dear but also not available in Gaza. She even uses hair spray to set the dye of the colors on the charcoal sketches. In *Middle East Eye*, Ismail recounts in "Gaza: Diary of Pain" the night both of his parents, two brothers, and four-year-old nephew perished from an Israeli air strike that descended on his home during the al Fajr (dawn) prayer. In the piece, he recalls a nostalgic moment when his mother was reciting her favorite poem to him and then suddenly everything turned white; a shell pierced Ismail's skull. Some time later he awoke dazed with a head trauma at Al-Shifa Hospital.[4]

Another student, Anise, speaks English with barely an accent and an astonishing familiarity with colloquial US English, given that he and other Palestinians in Gaza have little to no access to native American English-speakers. Inside the classroom he assumed a leadership position as my teacher's assistant, and outside as my chaperone across Gaza City. (There were very few women who could be escorts, as tradition dictated after 5:00 p.m. they return home to their families.) Anise and I shared a passion for cooking, so we would spend a couple of hours at the few gourmet stores available in Gaza City to select assorted delectables to cook along with the basics. Within the past year, Anise launched his own online publishing house; although in its nascent stage, it is showing positive signs of modest growth in terms of recruiting a marketing and development team. With the

---

4   Ismail Abu Aitah, "Gaza: A Diary of Pain," *Middle East Eye*, June 8, 2015.

support of my recommendations, Anise attended a master's program in international education in a New Delhi university, as well as a summer exchange program at a prominent East Coast university, which is designed to bring together Israeli and Palestinian students to engage in knowledge sharing, social networking, and finding mentoring to accelerate their individual start-up proposals. Anise has recently immigrated to Southern California, thirty miles from where I live in Orange County, and is seeking asylum in the US.

All the students have their own stories, which snowball into telling more stories about other students, as in Ismail's case. The portraits of Emani, Ismail, and Anise form an invincible buffer against the tone of racially patronizing questions often asked of me, such as the one by an Israeli hotel executive in Jerusalem: "How is the university where you teach in Gaza?" A presumptuous question, clearly a microaggression that assumes Palestinian students are plagued by a cultural deficit and thus branding them as low achievers. Absent from this biased assessment is the suffocating siege that brings electrical shortages up to eighteen hours a day. Some students switch on their home generators and resume their studies with the hum of the motor laboring in the background, and others less fortunate under the flicker of the gas lanterns by their side. A few students received propitious news of acceptance for study abroad, and even fewer obtain the pass from the Israeli army and COGAT[5] to exit Gaza. Yet while they are studying overseas, more students than not yearn to return to their homeland (*watan*). The following quote of Mahmoud Darwish embodies the paradox of the homeland and traveler: "My homeland is not a suitcase / I am not a traveler."

July 14, 2021

---

5   COGAT (Coordination of Government Activities in the Territories) is an Israeli unit that reports to the IDF and other Israeli governmental authorities. It also liaises with the Palestinian Authority and controls movement in and out of the Gaza Strip.

Fables of the Sea
REHAF AL BATNIJI

An Israeli blockade limits fishing off Gaza's coast to six nautical miles in the north and fifteen nautical miles in the east. Yet Gazan fishing boats a half mile out have been shot at and harassed by the Israeli navy. Rehaf Al Batniji is a self-taught social-documentary photographer from Gaza City. The photographs in the *Fables of the Sea* series combine oral testimony with portraiture of intergenerational fishermen and their catches.

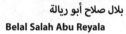
بلال صلاح أبو ريالة
Belal Salah Abu Reyala

جرع
Jarea

Rehaf Al Batniji, *Belal Salah Abu Ryala / Jarea* from *Fables of the Sea*, 2019. Series of twelve photographs, 70 x 90 cm (each). Courtesy of the artist.

As usual, I was far away and did not take part in the final farewell, 2004.
Courtesy of the filmmaker and writer.

More Photographs Taken from the Pocket of a Dead Arab

SAEED TAJI FAROUKY

1.

INT. OLD HAIFA VILLA—DAY

Saeed, looking tired, sinks deeper into the familiar chair.
His shoulders hang listlessly.

> **SAEED**
>
> Do you know what the homeland is, Safiyya? The home-
> land is where none of this can happen.

> **SAFIYYA**
> *(distraught)*
>
> What happened to you, Saeed?

> **SAEED**
>
> Nothing. Nothing at all. I was just asking. I'm looking for the
> true Palestine, the Palestine that's more than memories . . .

Memory is a burden, and painful. Memory is deceitful and falsely
comforting. But memory is also history, and nation. There is no true
Palestine. The Palestine of memories is often the only Palestine we have.

Memory is necessary. Like other cultures resisting ethnic cleansing,
we remember as a duty, though we would rather forget. Zionist soldiers
stole boxes, albums, entire archives of photographs and documents
from the homes of Palestinian families during the wars of 1948 and
1967 (and yet somehow I throw away old family photographs without
much hesitation). In 1982 the Palestinian cinema archive was stolen
by the Israeli army as they retreated from Beirut, and it has never
been recovered. Every so often footage from that archive appears in

an Israeli documentary, or a television news segment, then it's like watching a hostage video. Proof of life, yes, but a reminder that your loved one is still held captive.

2.

EXT. COURTYARD—DAY

A middle-aged Arab man, in a suit jacket and head covering, walks slowly toward camera with his hands above his head. He looks confused. Slightly scared but compliant. He glances at the camera awkwardly. Behind him, a long line of other men also walking in step. One of them smiles to camera. In the distance, a man in military uniform is loitering, holding a gun.

Other than these ephemeral scenes, the archive is gone, so we carry around in our heads an idealized, imagined archive. We complete the scenes ourselves, write our own conclusions to the stolen narratives.

An old black-and-white photo of the villa of Shukri Taji Farouky. This is my Palestine. I went to visit the villa in what is now Ness Ziona, south of Tel Aviv, but an armed guard stopped me: "I'm not even allowed in there," he joked with a shrug. The building houses the Israeli Institute for Biological Research, a secret government facility, reportedly the site of the country's biological weapons program. At the time, it wasn't on any map. I found it by stitching together pieces from various testimonies, articles, and memories. My archaeological rendition of Palestine.

My films are full of fragmented narratives because our narratives are fragmented. The map, too, is in pieces. My story is full of holes. Some parts have been generationally forgotten, some parts buried when my grandmother told me to forget them, not to research them, to ignore them. Then she died. So I revel in these fragments and I ask the questions I've been told not to ask. My memory is also full of holes, punctured by years of violence and the long legacy of resulting trauma.

This is why Raed Andoni recreated an Israeli prison from the collective memory of its detainees in his film *Ghost Hunting* (2017). Memory is our architecture, both giving us shelter and imprisoning us. And architecture is our memory. Often our most enduring recollections are of our houses: demolished, confiscated, hollowed out. We recall the walls of our grandmother's garden, the view from the top of the staircase in our uncle's house (we will, perhaps, never see these again). I can describe the texture of the bricks, how the light filters through the leaves of plants and brushes the window, but I can't explain to you how to walk from one room to another. I get lost too easily in buildings.

I get lost, too, in the plot of my own films, often forgetting—when I rewatch them—that this scene comes after that scene. It's as though I'm watching them for the first time. Eventually I thought the most elegant solution was to abandon plot, to craft films in the same way I experience life: a sequence of brief episodes, instances, evocations, atmosphere; specters of experiences, the remnants of events. (There it is again: archaeology.) In documentary film this is even more appropriate, because our lived experiences have nothing even resembling a plot. We are, instead, the collective echoes of our most salient moments.

At last, I even abandoned linearity. It happened when Thein Shwe, an oil miner in Burma, asked me, "I wonder why you traveled halfway across the world to film with me? Maybe we were related in a previous life." I realized then that it was impossible to tell a deterministic story with a man who believes he has lived, died, and been reborn thousands of times over tens of thousands of years. It was naive to say "*a* leads to *b*, which leads to *c*" to a family who believed this life is influenced by the accumulated karma of all their previous rebirths, and this life will—in turn—generate karma to influence the next thousand rebirths and the events in those lives, and on and on until enlightenment. An intricate web of fate, luck, karma, astrology, numerology, mythology, capitalism, and politics determines all the possible trajectories of their lives. So, we talked, instead, about cosmic time. We looked not only at the clouds in their sky, but at the universes beyond them. We looked not only at the soil into which they plunged their hands, digging for oil, but deeper into the core of the Earth and the primordial fire within. We told a story of cycles, coincidences, fated connections across time, a puzzle box in which every piece is in motion until the very last moment when they all fall into place.

This approach requires space. A form defined enough that we understand its boundaries, but ambiguous enough that we can move through it without a map. This is my preferred meaning of "plot": a piece of land, outlined but empty. You know the plot's outer edges, but within that framework, there is space through which to wander. And so I learned to love the architecture of Zaha Hadid. Her exploded, fractured designs give us the security and familiarity of a building but with the freedom to explore, unafraid. There are walls, yes, but any conventional sense of architectural language has been pulled apart, so we no longer feel the constraints of floors, walls, straight lines. Her spaces are ambiguous and liminal, constantly in transition between wall and nonwall, floor and nonfloor. Each wandering through one of her buildings is unique because each visitor defines their own route through the space, imagines their own journey.

It's like listening to a performance by Umm Kulthum, who recorded and performed hundreds of hours of epic songs and never sang a line the same way twice. Each performance was a new experience, a unique exploration with the audience. She would tease a phrase, repeat it, drag it out over minutes, hint at a resolution, imply to her listeners where she was going but then, at the last moment, she would hold back, change direction, return to another moment. She did this for hours at a time, her performances legendary in their length and intensity. Her audience—who had committed her songs to memory—would find her performance uncanny: both familiar and unfamiliar at the same time. They would be on their feet, standing on chairs, pouring with sweat, crying, cheering—a hysterical, ecstatic trance of anticipation. Sometimes she gave them what they wanted. But more often she withheld, leaving a phrase unfinished. And the more she withheld, the more she invited her audience to complete the phrase for themselves.

These were not linear journeys but spiritual dialogues spanning centuries of poetry, music, religion, and culture. When your storytelling is born of endless voyages across a featureless desert, the last thing you want is an efficient resolution. You don't want logic and conclusions. You want eternity and magic. Her most effective technique, the one that had her audience in the palm of her hand, was to simply stand back and say nothing.

*

Silence. Empty space.

This is storytelling: unpredictable, sweaty, inefficient, liquid.

In 2004 Abdelfattah turned to me—to the camera—as I was filming him for *I See the Stars at Noon* and asked, "What about me?" In that moment he shattered the received mythology of the objective documentary. He took a sledgehammer to the heavily constructed facade of the detached observer. His basic expression of humanity and demand for dignity changed my filmmaking and my understanding of documentary cinema forever. What about him? I would finish filming, fly back to London, edit the film, release it, move on, and make another. But what about him?

When I approached my friend, the editor Gareth Keogh, with the footage, I apologized, saying we'd have to cut all the shots in which Abdelfattah talks to the camera. But Gareth understood that those were the best parts.

And so we made a film about making a film. A loop.

Documentary editing is a process of reverse causality. Choices we make now define the events of the past. This is also how I write my films. I start with the feeling I want the audience to experience when it's all over and work backward from there. Because I always remember goodbyes.

Consider this ninth-century Arab folktale, "The Tale of Attaf." The ruler Haroun Al Rashid is reading a book in his vast library, and something in the text moves him. He laughs and cries at the same time. His adviser, Jaafar, is confused by this display of ambivalence and asks how a man can laugh and cry at the same time, and Haroun Al Rashid, incensed, banishes him from the kingdom until he can understand how such a thing could happen. Jaafar goes on a long journey, a series of adventures with a man he meets along the way named Attaf. When Jaafar returns, he goes to the library to look for the story Haroun Al Rashid was reading. He eventually finds it, and as he reads, he comes to the astonishing realization that it's the story of himself, on a long journey, a series of adventures with a man he meets along the way named Attaf.

The story, like most Arab folktales, begins with the line *kan ya ma kan:* "There was, or there was not," an unapologetic assertion of fundamental uncertainty. A liminal space in which the storyteller can be both honest and dishonest at the same time. A moral ambiguity that resists the purity and truth of a conventional heroic tale.

After all, why should I write a hero's journey when I don't believe in heroes? Why should I tell the linear narrative of a singular protagonist when our revolution is multimodal and collective?

The founders of the Palestine Film Unit (our godmothers and godfathers of militant cinema) made a distinction between their work and the conventions of documentary filmmaking. They were not merely detached observers, filming events as they happened, but were instead active participants in those events. The camera was not a tool to record but a weapon with which to fight for the resistance and the revolution.

This is why our cartoonists are shot in the neck; left to bleed to death on Ives Street, London. And why Israeli assassins fired twelve bullets into a literary translator in the lobby of his Rome apartment. And why a Mossad car bomb eviscerated the author of this essay's opening words. Try telling us now that culture isn't a weapon. Try telling Naji al-Ali that cartoons are just comic relief. Try telling Weal Zuatar that literature is simply entertainment. Try telling Ghassan Kanafani that writing is a distraction from politics. Culture is a crowbar with which we can pry open the prison gate and smash the windscreen of the limousine when our politicians pull up to the Wyndham Grand Hotel in Manama for the next normalization summit.

The Egyptian filmmaker Philip Rizk—in speaking about *Out on the Street* / برة في الشارع , codirected with Jasmina Metwaly—makes the distinction between reenactment and enactment. For most of the film, the actor-workers play themselves in a recreation of their factory strike. But near the end they leave the set. They congregate in the stairwell of the building and begin talking off script, joking with each other, a more chaotic expression of self-determination. They act out an idealized version of their factory strike, one in which the boss is gone and they win. But they can only achieve this because the architect-directors built with them a space in which they could roam, wander into the stairwell, disregard the set and enact their dream scenario.

My dreams are often elaborate films (ironically the kind of convoluted adventure films that I would never make). But when I try to write them down, they're meaningless. They were never really stories. Our dreams never are. They are only moments: jump cuts, nonlinear sequences, associations and dissociations, series of images that make no sense but that we retroactively turn into stories. They are stitched together from disparate parts, and in the gaps we fit our own experiences; we make the story about us. We've done the same with our nation and our map exploded into thousands of pieces.

I first dreamed of making films when I read the final words of Driss Chraibi's novel *Heirs to the Past* and immediately knew that I had to one day turn it into cinema. He describes an act of digging and building at the same time. Archaeology and architecture combined. I always remember goodbyes.

3.

INT. RABAT AIRPORT—DAY

The overly enthusiastic customs officer hands Driss a thin envelope. Driss turns it over in his hands. No name or address. He folds open the flap with only his thumb. His plane ticket back to France. He takes it out, but there's something else in there. A note. A single, small piece of paper with familiar tiny letters, scrawled but precise. Driss reads.

DRISS

(to himself)

Wells, Driss. Dig a well, and go down to look for water. The light is not on the surface, but deep down. Wherever you may be, even in the desert, you will always find water. You have only to dig, Driss, dig deep.

In the last few years of her life, my mother's memory became fragmented. She had false memories and would forget real events. She had been an archaeologist and had occasionally brought pieces of broken pottery home from her digs. As a child, I would feel their sharp edges, wondering how they fit together, where the missing pieces were. Once, our family dog tried to eat a broken flowerpot, cutting his mouth. Blood stained the pottery. I kept it for years as a memento, another fragment of history, a relic of his suffering like the prophet I believed him to be. I often fell asleep on his belly, inhaling his fur, whispering to him that he was the only sane one in the family. I remember this. Eventually that image will become a scene in a screenplay, no doubt. But it will be more than merely a reproduction of a memory; I will need to fill in the gaps, like the threads of gold in *kintsugi*. In this scene, reclining on his dog, the young man will be reading Kanafani's *Return to Haifa*. He will like the fact that the main character has the same name as him, and he will imagine one day turning the book into a film.

March 5, 2023

N31°44.3416' E035°09.4615'
ADAM BROOMBERG and RAFAEL GONZALEZ

Adam Broomberg and Rafael Gonzalez, *N31°44.3416' E035°09.4615'*, 2023.
Photograph. Courtesy of Adam Broomberg, Rafael Gonzalez, and MACK.

Every two years Al-Badawi, an olive tree in Palestine that is twelve
meters tall and approximately 4,500 years old, yields more than eight
hundred kilograms of olives. Since 1967 over one million Palestinian
olive trees have been burned to the ground or uprooted by Jewish settlers
or Israeli authorities. This tree comes with its latitude and longitude
as part of an initiative, by the collective Artists + Allies x Hebron, to
ward off marauders.

Victoria García, *Freedom for Palestine,* No. 1, 2023, detail. Series of five posters, high-res PDF, 11 x 17 in (each). Courtesy of the artist.

The Road to Jerusalem, Then and Now

RAJA SHEHADEH

It was eight in the morning, three weeks after the beginning of the Israeli occupation of the West Bank, when I left my house in Ramallah armed with my camera and began to cycle to Jerusalem. I had just turned sixteen and wanted to capture through photographs the damage that had been caused by the June war of 1967 to property along the Ramallah–Jerusalem road.

The road I cycled on was a minor two-lane thoroughfare, built in 1901 during Ottoman times, and had no military value. The approach to Jerusalem in the First World War was not through here. The Allies' path was well to the west of this, through the village of Nebi Samuel, with its imposing mosque that I was able to glimpse from various points on the road.

A few weeks earlier, on June 6, Colonel Moshe Yotvat's brigade, entering the West Bank through Latrun, captured Jerusalem Airport without a fight. Then the Israeli army moved toward what they believed was the road to Ramallah. To be sure, they ordered an old Palestinian man to be their guide. Meanwhile the conquest of Jerusalem was proceeding through the western part of the city.

The army entered Ramallah with a battalion of tanks in the evening of that accursed day. Perhaps to our good fortune they did not wait for a bombardment to soften us up. They crossed and recrossed the city several times, shooting in every direction. We were in the house, huddled in a corner, thinking the army would break in at any moment and shoot us all. As we waited Father told us: "The reason for the shooting is because the Israeli army is ascertaining whether there's resistance." I wondered how he knew this and was of two minds. I wanted the shooting to stop yet at the same time felt weighed down by the demoralizing expectation of defeat.

When no one returned fire, the shooting stopped. There was no resistance. In a few hours the Israeli army's conquest of my city was complete. Three weeks later I was on that narrow road cycling on my own toward Jerusalem, which had been captured a day after Ramallah fell.

For the previous nineteen years of Jordan's rule over the West Bank, this road was Ramallah's only link to Jerusalem. Eastern Jerusalem, under Jordanian rule, provided the villages to the north with specialized hospitals, good restaurants, and shopping outlets. When I was young we would take bus number eighteen to get to Jerusalem. It was bedecked with signs: "Do not spit," "Do not talk to the driver," and "No smoking of *shisha*." The turn signal was a manually operated metal rod. When it was returned to its place, I could hear it rattle. The whole bus clanked and rumbled as it made its slow way south to Jerusalem, making it possible for me to look out of the window and observe the fields surrounding the road. My grandmother had friends in the city, and I often accompanied her on her visits to them. She would warn me against touching the handrail in front of the seat because she said it was covered with germs from other passengers' dirty hands. Money also was full of germs, and I always had to wash my hands after handling it. When I was older I would take the shared taxi to Jerusalem, enjoying the drive with the lively music the driver played on his radio. I would listen to the animated passengers exchanging news about what they did on their visit to Jerusalem, being sociable, friendly, and open. In warm weather I relished the clean, fresh breeze blowing, especially at dusk as the colors were changing. There was much to look on the way: rock-strewn fields, grazing flocks of sheep, passing traffic, and the occasional fancy building proudly flanking the side of the road.

A short time after the end of the war, my father was one of the first Palestinians to go back to his beloved Jaffa, though only for a brief visit. But his sister, Mary, who had stayed in Akka after the Nakba, was long gone. It was a bittersweet experience. He was realizing what for a long time he had been hoping—to see, just to see, Jaffa—and yet his return was as a defeated Palestinian who had now lost the rest of Palestine to the enemy. Jaffa was in a dilapidated state, a sad sight so unlike the vital city he remembered. When later on we visited it with him he pointed out the various cafes, once so busy, now abandoned. It was difficult for me to imagine how it must have been in the past. Perhaps the visit made him realize that there was no possibility of a real return or compensation for what he had lost. How could that be? What could possibly compensate for the years of grief and deprivation that he lived through on the other side of the border?

After leaving Ramallah I first cycled to Bireh, Ramallah's sister city, passing by the Am'ari Refugee Camp, a crowded place with mainly concrete houses and narrow lanes where I had never set foot. I left the town and continued south to the old Ramallah–Jerusalem road.

Just after leaving Bireh I cycled past the Jubran family's arak distillery at the Maloufieh on the outskirts of the town. Drinking arak while nibbling on the numerous small savory plates of mezza in a garden cafe was a favorite pastime for residents of Ramallah. With all cafes and restaurants now closed, this pleasure was one of the casualties of the occupation and was bound to add to the mood of general gloom.

The distillery, which was also shut, lay at the edge of a low-lying valley surrounded by hills. Close to the top of one of these to my right stood a lonely stone house with pine trees next to which was a spring where young men came to hunt birds and visit the cave there. Just above this, at the top of the hill, was a plot of land Father had bought with the intention of one day building a home. When he took me to see the land, I had imagined the palatial house that we would someday own, perched over the hill overlooking the valley below. But Mother, who did not drive, felt she would be an exile atop that hill with no neighbors around to visit and totally dependent for her coming and going on Father. What also made it an unacceptable location for her was that the hill was "wilderness" and clearly unsafe. She rejected that project, and the house was never built. Except for a modest winter house in Jericho, my parents could not agree on the location, size, or any conception of their dream house. Nor could they agree on the sort of life they wanted to live.

After cycling some four kilometers from the start of my journey I arrived at the Samiramis Hotel on the left of the road, where King Hussein was rumored to stop to rest and drink lemonade when he drove from Jerusalem for his occasional visit to Ramallah. From there a narrow road led to the attractive village of Kufr Aqab up on a hill with a population of some 420. From the road the hill was visible, and one could just see some of the old houses and the minaret. We later learned that one of the officers in the Jordanian army who died defending Jerusalem, Muhammad Ali Suad Jamil, came from there. Opposite the modest hotel at the intersection, the road to the west led to the few houses in an area that had the unflattering name of Um Alsharayet ("Mother of Rags").

I cycled on, passing the Jallad flour mill, one of three in the whole of the West Bank. Wheat was cultivated and ground locally, supplemented by some imports of flour. There were several sifters one on top of the other, which had become so rusty that I imagined fine rust powder rather than flour now passing down from one platform to another. Jallad's daughter, Claire, and her family, the Kassabs, lived across the street from us until they moved along with their factory to Amman. They had three daughters, one of whom was exactly my age. They all called their father Papa—not like the rest of us, who said Baba. They relocated to Amman just before the occupation, as though they knew what was coming.

At the mill the road forked. I took the one going northeast. Just a few years earlier we used to drive straight ahead toward the runway of the Jerusalem Airport. When a plane was taking off or expected to land, we had to wait at the barrier. We would watch the propellers turning to gather steam, then the exciting moment would arrive when the plane was ready to move and it zoomed right in front of our car and began its ascent. We also had to stop to wait for an incoming plane. I relished these delays and watched carefully every movement of the plane, trying to remember how it had felt when I was in one traveling to Beirut for vacation. I always hoped there would be a plane to watch when we passed by on our way to Jerusalem. Often when we drove on this road I would look up at the landing planes that seemed like large birds about to swoop down and land on top of our car.

Then a new bypass was built to the east that circled around the eastern edge of the runway. This was the road I took. The triangle between the old and the new roads was full of greenery, mainly pine and citrus trees.

An Israeli customs checkpoint between the West Bank and Israel was checking cars for goods. The Israeli officials looked puzzled as I cycled past. I was not a car, and it was obvious that I wasn't carrying anything so there was no reason to stop me. Afterward I passed a car on the side of the road that had been flattened by an Israeli army tank driving over it. I stopped and photographed it then continued cycling up that incline. There were more destroyed cars along the way, more expensive models than those I had seen earlier, Opels and Mercedes-Benzes. I stopped to photograph them. But this time before doing so I took my time to examine them. I was certain that they were all crushed by a tank driving over them. How does it feel to exercise the power to turn a luxury car into a flat pile of metal in only a couple of minutes, I wondered. Did the tank driver and his companions cheer every time they drove over another car? Did they then direct the driver to another car parked next to another of the posh houses on this street that they can crush? The Palestinians on this street owned far more expensive cars than was within the means of most Israelis. Did they want to destroy them out of envy, or was it revenge? *We are the victors so we can do what we like to the vanquished.* Was this the point when the destructive attitude that has lasted for over half a century began? And what about the owners of these cars? Did the soldiers look at the windows to see their anguished faces as they watched their prized possessions being crushed? Did they enjoy that? Surely there were elements of all these emotions present because there was no military necessity for this activity. It was merely for the recreation of the Israeli soldiers at the expense of the Palestinians. The scary thought then came to me: whether from this point, having lost the war we didn't fight, we would become like putty in the hands of the Israeli military, which started to believe that they could do what they liked with us with full impunity? The more such thoughts passed through my mind the more apprehensive I became of the future. I had to put a stop to such debilitating thoughts and pedaled on.

Then the easternmost end of the airport runway came in sight. It was on slightly elevated ground from the road. Before I got there, I passed the United Nations Relief and Work Agency (UNRWA) Vocational Training Center across from which was Qalandia Refugee Camp, another crowded area of concrete houses crammed next to each other with narrow lanes in between. The contrast with the Center, which had a lush garden, was striking. I turned my eyes from the treeless area of the camp and looked through the wrought-iron gate of the Center at the trees, much loved by birds, which were always so plentiful on the trees that lined the long driveway leading to the school buildings further down that were not visible from the road. Except for the crowded camp that sloped downward to the east, there were no other buildings in that area.

The refugee camp was quiet, seeming to be in deep slumber. Or so I thought. I was totally unaware then of the emotions that were raging there among the refugees of 1948 in response to Israel's resounding victory over the Arab states. Nor was I prepared for the reactions to years of passivity that were to be sparked by the rise of the Palestine Liberation Organization abroad and the resistance to Israel. Voices would be raised that had never before been heard over the past nineteen years. For now it seemed quiet, defeated, despondent. I had never been inside this or any of the other refugee camps around Ramallah. To me they were closed areas outside my scope of vision or experience.

I passed by them so often yet never really saw them or was curious about the nature of life within them.

What I did see was the airport, the gateway for my anticipated escape from Ramallah, with its runway on raised ground reaching all the way to the new road that now encircled it. That new curving road built to avoid driving across the runway was poorly designed, rendering the turn dangerous if one was speeding. Father, who often drove too fast, once skidded on it but then managed to regain control of his car, arriving home with only a bump on his head.

Across the road I saw the blue flag of the United Nations fluttering over the camp school, also painted light blue, that bordered the road. My negative view of UNRWA was influenced by Father's position toward the organization. His opinion was that it was corrupt and that its main beneficiaries were the high-salaried foreign staff rather than the refugees themselves.

Immediately after the Nakba in 1948 and until 1954 my father had worked assiduously on the question of the return of the refugees. Until he gave up hope. His struggle ended bitterly. This was yet another area where he failed. Seventy-three years have gone by, and the refugees have still not returned home. By 1954 my father had come to understand that it was not only Israel whom one had to fight regarding this problem but also the Arab leaders and the United Nations, both of whom supported Israel in this while making a feeble effort at supporting the Palestinian cause, achieving little more than keeping the refugee issue alive.

Perhaps that was why I did not see the camps or the men, women, and children living in them. Father was blocking their presence from his sight, and I was following suit. This, despite the fact that we ourselves were refugees from Jaffa. Yet Father would not accept to register the family with UNRWA and never received any of the aid that the organization offered, so angry was he at the international organization for turning the case from one of rights to a matter of relief and humanitarian assistance, with all the consequences of long-term dependence.

Our house in Ramallah overlooked the distant Mediterranean coast, and I often saw my father looking toward his Jaffa on the horizon. He must have wondered what had become of his city. I can imagine how difficult it must have been for him coming from Jerusalem to a metropolis like Jaffa where he had no contacts, setting up a law office, and succeeding. He did that, then lost it all. The home he left was so close and yet so far, impossible to reach. Yet knowing him he never gave up hope. For a long time he thought the day would never come when he would be able to return.

*

The ancient village of Qalandia, which gave its name to the camp that stood on land that had once belonged to it, was some distance away, out of sight from the road. In the midst of the central highlands this was an unusually flat area. This feature must have been the main consideration for situating the airport here. Bordered on the east by a small hillock, the low terrain spread eastward unimpeded. The highest and most strategic point on the horizon was the hill of Nebi Samuel, over 885 meters high and visible from here. Fresh, gentle winds always blew across this open plain. This swath of lowland was so unlike the surrounding hilly terrain as to give a feeling of unbounded space to the landscape.

Before the war, when a plane was about to land, it was not uncommon to see boys from the neighborhood standing on the hillock overlooking the eastern end of the runway to watch the aircraft landing. No buildings were allowed here. The whole area around the airport was open and airy, and the runway ensured an attractive swath of empty, flat land with very gentle ripples extending westward into the distance. I enjoyed cycling around the eastern tip of the airport and welcomed the opportunity of taking a closer view of the abandoned runway. After circling its eastern border the road veered toward the southwest and continued down a slight slope.

From the early days of the occupation one of the principles that served as the basis of the expansion of Jerusalem's borders was to extend the borders of the city northward to include the Jerusalem Airport. Israel had hoped to turn this into an international airport. Although it was declared as such, no country would recognize it nor agree to operate international flights to or from it. This was because they refused to recognize the annexation of Jerusalem to Israel. The airport remained a small domestic facility serving regional traffic and sometimes planes used by UN officers and soldiers. Then during the first Intifada it served as a parking lot for cars confiscated by the army. There were very few houses by the side of the southward slope. As I cycled down I was enjoying the unimpeded openness of this area and the soft, refreshing wind that cooled me down.

Farther ahead, the land to the right of the road was separated by a small basin. Nearby, in an old building by the side of the road, a tense, wiry French Jew, years later, established a horseback-riding school where I and a few friends learned to ride. When we got more proficient we would gallop through the hills cultivated with olive trees until we reached the steep climb up to Nebi Samuel. Along the way we had to maneuver our horses to avoid getting knocked out of our saddles by the low-lying branches of the trees. It was an exhilarating ride. It was fortunate that I, an inexperienced rider, did not fall and break my back.

After 1948—and in the course of the nineteen years of Jordanian rule over the West Bank which Palestinians had with no access to the sea—roads went through the bean-shaped territory of the West Bank from north to south. The south was reached by passing through the northern section of Jerusalem, then circling around the southern parts of the city, which were under Israeli rule. Prior to 1948 Jerusalem had been connected to the coastal region by the road that went through Bab el-Wad. It was possible to travel to Jaffa from Ramallah without passing through Jerusalem, which really was peripheral and had no strategic importance for the rest of Palestine. But with the establishment of Israel on most of the land surrounding the West Bank, the Ramallah–Jerusalem road became vital as a main conduit between the northern and southern regions of the West Bank. As I was growing up, I knew no other road for reaching Jerusalem and the cities and villages in the south other than this Ramallah–Jerusalem road that I was cycling on now. And so I was intimately familiar with every detail of this short road. This of course was not the experience of my father. How often he must have traveled from Jaffa, where he had set up his office, to see his father in Jerusalem using the Bab el-Wad road. But when he came from Jaffa to take refuge in Ramallah in 1948, he must have traveled on the road directly linking the two through Latrun. After 1948 that road was closed.

Father's experience of Palestine was entirely different from mine. For him the whole country—the coastal region, lower and upper Galilee, Gaza, and the Jordan Valley—had been open, the country's cities and villages connected by roads that didn't have to circle around to avoid borders. I didn't know these past connections and so didn't miss them. How different and skewed has been my experience of the country and how reduced my existence. I grew up thinking the road I'm on now was the only road, life as I lived it in the landlocked West Bank the only life.

With the occupation of the West Bank by Israel, the whole of geographic Palestine was once again open to all the inhabitants, both Palestinian and Israeli. The place reverted to how Father's generation had known it. To me and my generation, it was all a new experience. Yet it was not to remain so.

*

If I were to cycle now to Jerusalem I would be stopped at the Qalandia checkpoint some five hundred meters from the Vocational Training Center. This has since come to mark the border between Israel and the West Bank. It was built near the eastern side of the runway, which is now enveloped by the four-meter-high annexation wall.

The once-nearly-empty strips of land on both sides of the road, from where the customs point had been to the Center, are now densely built and in a miserable state, the road going between them constantly clogged with cars either trying to enter Jerusalem or continuing eastward to drive to the southern part of the West Bank through the village of Jaba'. As you approach the checkpoint, you're confronted by the concrete four-meter-high wall that Israel built to surround the runway and separate it from the rest of the West Bank. This section is smeared with layers of graffiti. An image of Yasser Arafat wearing his keffiyeh can be discerned alongside another of the much younger imprisoned leader Marwan Barghouti. The wall then continues on the other side of the checkpoint. It looks like someone took a felt pen and drew a thick line around every area where Palestinians live. Then a concrete wall with watchtowers was constructed following the line encircling all the different communities and villages. What was once an open, unenclosed area has been turned into a series of isolated zones, trapping the Palestinian communities and separating them from Israel.

The hill that was used by the neighborhood boys as a lookout to view the runway has been mostly leveled to accommodate the offices and parking lots associated with the checkpoint. Only a small part of the hill remains; the rest is gone, transforming the area from an attractive expanse of land into one that is strangled by the wall with its watchtowers. From the road, no part of the runway is visible.

Qalandia checkpoint has become the new Mandelbaum Gate, which used to separate the two parts of Jerusalem. This barrier separates the West Bank from the expanded borders of eastern Jerusalem. Israeli fears of and callousness toward the Palestinians are amply evident here, both in the way the wall is designed and in the path it takes. It is a far more formidable wall than that which once divided Jerusalem after 1948. It has Israeli soldiers on both sides. Holders of Jerusalem residency cards are the only ones allowed to pass through the crossing point. Cars with West Bank license plates can no longer cross and must drive east. They must circle around expanded Jerusalem through the newly constructed bypass road that skirts the village of Jaba', then drive southward through Wadi Nar ("Valley of Fire"), never entering any part of expanded Jerusalem or the surrounding villages that were annexed to the city after 1967. Often the road from Ramallah leading to Qalandia gets clogged up with the lines of cars reaching all the way to Kufr Aqab, which I had passed near the start of my cycling journey.

A short time after I cycled past Kufr Aqab, Israel annexed this sparsely populated hamlet along with twenty-eight others, joining them with Jerusalem. The annexation followed a haphazard line avoiding the areas most populated by Palestinians while including undeveloped Palestinian land. The western side of the road I was cycling on was incorporated within the city while the eastern side, including the refugee camp, remained in the West Bank. This meant that those living on the eastern side of the road were considered residents of Jerusalem but not those on the western side.

The new border of expanded Jerusalem reaches to the outskirts of Bireh. Kufr Aqab and sections of Um Alsharayet, where only a scattering of houses once stood, were included in greater Jerusalem. With the scarcity of housing for Palestinian residents of the city, over the years many Palestinians who needed to live within the boundaries of Jerusalem to avoid losing their status as residents moved to these areas, causing a building boom and turning Kufr Aqab and Um Alsharayet—which the Israeli authorities did not care to plan properly, and chose not to prevent building violations—into virtual urban jungles. The mass of new buildings has swamped the small, attractive village that I could see in 1967 at the top of the hill to the east as I cycled by. This was also the fate of that solitary house on the hill surrounded by the pine trees on the western side of the road where Father's land lay. All the trees there were felled and replaced with a forest of stone buildings standing next to each other. It was fortunate Father had not built a house there.

That morning in June 1967, as I headed to Jerusalem, I could not have anticipated that the Mandelbaum Gate—which stood between the eastern part of Jerusalem, under Jordan, that I grew up thinking of as my Jerusalem and the western part, under Israel, that was totally unknown to me—would come to be moved to Qalandia.

My father had had his share of harsh experiences at that gate. His sister was living in Akka ("Acre"), and he could only see her at Christmas if she managed to get a permit from the Israeli government to cross over for a few days to celebrate the feast with us in Ramallah. The anxiety-ridden memories of that must have been on Father's mind when he heard of his brother's crossing to Amman. He feared being separated from and losing his brother as he had lost his sister. How would it be now; what would it take to get to see his brother again for a visit? Whom would he have to petition to obtain the necessary permits? Now once again his brother was forcing him into the position of a petitioner asking for favors to allow his return from across the new border. This made him very angry.

But I understood none of this that morning in June when I cycled to Jerusalem.

After passing the eastern tip of the runway, I coasted quickly down the slope where there were no houses on either side of the road. This brought me to the Halfway Bridge, so-called because it is halfway between Ramallah and Jerusalem. By then I had cycled nearly six kilometers, almost half the distance to Jerusalem.

The June sun was getting stronger, but a refreshing, cool breeze continued to blow. In rainy weather, a good stream flows under the bridge. The small village of Er-Ram ("Small Hill") rests on a mound just beyond this bridge to the north. By the side of the road near Er-Ram is a cluster of new houses known as Dahiet El Bareed ("Postal Service District"). This was one of the rare housing cooperatives, and it belonged to employees of the postal service in Jerusalem. The same man who was behind this pioneering initiative had also promoted another housing cooperative on a flat tract of land some four kilometers from the center of Jericho on the way to the Jordan River. Father had joined this project. After many years, the cement houses, each with a garden all around, were completed.

It was 1962 when our family became the owners of a winter house in the warm climate of Jericho, in which we spent weekends whenever we could manage it. I kept a bicycle there and would ride it around the project on the flat land that was so unlike hilly Ramallah. At times I would cycle all the way down to the banks of the Jordan River. We spent many a happy weekend in our winter house. Its garden had all kinds of citrus trees and vegetables, which, with the mild winter and plenty of water, grew like magic, so unlike our garden in Ramallah, where the pine trees made the soil acidic. After the 1967 war, we got news that the house had been broken into and looted. A number of the middle-class families who owned houses there were from Amman, and now they would surely not be able to use their homes. Many other owners from the West Bank had also left for Jordan. There was a sharp depletion in the middle class after the war. As is often the case, they are the first to desert. As for us, those times when we moved in winter between Ramallah and Jericho, along with other family friends, would surely also come to an end, as will my excursions to the river, the new formidable, unapproachable frontier. Such was the expected disruption of our old way of life with the onset of the occupation.

Close to Dahiet El Bareed, along the other side of the road, was the village of Bir Nabala, with its many springs and rich agricultural land, hence its name, which means the "well of Nabala." This village was reachable via a slight detour from the Ramallah–Jerusalem road.

For a number of years the Halfway Bridge was the location of the checkpoint before it was moved farther north to Qalandia.

I remember when the Annexation Wall was being built along this road. I saw the first blocks of concrete being placed right in the middle of the road. I didn't believe that was where they were going to build it. I thought it was impossible that it could be built there. Of course that was where it was actually erected and where it has remained.

This section of the Annexation Wall that begins at Qalandia continues southward, bifurcating the Ramallah–Jerusalem road right in the middle. Travelers to Jerusalem now drive in the shadow of the wall. At the bridge it curves eastward, separating Er-Ram from Dahiet El Bareed and encircling the former, leaving it on the West Bank side. It then continues eastward, keeping the settlements of Nebi Samuel on the Israeli side and the village of Jaba' on the Palestinian side. It also stretches westward, blocking the entrance to Bir Nabala and encircling the town. A highway passes above that closed entrance, connecting the Jerusalem settlements to Tel Aviv and the coastal region. In that cul-de-sac, an Israeli company, GreenNet, operates a large facility that sorts the waste collected from Jerusalem. A permanent foul smell permeates the area.

Before the wall was built, the town of Er-Ram had grown from a small, attractive village on top of a small hill (hence its name) into a small, sprawling city where many of Jerusalem's Palestinian residents reside because of the shortage of residential homes for Palestinians in eastern Jerusalem. Now that Er-Ram lies entirely behind the wall, in the West Bank, those who wanted to keep their Jerusalem residency had to leave and find a place to live within the area recognized as Jerusalem. The exact same fate has befallen Bir Nabala.

As I write this, fifty-three years later, the area where the Qalandia checkpoint stands, which used to be an open space, caressed by a soft wind, affording a welcome contrast to most of the landscape surrounding it, has now been transformed into a dirty, tortured place, littered with trash, enclosed by a wall smeared with graffiti, shackled by gates and miserable turnstiles too narrow to allow easy passage for many pedestrians who go through them. The Jerusalem Airport runway has become a parking lot hemmed in by the Annexation Wall and no longer visible from the road. Plans are in the making for the construction there of housing for Israeli Orthodox Jews, to complete the encirclement of eastern Jerusalem by Jewish settlements.

When Israel decided to close off Jerusalem from the West Bank after 1991, the process was gradual. At first they put the checkpoint much farther to the south. It slowly crept farther north, moving closer to Ramallah until it settled in its present position in Qalandia, where it assumed the role that the Mandelbaum Gate once played—only this time it has Israeli soldiers on both sides of the checkpoint, which has come to separate the expanded Jerusalem under Israel from the West Bank.

November 15, 2020

Shylock in the Promised Land
JO GLANVILLE

Sixty years before Shakespeare wrote *The Merchant of Venice*, Suleiman the Magnificent built the walls of Jerusalem. Even as the solid blocks of stone were being laid, Suleiman's Muslim army was thundering into Europe and threatening to topple Christendom. His greatness lingers on in Shakespeare's play, and when Portia's Moroccan suitor attempts to win her heart, he clearly thinks that he can impress her with a secondhand boast about the great warrior. He brandishes his scimitar and claims that it killed a Persian who once got the better of Suleiman. The reflected glory is not, however, enough to win him his bride.

My neighbor Nisreen was studying the play at school. As she read the Moroccan's lines she could look out at Suleiman's walls, which still form a mighty girdle around what is now the Old City of Jerusalem and Nisreen's home. The controversy that periodically accompanies European productions of the play pales beside its potential for fomenting discord in Shylock's spiritual home. That, at least, was the opinion of the Israeli authorities. Nisreen is a Palestinian and was reading the play in English, but the Israelis had banned *The Merchant of Venice* in Arabic, in the West Bank and the Gaza Strip. The miserly, vengeful, and bloodthirsty Shylock, reviled by the Venetians and rejected even by his own daughter, could be seen as a fine Jewish figure of hate for the Palestinians who lived so miserably under Israeli rule. As a ghetto diaspora Jew, he also represented everything that the Israelis had left behind in Europe.

There is no getting around the fact that Shylock is a villain. He is "the dog Jew," "a very Jew," "a faithless Jew," and, as I read those lines in my flat in the Old City, their sentiment chilled my blood. I had agreed to help Nisreen with her English studies, but I was now shrinking from the task. There is nothing like antisemitism for making an assimilated Jew, such as myself, feel Jewish.

At home in London, I had the luxury of a cultural Jewish identity without being a member of the Jewish community. I could not wholeheartedly call myself Jewish, since I had not been brought up in the religion, and its traditions were not part of my life. My mother is Jewish solely on her father's side, and I would therefore not be considered Jewish by the Orthodox, in any case. But there was no room for the niceties of my Jewish identity in Jerusalem and no possibility for half measures. Whose side was I on?

I met many Europeans who had come to Israel in aid of the Palestinian cause. They disliked the Israelis with a bitterness which I never encountered in the Palestinians themselves, who mostly displayed an astonishing generosity of spirit. When these Europeans posed the inevitable question—how could a persecuted people inflict such suffering on another?—I had a great desire to commit an act of violence. Since when, I retorted, did abuse beget anything other than abuse? But I realized that I too wanted the Israelis to be beyond reproach. I could not bear to hear them criticized, and yet at the same time I was deeply critical of them myself. It's okay for Jews to tell jokes against themselves, but if anyone tells a joke against them, it's antisemitism.

The young American Zionists were also intolerable. For them, Israel was one big summer camp. They considered the Palestinians to be the enemy, and when they talked about the Israelis, they said "we" and "us." The Israelis did not thank them for it.

*

By choosing to live in a Christian Palestinian neighborhood while studying at the Hebrew University, I was attempting to straddle both worlds and finding the exercise more difficult than I had anticipated.

It is not very comfortable sitting on the fence. Most Israelis were horrified when I told them where I lived. Was I not afraid? Was I stupid? Some nostalgically recalled the days when they spent Saturdays in the Old City and ate hummus in its restaurants. Arab East Jerusalem was the only place still humming with life on Shabbat when the western, Jewish side of the city closed down, but it had been off-limits to the Israelis since the Intifada began in the late 1980s. Some left-wing Israelis stayed away as a matter of principle, but most kept to West Jerusalem out of fear. One Israeli friend asked me to take her round the Old City, and so I found myself in the curious position of being tour guide to a native.

Israelis never took me for a Jew. They considered me wholly English, and I realized that they were right. I irritated them excessively with the number of times I said "sorry" in the course of a conversation. When it came to speaking Hebrew, I realized that I had great difficulty in asking directly for what I wanted. The English language serves as a very convenient cloak for one's needs and desires, which can be dressed up in numerous "mights" and "maybes" to disguise the fact that one actually wants something. But in Hebrew you ask directly for what you want, and there are no extra frills of language to hide the nakedness of your desires. That is why people so often consider the Israelis rude and abrupt: modern Hebrew was born in a hurry, and there was no time for trimmings.

It was the autumn of 1993, and at that time there was euphoria in the streets. In the build-up to the signing of the first Oslo Accord, Palestinian children marched round the narrow alleys of the Old City at night banging empty containers—a warlike sound that simultaneously thrilled me while chilling my Jewish sensibilities. Palestinian youths zoomed around the roads of East Jerusalem, which skirted the Old City, in open trucks waving the Palestinian flag, which had, until then, been illegal. When Yasser Arafat and Yitzhak Rabin shook hands on the lawn of the White House, I watched it on television and could hear my neighbors cheering. When I asked Nisreen what she felt, she shrugged her shoulders. She was a child when the Intifada began, and at seventeen she was already cynical. She expected nothing from the Israelis. It was rare in that heady atmosphere to encounter such coolness as Nisreen's. What would she make of Shylock?

I was torn. I wanted Nisreen to know that I was on her side, but I also wanted to defend Shylock. Should I start by sanctimoniously lecturing her about the bitter history of European Jews and thereby try to exonerate Shylock and the Israelis in her eyes? If she chose to identify Shylock with the Israelis, as I expected, what right did I have to preach at her?

Five Palestinian families lived in the courtyard where I shared a flat with two friends. It was on the cusp of the Jewish, Armenian, and Christian quarters. The Jewish quarter had been badly bombed in 1948 and later rebuilt by the Israelis after the Six-Day War. Crossing from the Muslim and Christian quarters into the Jewish quarter was a little like arriving in the Land of Oz from Kansas. The dark, discolored stone of the Palestinian streets gave way to the light, airy spaces and honey-colored stone of the wealthy Jewish neighborhood.

Shylock might not have attracted too much attention if he had happened to wander down these streets; there were enough people already in them in the antiquated fancy dress of their religions and denominations for him to mingle in the crowd: Franciscan monks, Greek Orthodox priests, Hasidic Jews, Ethiopian monks, Armenian priests. Then there were the groups of Christian tourists shouldering life-size crucifixes along the Via Dolorosa as they retraced Christ's footsteps and created a traffic jam. It was a religious theme park and going about one's daily business in a place so pregnant with symbolism seemed profane. I bought my stamps from a post office that faced the citadel where Pontius Pilate condemned Jesus, and I took a shortcut home from the butcher through the courtyard of the Holy Sepulcher, built, so they say, on Calvary. I would be struck down at any moment.

There were often strikes in East Jerusalem, commemorating clashes with the Israeli army or protesting against an incident in the West Bank or Gaza. The shops in the Old City would close, and the market streets would empty. Only a few defiant souls would carry on doing business behind their shutters. It was difficult to know how the owners of the tourist shops made a decent living, in any case. Trade had fallen drastically since the Intifada and most of the shops sold the same things: rugs, pottery, and olive-wood carvings.

When disaster struck the Palestinians—when Baruch Goldstein massacred the Palestinians in Hebron, when Israelis died in suicide bomb attacks—the depression and fear were palpable. Everyone was infected by a common sense of horror, and I became desperate to escape from Jerusalem, as though from the claustrophobic embrace of a family in the grip of catastrophe. Although I acclimatized quickly to the intensity of emotion and the burden of history that charged the atmosphere of the city, whenever I left Jerusalem for any period of time, I felt a sudden, physical release of pressure from my head, as if I had come down from a great altitude.

Nisreen was very down-to-earth. She had her own domestic troubles. Her father was a very sick man, dying slowly after a botched operation. He once lifted up his shirt to show me his stomach. There was a crater where his belly should have been. A tough rim of skin, like hide, surrounded a circle of softer-looking flesh. In desperation, he had gone to India for a kidney transplant. He was given no time to recuperate and flew straight back to Jerusalem. The wound had opened on the journey home, and the doctors in Israel had not been able to repair the damage. He would become deeply depressed and lie on his bed crying, "I want to die, I want to die."

Once, when I was visiting, he began cursing the Jews. It was in those situations that the question of my Jewish identity plagued me, and I wondered why I had been so naive as to think that I could live in a Palestinian neighborhood. My neighbors accepted me as a foreigner. They welcomed me and my flatmates into their homes. They fed us, entertained us, and made us feel as though we were part of their lives. My friend Cathy had found the flat. She spoke good Arabic and had lived in Jerusalem for several years. With her ebullient, forthright personality, she was more at home there than in the quiet English seaside town where she had grown up. She was a Christian. Palestinians were always attracted by her infectious warmth, and she had many friends.

One night, soon after I had arrived in Jerusalem, a group of Cathy's friends had gathered on our balcony. Someone told an antisemitic joke. I did not say a word. Suddenly, I had become a Jewish victim, shocked and alienated from their company. My grandfather had changed his name from Goldberg to Glanville to hide his Jewish identity, and here I was, hiding my Jewish identity and not daring to speak out in the country where Jews were supposed to be free. But perhaps my automatic response and inherited sense of persecution were not appropriate. For it was the Palestinians who were victims here, not me. They were the underclass. They had no reason to be friends with the Israelis, and if they chose to let off steam by telling crude jokes, who was I to correct them? They may have been guests in my home that night, but I was a guest in their city, just passing through their lives.

However, when Nisreen's father began railing against the Jews, I told him that I came from a Jewish family. "Ah, you Jews from over there," he said, gesturing in a direction that I assumed to be Europe. "You are different." I was amused, and I confess relieved, at how swiftly he reconciled his liking for me with my Jewish origins. Some Palestinian friends had advised me never to declare that I was Jewish in Palestinian neighborhoods; others said that I should choose my moments carefully. Whenever I did "come out," for that is what it felt like, I was always pleasantly surprised by the response.

Once I shared a taxi to the West Bank with a Palestinian. I had been told on no account to speak Hebrew there. My command of Arabic was poor, and my traveling companion spoke little English—Hebrew was the only common language, and we chatted merrily for the entire journey. I had the fearful sense of breaking a taboo, but I was never able to grasp the etiquette that governed the Israeli-Palestinian divide. Perhaps there were no rules, and this in itself was alarming. I often had the sense that I was walking through these two cultures blindly, endeavoring not to step on the cracks in the pavement without having any idea of where the cracks actually were.

*

No one surprised me and shattered my preconceptions as much as Nisreen. We spent the first few sessions on *The Merchant of Venice* unraveling Shakespeare's metaphors and deciphering the punning banter of the Venetian lads. In all my apprehension, I had completely neglected to consider that the language might pose a problem for Nisreen. Her English was good, but Shakespeare is difficult enough for British schoolchildren of her age. To my astonishment, Nisreen was wholly captivated by the poetry. She declared that she wanted to marry Shakespeare. Then she began to joke that she was Shakespeare's wife and called herself Mrs. Shakespeare.

"How is your husband?" I would ask her when she arrived for a session on *The Merchant*.

"He is well," she would reply gravely and then break into a smile. I was learning to read and write Arabic and had a children's ABC on the wall of my room. Next to each character was a corresponding picture: a rabbit for the letter *aleph*, a duck for the letter *beyt*. Nisreen would point solemnly at each picture, and I would have to name them correctly. Then we would begin reading *The Merchant*. Nisreen loved the story and became as involved with the characters as she might've if it were a soap opera. She tutted at Bassanio's recklessness and held her breath when Portia's suitors tried the caskets.

Then one day we read the passage where Shylock's servant, Launcelot Gobbo, curses his master and runs off to serve a Christian, Bassanio. As we read Launcelot's speech, in which he declares, "The Jew is the very devil incarnation," I inwardly cringed, fearing that Nisreen would applaud the sentiment. She looked at me and frowned. "Shylock will kill him if he hears him!" she exclaimed, entirely rapt in the plot.

I felt ashamed of myself and thought of the Israeli authorities who had banned the play in Arabic. All that we seemed to be able to see in the play was antisemitic feeling; all that Nisreen could see was the drama. Shakespeare and his art had triumphed over our own self-obsession. Nisreen pitied Shylock—she hated the manner in which the Christians reviled him and was horrified when they stripped him of his wealth and forced him to convert to Christianity. She responded to all the characters with equally human feeling. Shakespeare can rarely have had a better audience than Nisreen.

I gave her a book of his sonnets for her birthday. She proudly took the book to school to show her teacher and then became the most unpopular girl in the class when her teacher made all the students learn one of the sonnets by heart for homework.

When I heard that the play was being performed in Tel Aviv, I wanted to take Nisreen. But it was being performed in Hebrew, and she was not keen to go, so I went alone. Tel Aviv is another world. It is a modern city on the Mediterranean, and Jerusalem, in comparison, is a provincial town. I had begun to dress very conservatively since living in the Old City in an attempt to fit in with the cultural norm, and when I experienced a sense of shock at seeing the women of Tel Aviv so free and easy in their short skirts, I realized that I had not even appreciated how constricting life in Jerusalem had become. Tel Aviv was far closer to the life that I knew in London, and yet it felt alien.

The Merchant of Venice was playing at the Cameri Theatre, one of the best-known theaters in the country. To see Launcelot cursing Shylock in Hebrew, Bassanio and his chums bantering in Hebrew, and Portia's suitors wooing her in Hebrew filled me with awe. Surely this must be one of the ultimate triumphs for Jews—to produce *The Merchant of Venice* with a Jewish cast, before a Jewish audience, in the language and nation of the Jews. However, it was not enough of a triumph as far as the director was concerned. The production turned Shakespeare's play on its head.

Shylock was a sober, respectable businessman in a gray three-piece suit, while the Christians sported velvet and hung out in a hippie den. They were a dissolute bunch of layabouts, and you would not lend a fiver to a single one of them.

Worse was to follow. When Jessica eloped with Lorenzo, she appeared dressed in velvet, as if she had been brainwashed and joined a cult. She handed a suitcase full of money to Lorenzo and was then raped by his cronies while he kissed the bills of cash.

When Shylock made his famous speech—"Hath not a Jew

eyes?"—the Christians gathered round him and beat him up. At the end of the speech, as Shylock spoke of vengeance, they fell to the floor.

Here, in Tel Aviv, Shylock had finally had his revenge and corrected the wrongs of centuries of persecution. The stereotype of the money-loving, rapacious, lascivious Jew had been projected onto the Christians, and Shakespeare's play had been rewritten. If it had not been for Nisreen, I might have rejoiced in the Israeli production. She had the humanity to see both sides of the story and taught me a lesson about my own prejudice.

I rang the Israeli authorities to ask them why they had banned the Arabic translation of the play in the West Bank and Gaza. The Israeli official to whom I spoke was shocked to hear that the play was banned. He had had no idea and doubted that I had been correctly informed. Perhaps, he suggested, there was a particular Arabic edition of the play with an introduction that incited violence against the Israelis. Perhaps, but I was never able to find out. These days, it is Arafat who monitors the Palestinians' reading matter and bans books in the Palestinian territories.

Autumn 1997

We Will Never Leave
HANEEN NAZZAL

Haneen Nazzal, *We Will Never Leave*, 2021. Digital illustration, 36 x 51 cm. Courtesy of the artist.

We Will Never Leave was inspired by graffiti on the walls of Sheikh Jarrah, in occupied East Jerusalem. The poster was used in a campaign to save Palestinian homes that was launched by families in the area who were—and still are—facing ethnic cleansing by the Israeli authorities. Top right, the address on the poster reads: "13 Sheikh Jarrah Arab Palestinian neighborhood."

Sheikh Jarrah Is Burning
MOHAMMED EL-KURD

If "Israel" is venom in a snake's fang
our youth have defanged the snake.
—**Abu Arab**

If the first sentence is the skunk water, it's overwritten for the tear gas in Abu Ali's living room. The Nakba asserts Sheikh Jarrah is not an exception to the rule. A microcosm of settler colonialism, I've been telling the media, ethnic cleansing, apartheid, a hell, whatever you want to call it!

This is the second month of the blockade. The media won't call it illegal. Zionist philanthropy carves out its home in my spine. American settlers find their way into the front yard, and their billionaires take us to court. Their laws are daggers. Their laws are hungry. Armed colonizers peacock around my street with impunity.

After the protest, they put up cement barriers. No journalists, no medics. The pig calls me by my name before he asks for my ID. No entry. The settlers walk in, no questions. Barricades for them are hypothetical. I told an American reporter this is apartheid, but she's not entirely convinced. I look at the cuts she sustained, jumping over my neighbor's fence.

Early May: Mahmoud's head was under a fascist's knee. If only he didn't have the rifle and the baton! Jana was standing in her house, on May 19, when a Zionist shot her in the back. She is sixteen soon. Her spine will recover, I hope. It is those who are spineless who cannot buy themselves a spine. They broke Saleh's leg. Stun grenades turn midnight into dawn. Military horses storm through us. The skunk water truck shoots at our fruit trees. Skunk sticks, its evidence blistered on Muna's hands. They keep chanting for our death. Some of us sleep in our shoes, others sleep through the waged war.

A cavalry came to confiscate our balloons. They looked ridiculous getting off their high horses to climb up the settlers' ladder, untangling the balloons from the electricity wires. We laugh as much as we can before the tear gas. There's a circus in their brutality. At the interrogation they asked me how we dare paint Palestinian flags on children's faces. They asked what's my problem with the police? *Nothing*, I answered. Nothing but the cuffs on my hands and feet. The bruises and the rifle butts. They're arresting everyone and their mother. Arresting broomsticks and donkeys. Arresting schoolgirls with Palestinian flags. Our beloved speaker system. A kite, a hat, my threshold for shock.

A dozen Kyle Rittenhouses patrol my street. Cowards if not for their M-16s. They attacked us with rocks and dispossession. We retaliated with plastic chairs in lieu of the rockets. I stood in awe of the hail. The settlers stole our chairs, and the cops sat on them. I called this collusion. My journalist friend didn't believe me until a settler gestured to a cop to kick her out of the neighborhood. I gave her a cigarette in lieu of an "I told you so."

The youth remind me with firework spectacle: decolonization is not an abstract theory. See: The solider with a stone in his fascist face. The colonizer car in flames. Surveillance cameras smashed. "Checkpoints" emptied out of their gatekeepers. I stand in awe of the hail.

Conversation
Palestinians and Israelis
Commemorate the Nakba Together
RANA SALMAN and YONATAN GHER

The two CEOs of Combatants for Peace, one Palestinian, the other Israeli, discuss their organization's participation in Nakba Remembrance Day on May 15, 2022. Combatants for Peace is a group of Palestinians and Israelis who have taken an active part in the cycle of violence in their region: Israeli soldiers serving in the Israeli Defense Forces and Palestinians as combatants fighting to free their country, Palestine, from Israeli occupation.

٭

Yonatan Gher: We should probably tell our readers from the start that in writing this article, we are violating Israeli law. According to Israel's 2011 Budget Foundations Law (known as the Nakba Law), it is forbidden to relate to the day of the founding of the State of Israel as a day of mourning.

Rana Salman: It's a law I'm happy to violate. The Nakba Law violates the right to freedom of expression for citizens in Israel and the rights of the Palestinian minority in the country and aims to erase the memory of the most mournful day in the lives of Palestinians. Nakba literally means "catastrophe," but the Palestinian Nakba was not a natural disaster. It marks the destruction and displacement of more than seven hundred thousand Palestinians during the creation of the State of Israel, in 1948. Today, the total 1948 refugee population is estimated at some 5.5 million, including 4 million registered with United Nations Relief and Works Agency and 1.5 million not registered. Most live in

Jordan, followed by the Gaza Strip, the West Bank, Syria, Lebanon, and East Jerusalem.

YG: These are things I should know. Growing up in the Israeli school system, at no point did I hear the word Nakba from any of my teachers, let alone the perspective it represents. In Israeli history class we learned that the waves of Jewish immigrants that came to Israel in the late nineteenth and early twentieth centuries arrived in a barren land. There was no local population to speak of, other than those who tried to kill us. So we defended ourselves, and they ran away. Later in life, when I learned of the term Nakba, it was in the context by which many Israelis have come to understand the term: an antisemitic desire that Israel should cease to exist and that we all should die.

RS: That's not what I want. But I do want Israelis to understand what the Nakba really is. As for me, I didn't have to learn about Nakba at school to understand how painful it was, as I am a descendant of a Palestinian refugee family that was expelled from their home in Haifa in 1948. I grew up imagining how difficult it must have been for my family to lose their home and become refugees. My grandparents were never allowed to return.

YG: Many nations have gone and continue to go through a reckoning of their past and the devastation that their founding brought upon the Indigenous communities that existed prior. Australia changed its national anthem to reflect its understanding and respect toward the Aboriginal communities that lived on the land long before the European arrival. Israel lacks the ability of these other nations to look at their history and say, "Yes, we did wrong, we now wish to rectify," to a large extent because in our case—this has to be said—the wrongdoing is still taking place. So while my position might not be popular in my country right now, I would like to think that when future generations learn about this period, my actions will be ones for which they will not need to apologize.

RS: That will take commitment and a lot of work. Learning about the Nakba is not only a matter of learning facts, although having this knowledge is of great importance. It is essential to comprehend the meaning of these facts to cultivate sympathy and compassion. Israelis should learn about the traumatic event of the Nakba and acknowledge it as a historical reality. It is necessary for Israel to recognize the ethnic cleansing that was (and still is) committed; it is the only way that we will overcome it. Educating Israelis about the Nakba is still relevant today, as tensions continue to escalate. In 2021 Israel was carrying out the most brutal displacement operations in Sheikh Jarrah neighborhood in East Jerusalem, while the international community was not only witnessing and ignoring but allowing Israel to continue its human rights violations and international crimes against the Palestinian people. In 2022 the communities of Masafer Yatta, an area in the South Hebron Hills of the West Bank, are also facing the threat of expulsion.

YG: If we are to make peace between Israelis and Palestinians, we must be able to understand where the other is coming from. We don't need to accept or agree with the other's narrative, but we need to recognize that it exists. One side's terrorists are the other side's freedom fighters. One side's occupation forces are the other side's defense forces. One side's independence day is the other side's Nakba. Both sides have their dignity and their determination, and no side will be defeated into submission. At the same time, we must also recognize the facts on the ground: the apartheid and oppression are very real and cannot be ended until we have a serious reckoning with both history and the current reality. Israelis are participating in the Nakba ceremony because we want to learn; we want to understand; we want to reckon; we want to end the bloodshed and live here together with equality and peace.

RS: Learning each other's narratives is why Israelis participate in the Nakba ceremony, and also why Palestinians participate in the joint Israeli-Palestinian Yom Hazikaron Memorial Ceremony. You can't truly connect with someone without sharing things about yourself.

Palestinians participate at the joint Memorial Ceremony because we want to connect with the "other" on a human level. We want to prevent further pain, grief, and loss. It is through this approach that Palestinians and Israelis realize war is not a decree of destiny but a political choice.

And that's what we hope to achieve with the Nakba Remembrance Ceremony. It builds empathy and awareness of the suffering caused by the events of 1948 and the creation of the State of Israel—pain that continues to this day. A peaceful future can only be built when together, we honor and acknowledge the pain of the past and its influence on the present.

April 25, 2022

Return Is Possible
The Status of 536 Palestinian Villages
Depopulated by Israel
VISUALIZING PALESTINE

Posters by Visualizing Palestine highlight genocide, torture, imprisonment, and the inhumane treatment of Palestinians, such as the number of children in Gaza killed by Israeli forces. VP also produces and publishes its posters in Arabic, Hebrew, French, and Spanish. *Return Is Possible: The Status of 536 Palestinian Villages Depopulated by Israel* visualizes complex data effectively and graphically. On the poster, Visualizing Palestine notes: "Today, Israel systematically denies Palestinians their right to return, yet the sites of their original homes remain largely empty. Seventy-seven percent of former Palestinian towns and villages in Israel have never been built over."

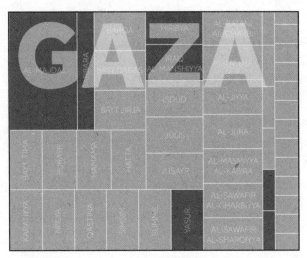

Visualizing Palestine, *Return Is Possible*, 2017, detail. Data Sketch. Courtesy of Visualizing Palestine.

RETURN IS POSSIBLE

THE STATUS OF 536 PALESTINIAN VILLAGES DEPOPULATED BY ISRAEL

In 1948, the UN General Assembly declared that Palestinian "refugees wishing to return to their homes and live at peace with their neighbours should be permitted to do so at the earliest practicable date".

Today, Israel systematically denies Palestinians their right to return, yet the sites of their original homes remain largely empty. **77% of former Palestinian towns and villages in Israel have never been built over.**

77% NEVER BUILT OVER   **23% BUILT OVER**

RAMLE · BEERSHEBA · GAZA · TIBERIAS · BEISAN · SAFAD · HEBRON · HAIFA · JAFFA · ACRE · JERUSALEM · TULKARM · JENIN · NAZARETH

Depopulated towns/villages organised by British Mandate districts. The size of each is relative to population in 1948. 'Never built over' refers to the original built-up area of the village. Precise location of some communities in Beersheba district unknown, but assumed not to be built over as region is sparsely populated.

VP DATA SKETCH   **SOURCES** bit.ly/vp-return · **V1** May 2017 · f fb.me/visualizingpalestine · 🐦 @visualizingpal

Visualizing Palestine, *Return Is Possible*, 2017. Data Sketch. Courtesy of Visualizing Palestine.

Driving in Palestine
Now Is More
Dangerous Than Ever
FADI QURAN

Driving in Palestine now is more dangerous than ever.

Yesterday, I drove from Ramallah to Dura, a village near Hebron, to attend the funeral of Ahed, my friend's baby sister, who had just become a mother. She was shot by an Israeli sniper. A heartbreaking loss.

If I could use Israel's apartheid roads designated for settlers, it would be an eighty-to-ninety-minute drive, but it took me four hours. Why?

First, we're forced to take segregated Palestinian-only roads, which make it a two-and-a-half-hour drive because of checkpoints.

But these days it's even worse, as Israel has imposed an even more strict strangulation policy over the West Bank, which means even some of those segregated roads are blocked, and there are ten times as many checkpoints.

Taking this drive outside our village and cities of residence is extremely dangerous for three reasons:

1. **Settler attacks:** Israeli settlers are in rampage mode, and you don't know when you could get hit by a rock or bullet from one of their raging mobs.

2. **Soldiers at the end of a wrong turn:** There are no signs for which "roads" are currently opened or closed for us—you have to guess or stop to ask locals every few miles. If you make a wrong turn and end up face-to-face with soldiers, they can shoot you and claim you attacked them.

3. **Arrests for social media posts:** If you're stopped at a checkpoint, soldiers these days are taking folks' phones and checking their WhatsApp, Telegram, and Instagram. If you

have a message standing in solidarity with Gaza, or anything the Israeli soldiers see as offensive, they'll beat you to
a pulp and could even arrest you. My friend Diala, a human
rights lawyer, was just arrested at one of these checkpoints
this evening. We don't know why, but it likely relates to her
work and messages they found on her phone about it.

On my end, driving back at night was a nightmare, mainly because
I had a friend in the car and was worried about him.

As we drove back, these historically busy streets were ghostly empty
because nobody is taking the risk of driving at night unless absolutely
necessary. Every turn I'd take, I'd slow down to a crawl to make sure
there was no trigger-happy soldier or angry settler ready to pounce.

I got lucky, for although we waited at a checkpoint for an hour,
the soldiers got bored and literally opened the checkpoint for all the
cars to pass without any security check—proof they're using these
checkpoints arbitrarily as collective punishment.

*

In Dura, I saw where Ahed was shot.

The soldiers had stormed her village as part of their intimidation
tactics in the West Bank to keep people anxious. Ahed ran to her roof to
warn her husband to come home. An Israeli sniper shot her in the head.

As I drove home, thinking of Ahed, her heartbroken family, the
families of my friends in Gaza, all the souls we've lost, and how easily
my life could be taken for simply driving across my ancestral lands to
help my friend in her grief.

It shouldn't have to be said, but our lives are precious. They're
beautiful. They're equally worthy of joy and basic dignity.

I'm committed to one day being able to drive across my people's
ancestral land a free man, surrounded by my liberated people.

If Israel's death machine is haunting us around every corner, we
might as well live fighting for a life worth dying for.

January 19, 2024

Unembedded
Reporting from the West Bank
CHLOÉ BENOIST

The news agency's English desk consisted of four foreigners—three Americans and me—and three Palestinian translators, working side by side in a nondescript office with our Arabic-language colleagues, with whom we shared tea, coffee, and jokes throughout the day. My favorite Palestinian colleagues were the news agency's translators of Hebrew, a language they picked up in Israeli prisons in the late 1980s. I won them over by telling them I was born in 1987, "like the First Intifada."

Unlike most foreign journalists reporting for big international newspapers from Jerusalem, I wasn't registered with Israel's Government Press Office. To have a GPO-issued press card would have opened many doors, including the option of reporting outside of the occupied West Bank, but I would have had to abide by Israeli gag orders, which prevent journalists from reporting on certain cases. I never got to see Gaza, despite it being only seventy-five kilometers away from where I lived in Bethlehem.

I soon got the hang of the daily routine at the news agency. Most mornings would start the same: looking up the Palestinian Prisoners Society's latest statement on overnight arrests and calling the Israeli army spokesperson's office to cross-check how many Palestinians had been detained and where. On average, we would record between twelve and twenty Palestinians detained per day; the times when that number fell into the single digits were rare enough that we would comment on it in surprise.

A key part of the English desk's responsibilities was to call Israeli government bodies for comment. Many of our Palestinian colleagues were nervous about speaking to them, and so it was up to us to get the official Israeli version of events firsthand—and challenge it when necessary.

The first time I called the army, I was tense. I expected a stern older man who would refuse to answer my questions.

Instead, I fell on a young woman with a flawless Valley girl accent who chirpily mangled the names of Palestinian villages that soldiers had raided overnight. I would write them all down, then walk over to the map of the occupied West Bank pinned to the office wall, trying to decipher which locations she may have meant.

I surmised that the spokesperson's office was staffed almost exclusively by very young women originally from the US who had leveraged their impeccable English into a more comfortable military service than manning a checkpoint. Soon I would come to mirror their tone, learning that it would yield the information I needed much more quickly and painlessly.

One day, I reached a familiar voice, the bubbliest one of them all. "Hi," I said, "I'm calling about a report that a Palestinian was shot and injured by Israeli forces near the borderline in the Gaza Strip. Can you confirm whether you have a record of this?"

The spokeswoman made me wait for a minute while she looked, then got back on the phone to say that yes, someone had indeed been shot. "Do you have any more information as to why?" I asked, leaning into my upspeak.

"No," she said. I could almost hear her shrugging. "It's nothing out of the ordinary."

Nothing out of the ordinary.

She wasn't wrong, of course. That was precisely the problem. I wondered how young she was—probably eighteen to twenty years old, if this was her military-service posting. Did she grapple with the full weight of the information she conveyed day in and day out, or did this all feel abstract to her—data on a screen and memorized talking points? Had I let her feel so comfortable speaking with me that she felt she could let such a callous statement slip?

So much of life in Palestine, as it turns out, depends on teenagers in army uniforms.

By contrast, the police spokesman was the one we dreaded contacting the most. Every time a story took place in East Jerusalem, within Israeli police jurisdiction, we would pray that he wouldn't pick up the phone—and most of the time, he didn't.

But if he did, he would abruptly ask who was calling in his terse British accent, making it clear that we were wasting precious minutes of his life with our inane questions. I would soften my pronunciation of the news agency's name, turning the ع into an a in hopes that its Arabness would go unnoticed and grant me more information—in vain.

I once made the mistake of asking for comment about a report that Israeli police had attacked some Palestinian youths in Jerusalem. "Why would you use that word? Police don't *attack* Palestinians," he barked at me. This taught me to carefully weigh my words and rehearse my script before I dialed his number. It also made me take notice of when other news outlets would adopt the terminology of Israeli spokespeople as if it were their own.

The Coordinator of Government Activities in the Territories, the euphemistically named military body in charge of governing "civilian" matters for Palestinians in the occupied territories, was another story. Getting a straightforward answer was like trying to draw blood from a stone, as they could take up to a week to get back to us on even the simplest cases (a demolition order issued against a Palestinian home, the announcement of tenders for the expansion of a settlement)—if they answered at all. We got in the habit of including in our articles the line: "A COGAT spokesperson did not respond to a request for comment at the time of publication"—a common journalistic turn of phrase to show that we had done our due diligence.

Until one day a colleague received an angry call from a COGAT spokeswoman. People had been asking her why they kept seeing that sentence in so many of our articles, she screamed. We were the only news outlet who didn't wait to hear back from them before publishing, she went on to say—an unbelievable claim, given how nakedly they were trying to bury stories with their silence. For how else could we explain their unresponsiveness to us on stories that Israeli media had already reported on?

So we switched tactics: every request for comment included a specific deadline by which we would need a response. COGAT adapted to that too, meeting our questions with requests of their own. Once, we were told that we hadn't provided them enough information for them to respond to questions about a recently issued demolition order—leaving us to wonder: Exactly how many one-story carpenter workshops owned by an Iyad D. in this specific northern West Bank village of two thousand inhabitants had received demolition orders that very day for there to be any room for confusion?

We were once told that COGAT couldn't confirm whether it had detained a Palestinian man, whose full name we had supplied, at the Erez crossing that day unless we supplied them with his ID number—as if we journalists had better access to a Palestinian's private information than the state that boasts some of the most advanced surveillance technologies on earth.

The same road would be simultaneously open or closed depending on which Israeli governmental body you spoke to or how you phrased your question. Alleged Palestinian attackers would be described as "neutralized" on the scene with no further elaboration—neither living nor dead, like Schrödinger's cat. (Although, more often than not, they would be dead.)

These anecdotes would be added to our collection of surreal Israeli responses, which we shared among ourselves to laugh out of frustration and despair. "Did not respond to a request for comment at the time of publication" became a small act of rebellion amid the Orwellian doublespeak we found ourselves navigating every day.

The truth is, the Israelis weren't the only ones we had to worry about when doing our jobs. While the news agency I worked at was nominally independent, it wasn't rare for members of the Palestinian Authority security forces to stop by the office in full uniform for tea. And a simple phone call could suffice for an article to be taken off the website.

The English desk was submitted to a lesser degree of scrutiny than our Arabic-speaking colleagues, but we knew we were also being watched. A PLO official once called and complained to a hapless colleague that while the Arabic website read like "it came straight from Mahmoud Abbas's office"—something he said he didn't agree with—the English site, on the other hand, sounded like the leftist Democratic Front for the Liberation of Palestine opposition party.

We foreign staff laughed it off, wearing this critique as a badge of honor—but we also knew that the Palestinians on our team were bearing the brunt of this pressure.

These regular run-ins we, as foreign journalists, had with various authorities were of course only a small taste of the death by a thousand bureaucratic cuts inflicted on Palestinians. Under the guise of law and order, Israel gaslit the world into believing Palestinians were unreasonable for repeatedly building homes illegally (when 98 percent of their construction-permit requests are denied), or for raising entire generations of violent terrorists (tried in military courts with 99.7 percent conviction rates)—a conception of "law and order" that, conveniently, happened to forget about international law as far as Palestinians were concerned.

Looking back years later, my time in Palestine appears relatively uneventful. Yet a perusal of my notes from the time reminds me that I bore witness to the so-called Knife Intifada; the cold-blooded murder of Abd el-Fattah al-Sharif by Elor Azaria, in Hebron; a mass prisoner hunger strike; the death of Bassel al-Araj; increased settlement construction in the E1 area around East Jerusalem; the surveillance camera crisis at Al-Aqsa; the imprisonment of then sixteen-year-old Ahed Tamimi; Trump's recognition of Jerusalem as the Israeli capital; the opening of the US embassy in Jerusalem; the early weeks of the Great March of Return in Gaza; ten years of blockade on Gaza; the thirty-year anniversary of the First Intifada; seventy years of the Nakba.

Beyond these momentous events were the countless daily indignities of life under the occupation that most abroad never hear about: the uprooting of olive trees, the demolition orders that homeowners have to carry out with their own hands to avoid being billed for the Israeli bulldozers tearing down their houses, the confiscation of Palestinian bodies, the army raids, every single night of the year without fail.

Each one a crisis in its own right, most of which barely registered in the international consciousness. Each one a crisis, and yet "nothing out of the ordinary."

*

I couldn't escape these uncanny reminders of the occupation anywhere. Every passage at the Ben Gurion airport, in Tel Aviv, meant thorough questioning to the point of absurdity: Do you work in an open space or do you have your own office? Do you have Palestinian friends? What are their names? Do you live alone? What is your roommate's name? There's a Jordanian stamp in your passport from last summer—what was the name of the hostel you stayed at in Amman that one time? What do your parents do for work? Without fail, I would get a sticker with the number six affixed to my passport, the highest-level security check.

One day I set out on the 231 bus from Bethlehem to Jerusalem with a Frenchman I was seeing that summer, hoping to spend a weekend together in Haifa. The bus went through the Beit Jala checkpoint, where Palestinians were made to get off the bus to have their IDs checked while foreigners and the elderly stayed on, an uncomfortable segregation.

Two young Israeli soldiers, no more than twenty years old, climbed aboard, encumbered by their bulky weapons and protective gear in the narrow aisles. One of them took my passport and flipped through until he found my full-page visa.

"What do you do?" he asked me.

Not wanting to volunteer the fact that I was a journalist up front, I responded: "I work in the West Bank."

"Which bank?"

I stifled my laughter when I realized he wasn't joking. It dawned on me: To him, this is Judea and Samaria, and the only bank I could be conceivably speaking of at this moment is a financial institution. Two parallel realities superimposed on top of the same land, colliding in this unbelievable misunderstanding.

Ignoring my explanations and my companion's very French outrage ("Ouat eef she 'ad to go to zee embassy?!"), the soldiers said my visa, which I had used countless times to fly into Tel Aviv, did not allow me inside Jerusalem or Israel, and that we had to get off the bus and turn back around.

We decided to try our luck through Checkpoint 300, on the other end of Bethlehem—a commuter's nightmare for thousands of Palestinian workers at the crack of dawn; its spooky maze of concrete corridors felt like an abandoned slaughterhouse during the day. I took off the jacket that had been covering my tank top and gave the soldiers, all hidden behind Plexiglass and two-way mirrors, the best impression of a clueless tourist I could muster. I was let through, free to spend the weekend frolicking by the Mediterranean Sea that many of my Palestinian friends weren't able to visit for themselves.

The inconsistency I experienced that day from one checkpoint to the next was a key part of the occupation: never knowing when a rule would be waived or strictly applied gave the impression of Israeli leniency while making sure we always felt uncertain about what our luck would bring that day.

*

It's always been a strange experience trying to explain what it was like living in the West Bank. Some people expected me to witness absolute misery and devastation (I think it was a sobering moment for my friends in Lebanon when I told them that, unlike in Beirut, I had twenty-four-hour electricity and solid internet). Others believed I was living in an all-out war zone and appeared almost disappointed that I couldn't regale them with stories of dodging bullets or seeing someone die in front of my eyes.

Reality was more complex than that. Bethlehem had plenty of bars and restaurants and a hotel with a pool where we would spend sunny afternoons eating watermelon and smoking *shisha*. There were late-night bonfires where someone played the oud. Warm Ramadan nights when the streets would cheerily fill up with families out for some ice cream. Christmas lights on cobblestone streets. Profound friendships and love stories, tedious office drama, nights spent playing cards games like *trix* or *tarneeb*. Lemon and *askadinya* (loquat) trees stretching their branches over onto my balcony as if hand-delivering me fruit, while a flock of sheep grazed nearby.

And all of that existed in concert with the apartheid wall. The Israeli military base looming on the edge of the city. Bethlehem's three refugee camps—Aida, Azza, and Dheisheh—whose residents carry the memories of Jerusalem-area villages destroyed in 1948. The night raids. The tear gas. The checkpoints. The ever-present fear, until this day, for the safety of the people I know.

And so I learned to live with it. I learned to check the local Facebook pages at the end of the night to see if the army was out or if it was safe to head home. I learned to sit in the front passenger seat because Israeli soldiers were less likely to shoot at a car if they saw a white girl on board. I learned which side streets to escape through when the tear gas on Jerusalem-Hebron Road got too bad. I learned to smile and keep my voice upbeat at checkpoints and maybe even take off my jacket and show a little cleavage. I learned which people in the community had lost a son or a friend and whose bodies still carried pieces of shrapnel. I learned the spokespeoples' phone numbers by heart. I memorized statistics. I eventually had paragraphs of background information on the Gaza blockade, on the Al-Aqsa Mosque, on administrative detention flowing automatically from my fingertips.

Speaking to friends and family back in France or the US, I struggled to convey the reality of what I was witnessing. The sentence "Israeli settlers uproot three hundred olive trees" cannot carry in six words the enormity of the loss of each and every tree. I realized how the mention of a Palestinian being imprisoned under administrative detention would trigger some people's cognitive dissonance—surely these people must have done something wrong, they reasoned, for we cannot conceive of hundreds of people thrown into prison each year without trial or charges. That this specific policy is a remnant of the British mandate only makes such disbelief that much more ironic.

I thought that I was as prepared as I ever could have been when I first set foot in Palestine—that I knew enough not to be surprised. There are many days when humor helps you cope. And there are days that break you, when the callous, intentional cruelty is too much to bear. This may all become routine, but it never feels normal.

January 22, 2024

Negative Incursion
RULA HALAWANI

On March 28, 2002, Rula Halawani took photographs of the IDF invasion of Ramallah and printed the negatives. She told the journal *Art Radar*, "In negative, the pictures were able to express my own feelings merged with the feelings of my people, to explain what had happened to us and to Palestine. As negatives, they express the negation of our reality that the invasion represented."

Rula Halawani, *Untitled VI* from the *Negative Incursion* series, 2002. Archival print, 90 x 124 cm. Courtesy of the artist and Ayyam Gallery.

Water-Deprived Palestinians Endure Settler Rampage while Army Punishes NGO Protesters

BRETT KLINE

In the last days of September, violent incidents in the South Hebron Hills area of the occupied West Bank attracted media attention across the political spectrum in Israel but scant mention in mainstream Western press. The incidents involved a small army of radical settlers who attacked a tiny but strategically placed Palestinian village, where several days earlier soldiers in the Israeli Defense Forces had beaten middle-aged peace activists with Combatants for Peace and members of two other nongovernmental organizations who had been bringing water to the village.

Some sixty masked settlers rampaged through the tiny village of Khirbet al-Mafaqarah, destroying cars and water carriers and smashing windows in homes. A dozen Palestinian residents were injured by the attackers, including a three-year-old boy. Palestinian residents said such a highly organized level of settler violence is rare, though incidents involving throwing stones and cutting down olive trees take place regularly.

Washington expressed strong criticism of the settler rampage, as quoted in a number of Israeli dailies, though as of Friday, the comments had not been picked up by the *New York Times* or other mainstream US media outlets. "The US government strongly condemns the acts of settler violence that took place against Palestinians in villages near Hebron in the West Bank," a US embassy spokesperson said on Friday.

Israeli foreign minister Yair Lapid remarked, "This violent incident is horrific and it is terror. . . . This is a violent and dangerous fringe and we have a responsibility to bring them to justice." The quote ran in the center-right *Jerusalem Post*, the centrist *Times of Israel* and the left-of-center *Haaretz*, which has an important international audience for the English-language internet edition, as well as in other Israeli media in Hebrew and English.

The leftist Israeli activist group Peace Now called the attack a "pogrom."

The Israeli government arrested at least six settlers, including a minor, and a Palestinian who was almost immediately released. At least four of the settlers are still being held, according to the *Jerusalem Post*. The government rarely arrests any Jewish settlers involved in violence against Palestinians in the West Bank. Even more rare are convictions of settlers for frequent violent incidents.

Extremely disturbing videos taken by Palestinians were published by the well-known and internationally respected B'Tselem, the human rights organization, in *+972 Magazine*, the *Jerusalem Post*, the *Times of Israel*, and other media outlets. They show masked settlers in their late teens and perhaps early twenties smashing windows of cars and homes, many with residents still inside.

Heavily armed IDF soldiers can be seen standing idly alongside the settlers. The soldiers then throw tear-gas canisters at the Palestinians and call them "*sharmouta*," or whores, in Arabic.

In one Palestinian home, three-year-old Mohammed was hit by stones. He was taken by soldiers in a military jeep with his uncle to a nearby ambulance. After reportedly being attacked by settlers, the emergency vehicle managed to leave and take them to an Israeli hospital in Be'ersheva. Though suffering from a fractured skull and internal bleeding, Mohammed is reportedly in stable condition.

Khirbet al-Mafaqarah sits between two settler outposts, Avigayil and Havat Ma'on, both illegal under Israeli and international law. The previous Israeli government under Benjamin Netanyahu had sought to force residents there and in other nearby villages to leave by seizing their lands and demolishing buildings and structures.

For resident Mahmoud Hamamdah, quoted in *+972 Magazine*, the assault serves a clear purpose. "The settlers want to create territorial contiguity between Avigayil and Havat Ma'on, with us in the middle," he said. "That is their goal now: to use violence to force us to leave. They are always taking over more land and attacking us.

It's like the army, which destroys our homes. [They do] everything so that we leave."

Several days earlier, Israeli Jewish and Palestinian activists from Combatants for Peace and two other leftist NGOs had brought a water carrier to village residents, who are not connected to the Israeli West Bank water grid. Captured on video, IDF soldiers, led by their battalion commander, attacked several middle-aged Jewish activists, knocking them to the rocky ground. Two Palestinian activists also reported minor injuries.

In one incident, Tuly Flint, a former commander in the IDF reserves and currently the Israeli coordinator for Combatants for Peace, said he was standing with a sign in one hand and a megaphone in the other when a soldier came at him from behind and pinned him to the ground in a choke hold. The soldier then placed his knee on Flint's head, a scene often repeated in other West Bank videos, shot by B'Tselem volunteers, in which Israeli forces hold down Palestinians. To anyone who has seen the photo, it is immediately reminiscent of the Minneapolis police officer holding his knee on George Floyd's neck, in the summer of 2020.

Soldiers accused the NGO activists of blocking the entrance to one of the settler outposts and of attacking them. Calling the soldiers liars, the activists said their sole interest is the fundamental issue of water rights for Palestinians.

IDF officials reprimanded the battalion commander and his unit for their violent response to the protest, but none of them were taken out of active service during the subsequent so-called investigation. There has reportedly been no follow-up by the IDF concerning the unit.

Israeli right-wing prime minister Naftali Bennett heads a government made up of an unusual coalition of right- and left-wing political parties, including, for the first time in Israeli history, an Arab party. And—of all things—it is an Islamic party. Bennett has adopted a strategy reportedly called "shrinking the conflict." While refusing to even talk about a future Palestinian state, he seeks to offer Palestinians more job opportunities in Israel but also in the West Bank and to increase their quality of life.

Leftist critics say it is a scam to cover up increased settlement building, land seizures and demolitions, and arrests or killings of radicals. At the recent United Nations General Assembly, Bennett focused on the need to contain or destroy Iran's nuclear infrastructure, talk that Arab Gulf countries like to hear. He also praised the opening of diplomatic and business relations with Bahrain, the United Arab Emirates, and Morocco. Except for a moment of criticism of Hamas and Islamic Jihad radicals, he did not mention Palestinians even once.

Combatants For Peace, along with other activist NGOs including Breaking the Silence, All That's Left, and Peace Now, held a demonstration on Saturday near Khirbet al-Mafaqarah, the village attacked by settlers in the South Hebron Hills. According to Beth Schuman, director of the American Friends of CFP, the fundraising arm of the NGO, some six hundred people attended—about four hundred Israelis and two hundred Palestinians.

"The focus of the protest was fundamental water rights for Palestinians," Schuman remarked. "We are a human rights group. We don't take a position on the one-state or two-state solutions, for example. Members have different opinions on a number of issues."

Schuman said that IDF soldiers watched the protest from a distance but did not intervene. One might assume that, after the bad press and criticism the soldiers got from army higher-ups for their recent over-the-top pummeling of Israeli Jewish activists bringing water to Palestinians, they were given orders to stand back.

And there might be good news. Following the violent incidents, the IDF general in charge of the area went to the village and, during a very short visit, spoke with residents. He reportedly promised them the same access to water as the nearby illegal settler outposts. What follows his words, of course, remains to be seen. It would certainly be about time. Depriving off-the-grid Palestinian villages of running water, forcing them to buy tankers from private sources at high prices, and kicking residents off their land are all part of an Israeli strategy of ethnic cleansing. They are examples of why so many people view this conflict as a zero-sum, good-guy-bad-guy situation. But the sight of Israelis and Palestinians in Combatants for Peace and other NGOs working together may be proof of the contrary.

October 4, 2021

Lines
MOHAMMAD SABAANEH

Arrested by the Israelis in 2013, Mohammad Sabaaneh spent five months in prison. He was charged for cartoons published in a book about political prisoners by his brother. Sabaaneh's cartoons of assassinated Hamas leader Ismail Haniyeh, the Palestinian Authority's Mahmoud Abbas, and the Prophet Muhammad have drawn the ire of Palestine's political establishment. In addition to his work in brush pen and ink, he began making linocuts inspired by Sudanese artist Mohammad Omar Khalil and radical comic-book artist Seth Tobocman. In 2018 the Israelis confiscated artworks by Sabaaneh.

Mohammad Sabaaneh, *Lines*, January 4, 2019. Engraving and printing, 3 x 4 cm; linocut 30 x 40 cm. Edition 50/50. Courtesy of the artist.

Elderly Woman Falls Asleep on My Shoulder

MOHAMMED EL-KURD

Elderly Woman on the bus falls asleep on my shoulder.
                     No adjectives in the wind.
Her whistles asleep are choppy, her lungs—I assume—were
        embroidered with
screams, grainy and grayed.
                 Her phone wakes her up,
her waking up awakens me,
makes me aware of my pocketed-indulgence.
Alert, she asks *Where are we?*
Right before the checkpoint, I say. She responds:
Thank you.
الله يحميك من شر اليهود
ومن شر المسلمين
Through her scarf I see the Wall;
it exiles her livelihood: selling figs behind a two-hour-something
        bus ride,
travel permits,
searching and questioning,
tessellated behind bars,
into other bent bodies,
waiting.

Elderly Woman on the bus gets up,
her plastic bags filled with seventy mountains and a river.
I offer a hand. She is concerned about my spine
Women like her have spined me. I insist, *Let me help you, please.*

She wants to carry thirty-five mountains. I tell her I've got both
bags, not as heavy as they seem

                            not as heavy as she's lived.

We exit the bus, walking toward the military barrier.
Under occupation, walking feels barefoot.
Here, walking feels like attempting to run
                        in water.

The soldier, blonde and sunburnt, asks her for her permit.
My permit: these wrinkles
older than your country's existence.
My smile is a sun.

The soldier, accented and unhebrew, asks her what's in the bag.
Figs, bitch. What else you want to know?
I stuffed them with storms
and bombs and blows.

            My smile, a gloat.
            I know she had a gun someday, hidden in a wheat bag,
            and I know she hid freedom fighters in her closet—
                 warrior woman, za'atar diva.[1]
                She   may have
                    hid   in her closet, too.
Elderly Woman and I pass the checkpoint.
                       Violent vowels in the wind.
Her back, hunched—her spine, spined me.
She takes the bags from my hands. *Thank you.*
                   My daughter's waiting to pick me up.
                   May God protect you and the youth
                   around you.
And before my breath could take a seat,
she walked away as if she once knew purple shrouds.

----

1   After Suheir Hammad.

Culinary Palestine
FADI KATTAN

Beloved Mansaf
Jericho Sheikh Daoud and the Battle of the Chicken

When I think about food and incarceration, the stories of the late Palestinian community leader Daoud Iriqat immediately come to mind. He was always a lesson in optimism and perseverance, carrying his political ideals high and proud through the shifting sands of our regional history.

Spending long years in prison and then more in exile, food represented his sense of identity as well as his intense longing for home. However, at times his pursuit of food behind bars was itself all-consuming; it was a practical necessity, a matter of life and death.

Daoud's mother was from an old Jerusalemite family while his father was a landowner in Abu Dis, so he grew up between the city and the village. As a young man, he was religious and would go to pray at Al-Aqsa Mosque. Because his friends and peers were not religious, they would often taunt him, calling him "the Sheikh"—a nickname that followed him throughout his life. He liked to joke that his parents had sent him to Egypt to study theology at Al-Azhar and had expected him to come back a scholar, but when he got off the bus, he was carrying an oud and singing.

When he would walk around Jerusalem, Daoud's elder brother, Ahmad, who was a teacher and an intellectual, would task him with distributing the Communist Party's newspaper. He started reading the paper and discussing it with his brother. Thus, he shaped his own communist Leninist ideology.

Daoud joined the Jordanian Communist Party in the 1940s and, after the party split, stayed on in what became the Palestinian Communist Party.

He famously used to tell his family a phrase that encompassed his entire relationship with food: "I hate the empty plate!" It was a refrain pinched from his mother, who, like so many Palestinian mothers, was an accomplished cook and generous host.

Daoud's memories of food were dominated by his mother's sumptuous *mahshi*, "stuffed vegetables." In Palestine, Jerusalemites are well-known for the different *mahshi* they prepare: zucchini, eggplant, vine leaves, cabbage leaves, and so many more. However, Daoud's favorite meal was *mansaf*, that hearty dish shared in Jordanian and Palestinian traditions—melt-in-the-mouth lamb in a tangy fermented yogurt, served with rice.

But *mansaf* was something that Daoud could only dream of after he was imprisoned in Jordan's Al-Jafr prison in 1957. He was condemned to sixteen years: one for participating in a demonstration and fifteen for being a member of the Communist Party.

Imagine how it must have felt for a man who thrived on culture, music, and eating well to be in a prison in the harsh, barren desert.

Very quickly, as Daoud would recount, he and the other prisoners focused on what they saw as the necessities of life: education, food, and alcohol.

They organized themselves to teach classes of party politics, languages, and music. For musical performances, Daoud dried the shell of a squash and made an oud out of it.

However, improvements in food required more imagination and hard work. The rations the prisoners were given were low in protein and iron, and they had begun to feel the deficiencies. This motivated them to carry out what they called "the chicken operation."

A driver came regularly from Amman with stocks for the jail, and the inmates managed to pass him some money to buy things for them. They ordered fertilized chicken eggs and then set about building egg hatchers with cardboard and other scrap materials—anything they could lay their hands on. Finally, when twenty-eight eggs arrived, Daoud and his comrades attended to them on a relay system. They were elated when these hatched into twenty-seven healthy chicks.

Meanwhile, an agricultural engineer who—conveniently—was in jail with Daoud had managed to grow *fasouliya* ("green beans") and a few other vegetables.

As the prisoners had no access to utensils, oils, or spices, they improvised. They used any metal tin to soft-boil eggs while the chicken meat was often boiled into a broth and eaten. When any *fasouliya* had grown, they would celebrate with a delicious *fasouliya* and chicken soup.

Then came the great setback for the prisoners: what was known as *Al Maraket Al Jaj*, "the Battle of the Chicken." The prison warden had witnessed the great success of the poultry farm and, most probably getting no fresh meat himself, demanded a chicken from the inmates. After a meeting, the prisoners collectively decided to oppose the move, which they saw as pillage or extortion. Daoud would recall how he tried to reason with them—reminding them that they were ultimately powerless—but it was to no avail.

When the warden was told he could not have his chicken, he raided the farm with his guards and confiscated all the birds and the prisoners' books. To add insult to injury, he broke Daoud's oud.

Not to be deterred, the prisoners restarted their chicken project from scratch. It was an endeavor that continued until they were released.

Despite all the tremendous creativity and efforts of the jailed men, alcohol was always much more difficult. On only one occasion, after a long, drawn-out process, did they ever manage to distill one bottle of an alcoholic drink. Daoud would call it—one imagines euphemistically—*arak*.

He always remembered the heady party the prisoners had, fueled by that single bottle, and the sound of his new oud echoing across the vast desert late into the night.

Freedom finally came in 1965, when King Hussein of Jordan issued a pardon for the Communists of Jafr prison. All of the comrades were allowed to return home.

For Daoud that meant moving to Jericho to be with his family, and when he arrived back it was clear how they would celebrate: with lashings of the *mansaf* he had so desperately missed.

However, freedom did not last.

Less than a decade later, in 1974, Daoud was arrested once again, this time at his home in Jericho by the Israeli forces. He was to be punished for having signed the petition recognizing the Palestine Liberation Organization as the sole and unique representative of the Palestinian people.

But instead of imprisoning Daoud, the Israeli soldiers forced him across the Lebanese border, sending him into exile. His provisions—which he had at first refused—were only a sandwich and an apple.

After some time, Daoud made it to Beirut. A year later, he settled in Damascus. Amazingly, in Syria, he found ways to get sent some of the distinctive flavors of Palestine: salty Nabulsi cheese dotted with nigella seeds, pungent za'atar, and even fresh guava. But throughout his exile, he would complain of missing the huge, juicy pomelo from his garden in Jericho.

Daoud's second homecoming was not until 1993. Once again, he was welcomed back with lovingly prepared *mansaf.*

Until his untimely death in 2020, the large table on the Sheikh's terrace in Jericho was always a place to delight his guests with his favorite foods—and to serve up food for thought. His belief in humanism, universality, and the equal division of wealth between citizens and between countries, as well as his staunch fight for critical thinking and education, always endured.

His morning ritual was a sacrosanct time when he would listen to the radio and run an ongoing commentary with his lashing tongue while sipping his Arabic coffee.

But Daoud's gatherings always revolved around lavish meals; he believed in the power of delicious tastes and flavors to bring people together. It was always an honor to be invited to his home, but the greatest honor came if he really liked you. Then it would be your turn to be treated to *mansaf*!

Gaza Fatteh

Food from Home

Food memories are a tricky thing! It has been so long since I've been to Gaza, yet I still have wonderful memories of the Gaza *fatteh* prepared by the late Im Khader, my uncle's mother-in-law. In my childhood memories she was quite possibly the best cook in Gaza—an impressive woman who prepared delicious feasts, had the best *shatta* recipe ever, and was also known for her celebrated lamb meat.

For non-Arabs unfamiliar with traditional fatteh, it's a popular dish of toasted and often crumbled pita covered in diverse toppings, depending on whether it's prepared in Palestine, Lebanon, Egypt, Jordan, or Syria. Sometimes it's simply pita covered with chickpeas and yogurt (in the vegetarian version), but there are also varieties made with chicken, lamb, or beef.

When I delve into my food memories around the Gaza fatteh, I still feel the combination of that first mouthful of rice, bread, meat—very deep, intense, earthy—and the refreshing piquant of the *dugga* (or *dukkah*, similar to za'atar, albeit made with nuts and spices rather than sesame seeds).

There was always the Gaza dugga but also, always at my aunt's house, a few green chilies on the lunch table. Gazan cuisine is very different from Bethlehemian cuisine, bringing with it that marine air, that spiciness of the chilies and the long meals on the coast always rounded off with an unctuous *mouhalabiya* served with date jam.

Those memories of more than thirty years ago seem so unreal today.

Fatteh Ghazawiya

serves 8

MEAT & BROTH

8 pieces of lamb meat with bone (each 250 g)

10 cups water

2 tablespoons olive oil

1 onion, quartered

4 garlic cloves

2 bay leaves

2 teaspoons black peppercorns

10 cardamom pods

2 cinnamon sticks

1½ teaspoons allspice berries

3 teaspoons salt

RICE & BREAD

2½ cups short grain rice

2 cups water

1 cup strained broth

2 tablespoons ghee

3 shrak bread or rkak

DUGGA

2 garlic cloves

6 fresh red chilies

5 teaspoons lemon juice

GARNISH

1 cup almonds

2 tablespoons pine nuts

METHOD

FOR THE MEAT AND BROTH:

1. In a large pot, heat the olive oil, slightly cook the garlic and onions, and then brown the meat.

2. Add the spices and toss the meat well.
3. Add all the spices, cover with water, and bring to a boil.
4. Reduce heat, cover, and let cook for an hour and a half.
5. When ready, taste the broth and add salt to your liking.
6. Strain the broth to use both for cooking the rice and for serving.

FOR THE RICE:

1. Soak the rice for 30 minutes.
2. In a pot, melt the ghee, then add the rice and stir for a minute or two.
3. Add the water and strained broth.
4. Once the liquid boils, reduce the heat to low, cover, and let cook until the liquid is absorbed.
5. Fluff the rice grains with a fork and reserve on the side.

FOR THE NUTS:

1. In a pan, fry the almonds and then the pine nuts separately.
2. Leave each one to release the excess oil on a paper towel.

FOR THE DUGGA:

1. Peel the garlic and chop off the heads of the chilies.
2. In a mortar and pestle, pound the garlic and chilies with a pinch of salt until you have a rough paste.
3. Add the lemon juice and salt to taste.

SERVING

1. Preheat your oven to 180°C (350°F)
2. Tear the bread into large pieces and toast in the oven for a few minutes.
3. On a large serving plate, arrange the bread and soak with the broth until the bread has absorbed the broth.
4. Add a layer of rice over the bread.
5. Arrange the meat pieces over the rice.
6. Garnish with the almonds and pine nuts.
7. Serve the dugga on the side for people to sprinkle to their liking.

An Oral History of *Mouloukhiya*[1]

Mouloukhiya, that magic verdure, hated or loved across the shores of the southern and eastern Mediterranean, is an abundant green herb that often ends up in a stew with varying consistencies and a long history of conflict. We hear words in a multitude of dialects: *Warak willa na'ma?* ("Leaves or chopped?") *Basal o khal willa busul o leimoun?* ("Onions and vinegar or onions and lemon?") ringing in conversations about this divine stew. But to the eyes of the uninitiated, mouloukhiya looks like a deep green stew that is viscous and many times repulsive. Why do we celebrate it to an extent that it becomes cult like!

Across Palestine, mouloukhiya is prepared differently, from the chopped tradition served with rice to the whole-leaf tradition served with bread. Then come the subtleties: With meat? With chicken? With rabbit? And the fine details that are game changers are the tasha garlic or garlic and coriander; do you place a tomato in the stew to remove the viscosity or do you leave it? In Umm Al-Fahem, mouloukhiya is cooked whole and served with *khobz*, "bread," to dip in; in Jericho, it is chopped and cooked with generous amounts of chili and garlic; in Jerusalem and Bethlehem, it is cooked either whole or chopped with lamb meat or chicken and served with chopped onion in vinegar or chopped onion in lemon juice.

And the essential questions: Do you cook mouloukhiya only in season? Do you dry it? Or do you succumb to modernity and freeze it? For me, the dry and fresh mouloukhiya are two different experiences, each rich in flavors and creating two different memories: one of the celebration of summer and the other of a winter stew cooked with a combination of the nostalgia of sunshine and the smell of the *mouneh* room (a pantry where all produce was stored and where the smell of the dried mouloukhiya would reign).

When I remember mouloukhiya, I have this memory of a dark

---

[1]   From "An Oral History of Mouloukhiya from Egypt, Palestine, Tunisia and Japan," by Fadi Kattan, Nevine Abraham, Ryoko Sekiguchi, and Boutheina Bensalem, *Markaz Review*.

room where I could smell the dried mouloukhiya, but I still cannot remember if it was in Sido Nakhleh's house or Teta Julia's house or maybe both. And yet I remember the serving of the mouloukhiya, in a celebratory ceremony, with the right soupière for the stew, the long dish for the rice, the small bowls for the toppings, and then the soup plates, the generous spoons, and then the happy nods from everyone around the table when asked if they wanted seconds. I also remember Khadra, a woman who worked at my grandfather's place, sitting with my great aunts Victoria and Regina, cleaning the mouloukhiya off its stems, on the terrace overlooking Bethlehem. I also remember when my aunt May, from Gaza, taught me the love of green chilies served next to the mouloukhiya and the sound of the crunching when you bite into one, the mixture of flavors, the quite earthy mouloukhiya, the rice, the acidity of the lemon and the vividity of the chili scent. As much as I enjoy cooking mouloukhiya, I have to confess that when I want to enjoy mouloukhiya, I ask my mother to prepare it. Her mouloukhiya renders the initial Arabic sense of a royal dish to the utmost—the fresh coriander and the garlic, the fried bread, the wise dosage of the stew is like no other.

As a chef rethinking Palestinian cuisine and focusing on highlighting local produce using untraditional methods, the plethora of preparations for mouloukhiya challenges me to explore its texture and the possibilities. The simplest game changer was frying the fresh leaf in a shallow hot-oil bath and serving it as chips, with a dash of salt or with a dip made of the traditional vinegar and onion but whipped into a creamy consistency, a bit like an onion-and-vinegar mayonnaise. But my favorite is based on a traditional mouloukhiya recipe, where I create a rice ball stuffed with a bit of mouloukhiya and meat, serve it on a small portion of stew infused with lemon and vinegar, and top it with fried fresh cilantro and garlic—a bite-sized Loukmet Mouloukhiya!

Desire and the Palestinian Kitchen

Wait for her and do not rush.
If she arrives late, wait for her.
If she arrives early, wait for her.
— Mahmoud Darwish, "Lessons from the Kama Sutra"

When I think of desire in the kitchen, I think of that tingling sensation when one develops a recipe and waits . . . waits for it to translate from an idea into the actual preparation . . . then the cooking moment. Then the plating. And after that, the first time you taste it. And the first time you serve it and wait for the first guests to taste it.

Nothing more than that stanza from Mahmoud Darwish's poem, put into music by the fabulous Le Trio Joubran, captures those moments of waiting. And yet he talks about a man waiting for a woman, not a cook in a dark kitchen waiting for a dish.

All through the ages, chefs were perceived as having somewhat strange personalities, huddled up in dark kitchens, often in noble or royal mansions, in the basement. They would conjure a sort of mystical, unholy magic to create dishes served with great pomp at the hosts' table.

The desire to excel and then the desire to share the pleasure of the flavors with the guests and the world at large fill the chef with such anxiety that often they go mad. This pushes them over the edge and a frenzy of feelings and thoughts rush through the chef's mind and nervous system in this instant where the culmination of the courtship of the dish and the deep desire to please.

Despite their airs of big bullies and insensitive beasts, chefs are a funny breed, mixing a lot of this authoritarian, quasi-rigid command in a kitchen while within themselves being, I believe, the most sensitive and fragile beings.

The art of the table is close to the Kama Sutra—despite its different relations, protagonists, and elements, they are similar in the rhythm and the wait; the build-up and the tension; the meeting of flavors, textures, and soul in a dish; the reveal of the final dish and then the pleasure; the chefs become the creators and at the same time the naked souls waiting for the pleasure of sharing with others an illumination.

Desire is an expression of many states and contexts, and yet in the kitchen, they morph into one—the desire of a mother to share nourishment with her child, the desire of a lover to seduce, the desire of a patriarch to ensure the perpetuation of a craft, the desire of a child to have fun, and the desire of longing to re-create a taste from nostalgia with the intense yearning to create for the future an enlightened idea, all wrapped up into a small vessel, a dish, a plate, a bowl that contains all those desires.

And the desire for beauty! Which chef does not try to arrange, prepare, dress their plate in its finest? Which chef does not agonize before a rendezvous about the choice of the outer layer of their dish, about the finest details of the vestment and the most precise detail of the garnish? Which chef does not, in a moment of folly, sense that their dish does not look good enough for that rendezvous and in that instant let their primal cravings run wild in deconstructing the dish, splashing the sauce in a fit worthy of a desire-struck creator?

July 15, 2021, to March 15, 2022

Vera Tamari, *Woman at the Door*, 1994. Clay relief and engobe colors, 33 x 17 x 1.5 cm. Courtesy of the artist.

Vera Tamari's Lifetime of Palestinian Art
TALINE VOSKERITCHIAN

Rooted in the everyday life of Palestinians under occupation, Vera Tamari's art looks out onto a violated landscape from her ancestral seaport of Jaffa, on the Mediterranean, and centuries of Islamic art, to the invasion of her native land by successive armies, and more. She uses clay, paper, fabric, metal, Plexiglass, wood, paint, stone, film, wire screen, and photographs to create a body of work that is as varied as it is defiant of political and aesthetic categorizations.

Over a lifetime spanning the Six-Day War, in 1967; two Intifadas; innumerable Israeli incursions into the West Bank; and war on Gaza, Tamari has also been witness and chronicler, educator and engaged artist, observer and creative force.

Clay is one of her most pervasive materials. In *Woman at the Door*, from the series *Family Portraits*, the photographic image acquires the heft and bulk of sculpture. Without facial expressions, the figure acquires the universality of form but also a curious anonymity, which is complicated by the specificity of the Arabic inscription on the left: Jaffa, 1939.

Her impulse is to bring mutually exclusive opposites together, especially in the installation pieces, which, as grounded material objects of art, are intended to withstand the ravages of time and invasion. They are also at the mercy of the invader's violence. *Home* (2017), a Plexiglass stairwell caged by wire screen, sits in the Palestinian Museum Gardens, in Birzeit. Tamari says that the stairwell recalls the stairwells of pre-1948 Jerusalem homes, which connect homes and families to each other. *Home* embodies a subversive ambiguity, too. The stairwell is a defiant upward movement against the lateral expansion of the settler. Stairs are not meant to end in midair. *Home* begs the question: what hope, what "home"?

As a public art installation, *Going for a Ride?* no longer exists except in photographs and in the memory of its creators—workers, Birzeit University students, and Tamari. Between March and June 2022 Israeli tanks repeatedly invaded Ramallah and the nearby town of Al-Bireh, smashing some seven hundred cars in the process. "Vera graded, steamrolled, then tarred the road in a playing field belonging to the Friends Boys' School," writes the artist and curator Ala Younis.[1] Within a few hours of its opening, on June 23, 2022, one hundred Israeli armored vehicles returned, causing more destruction, including that of the installation itself.

The artist insists that her intent is not "merely to fashion junk as an art form or an anti-gesture." She wanted to show how "the war machine" turns "a mundane logical reality"[2] into something illogical and grotesque.

"Representing Palestinian life or a Palestinian landscape," maintains Tamari, is "in itself a subversive activity."[3] For people under occupation, art that is both subversion and solace is also a source of renewal.

October 16, 2023

1   Ala Younis, "Obliquely Political," in *Intimate Reflections: The Art of Vera Tamari*, eds. Penny Johnson and Anita Vitullo (A. M. Qattan Foundation, 2021), 98.
2   Vera Tamari, Presentation. Art and War Conference, Goethe-Institut, Ramallah, 2004. TPFF (Toronto Palestinian Film Festival), 2021.
3   Yazid Anani in conversation with Vera Tamari, "The Virtual, the Sensory, the Unrealized," in *Intimate Reflections*, 130-154.

These are the only photographs that Vera Tamari took of her installation Going for a Ride? *She had expected to take more during the exhibition, but on the night of the installation's opening, the Israelis returned and destroyed it with their tanks.*

Figure 1: Vera Tamari, *Going for a Ride?*, 2002. Site-specific installation, crushed car on tarmac. Installation view, Friends Boys' School, Ramallah. Courtesy of the artist.

Figure 2: Vera Tamari, *Going for a Ride?*, 2002. Site-specific installation, five crushed cars on tarmac. Installation view, Friends Boys' School, Ramallah. Courtesy of the artist.

Vera Tamari, *Home*, 2017. Plexiglass, wire mesh, 3 x 3 x 3 m. Installation view, Palestinian Museum, Birzeit. Courtesy of the artist.

The Diplomats' Quarter
of the Palestinian Authority

RAJA SHEHADEH

After the glorious peace agreement with Israel known as the Oslo Accords was signed in 1995, all that remained to do was to find an appropriate manner to express the nation's gratitude for the hard and successful work of the Palestinian diplomats.

Serious thought was given to the matter, until eventually the head of the new Palestinian Authority determined that the grant of a house was the best reward to give Palestinians whose homes were repeatedly stolen or destroyed time and again by Israel. And so a neighborhood dubbed the Diplomats' Quarter, dedicated to the hardworking heroes, came into being.

During its long occupation of the West Bank, Israel had taken huge tracts of Palestinian hectares, which it first proceeded to declare public land. Only Jewish settlers could benefit from these areas. Yet after investigations were undertaken by the PA, it was revealed that there remained a few tracts of public land here and there within "Area A" that the diplomats had succeeded in wrenching from Israeli hands and placing under the exclusive territorial jurisdiction of the Palestinians. These plots were registered in the name of the treasury from the time when Jordan was responsible for the area. Whereas it was within the power of the PA to dispose of these lands as it deemed fit, it was decided that there was no better use of this scenic land than to grant it free to the diplomats.

And so, on the slope of one of the still-untouched hills north of Ramallah, the work of digging up this pristine hill began. To save money, no retaining wall was built, and the rubble extracted for the foundation and infrastructure was instead deposited on the lower terraces, which were still in private ownership. What had stood as a gently sloping hill in the open area north of the city soon turned into a construction site. With the gorging that was taking place it looked like a wound in the landscape, which, along with the piling rubble, seemed like it was lacerating.

Those responsible for the project were pleased with their choice of location and could not stop marveling at how wonderful it would be that, once the work was completed, the face of the hill visible from the city would be the site of the diplomats' neighborhood standing there for all to see—a shining trophy of how the PA rewards its officials for their successes.

The guidelines given to the architect were in line with the PA's espousal of the principle of egalitarianism and nondiscrimination; thus, each of the houses would have to be the same size as the other. And so the diplomats' houses came to be built in rows, with one identical house snuggled up to the one after it. The architect who conceived of the plan for the project came up with a design of reams of buildings strapped along the belly of the hill, with one row of houses behind another.

When the contractor finished his work, the area looked just like an Israeli settlement, with rows of similar houses rolled out side by side. The PA seemed to think this was fine. But among the city's inhabitants, opinion was divided. Those who were enthusiastic about the likeness thought that it proved that the settlements Israel built on our hills were no longer to be an exclusively Israeli trademark. Palestinians were just as competent in conferring their own claim to the land and just as capable of transforming the Palestinian landscape. Others, however, felt pained that the Palestinians of all people were copying images of American suburbia. But what distressed this group even more was the visual similarity between the Diplomats' Quarter and an Israeli settlement.

When at long last the contractor was ready to hand over to each of the diplomats the keys to their new homes, a number of them who were accustomed to more sumptuous living conditions, found that the workmanship was so shoddy that they did not want to move to these homes granted to them free of charge. So for hefty amounts they sold their homes to others who were anxious to move out of the busy and crowded city and live in what they believed was superior housing fit for diplomats, in a quarter that continued to bear their name even after only a minority of diplomats opted to live there.

One of those who bought a house in the diplomats' neighborhood was an acquaintance of mine. He told me that he found the state of the house he paid for so handsomely so atrocious that he had to demolish most of the inside and start all over. This was costly, but given the astronomical price of land in Ramallah, he still thought he'd struck a good bargain.

All was going well with the remedial work until a pernicious problem with the piping surfaced that seemed impossible to resolve. The water flow was very weak, really only a trickle, despite the fact that the water coming into the house from the outside entered the main pipe in strength. He consulted a number of plumbers, and still the problem persisted.

One day he was standing outside his house inspecting the garden when his next-door neighbor passed by. He greeted him and asked how he was enjoying living in this grand neighborhood.

Grand it might be, he grudgingly agreed, but what sort of life can one have when the water coming through the taps is only a trickle? I wonder, he asked his neighbor, do you have the same problem in your house?

Ah, said the neighbor. We did until we discovered the source of the problem.

Why don't you tell me—perhaps it might be the same in my house. And indeed it was.

When the main pipe was dug out, as the neighbor had advised, the problem was identified. The laborers who built these diplomats' homes had decided to reward those heroes of the Palestinian cause with an appropriate national symbol. They saw the Palestinian flags fluttering proudly over the area of the project and decided to pull them down and stuff them into the main pipe through which water flowed into each unit. That way this project would be permanently stamped with the nationalist credentials it deserves.

As the owner proceeded to pull out from the narrow main pipe one crumpled flag after another, he told me he felt no anger—only great relief when the water began to flow in great force to his house. He harbored no rancor at the workers who impressed him by their determination to make known their feeling about how the nation rewards its heroes.

June 14, 2021

Return
MAYA ABU AL-HAYYAT

1.

On Highway 6
between Tel Aviv and Jerusalem,
drivers pay a toll for the well-paved road,
busses on either side
transport passengers who've returned at last
to Ramleh or Lod, the latter in peace, with jars
for the holy festival of Prophet Saleh.
Justice was walking on the shoulder
of the road outside the yellow line
giving back to the streets their names.

Rahmeh (Mercy) was seven
when she escaped a fire with her quick feet
at the family's annual grill reunion
in At-tirah. Now she leans on a cane she rented
from Bashir hospital
but won't give it back. She's gazing through
the air-conditioned bus: dreams
don't come true through will
or the passage of years that come undone
like rosary beads or a grape cluster
loosened in a bowl for kids.
Years that roll under the bed.
Dreams propel the body forward instead.
Decisions are taken by need—

no matter the arthritis, expenses,
plethora of adolescents, damp walls, and old cots
— because need clips the wings of dreams
and the legs of the righteous.

Rahmeh (Mercy),
who could run barefoot as fast and for as long
as a Kenyan runner might
in the Sydney Olympics,
didn't succumb to dementia or Alzheimer's.
She can still rise to her feet to smell Yaffa's sea,
but the smell of grilled meat and hair spray
plug her nose. Death,
the beast we wrap in romance novels
as terrible texts are wrapped
in ornate words, peers
from the other side of the window.
The reflection almost defines
the form of the end.
This may be the last chance.
Highway 6, whose toll you paid,
is your road.

2.

Sunlight penetrates green leaves
like an old lux on a dark night.
Al-badhan road is winding and treacherous.
Accidents can happen.
A car or rocks may fall
from the top to the bottom.
A flash pierces my sleeping eyes.
This road that leads me to Nablus is astonishing,
this road to my father's return from his exile

to the place I left behind.
A dark-skinned man drives
the seven-seater Mercedes from Jericho.
The vehicle won't stop vibrating.
Badhan road: what word is this
whose cold waterfalls give
small parks their names,
fill plastic chairs with bottoms that hover
over floating watermelons in a chilly stream?
What world is this
between Jericho and Nablus,
the lowest and highest points?
"This is return," my father says,
with tears in his eye
that a shrapnel from an old war had damaged
back when he used to wear khaki.

My father falls
asleep with a pistol,
eats his watermelon slices
without fork or plate
in the Mercedes where other passengers are
scared or asleep. The dark-skinned driver
from Jericho doesn't recognize their fear.
He wants to make it back in time
to add his name on the long list
of drivers for tomorrow's work.

3.

"Are we human?"
The book's yellow cover asks.
We live in what others have designed and dreamt.
We live in what the wind has done to a tree

thousands of years ago
above animal and scorpion urges,
in the belly of whales, within roots
and echoes, the nightly chatter of cave dwellers.
We roam the streets of engineers and the debris
of sharp axes in drawings
of ancient municipalities
and inside the head of a hasty old man.
Our words about the free soul,
beliefs, and the innocent
land is part of the design.
A screw in the mind of the rocking chair
that grants the universe a burst of passion.

4.

They wrote thousands of letters,
hung them to dry
on laundry lines,
and when the wind arrived
it did what it usually does:
erosion, corrosion,
then transfer of the body
and alphabet parts it could carry,
as the heavy parts are left behind disfigured.
This is the reason why
whenever they searched their memory
for a road,
an orange,
an olive,
a view from a window,
they couldn't find it.

That's how myths are made:

erosion, corrosion,
drop by drop,
doggedly, bitterly
they draw memory out.
You don't know how bitter
it is to search
a map for a memory
and find a cadaver.

Translated from the Arabic by **FADY JOUDAH**

Protest Stencil, *One Day*, 2018. Poster and London bus shelter, 120 x 180 cm. Courtesy of the collective.

One Day
PROTEST STENCIL

In a book for activists, accompanying this "subvertising" poster on a London bus shelter, the anonymous collective Protest Stencil included a 2017 testimony from an unidentified Palestinian friend: "Three years ago I'd just been deported from Palestine after being denied entry and detained, for trying to visit for a week. . . . Two years ago, my mum's cousin was shot and killed by an Israeli soldier in Hebron. . . . There are Palestinians who became refugees in Syria, and who are now again refugees in Jordan or Lebanon. There are those without any citizenship, who remain perpetual guests in a country. There are those living in cities like Hebron who have to walk down a segregated street to visit family, and who, like my mum's cousin, can be killed at any moment."

Where is the Palestinian National Museum of Modern and Contemporary Art?

NORA OUNNAS LEROY

At the tail end of the MO.CO. *Museums in Exile* exhibit,[1] visitors find the last room of the collection reserved for the *Palestinian National Museum of Modern and Contemporary Art*.

However, let's be clear: this museum does not exist, at least physically. For now, it is a project, a dream, a prayer, and a challenge to time, to nations, to History . . . to silence. Far more than the other two collections devoted to Chile and Sarajevo, this grouping of paintings and other works perfectly illustrates the concept of a museum in exile, putting one in mind of André Malraux's axiom, "A museum is first of all an idea."

The first batch of pieces supporting this collection were gathered in Beirut, in 1978, by members of the Palestine Liberation Organization, but soon disappeared under the bombs in 1982. In 2005 Gérard Voisin, the United Nations Educational, Scientific and Cultural Organization's artist for peace, and Mounir Anastas, member of the Palestinian delegation, came up with the idea of a fund of works for Palestine, but this collection would remain available for viewing only to UNESCO members during internal conventions. The artist Ernest Pignon-Ernest,[2] who had already led the Art against Apartheid campaign of the 1980s, launched the idea of a solidarity collection for Palestine in 2015, with Elias Sanbar, historian and writer, who was then Palestinian ambassador to UNESCO. A year later, a partnership agreement was signed with the Institut du Monde Arabe, in Paris, to conserve, classify, list,

---

1   MO.CO.'s exhibition, *Museums in Exile*, from November 11 to February 5, 2023, in Montpellier, France, included art from Chile, Sarajevo, and Palestine.

2   In 1996, Pignon-Ernest presented Nelson Mandela, then president of South Africa, with a thousand works of art. The project had been developed while Mandela was in prison.

and enhance the works offered. Until now, the collection's new acquisitions were exhibited once a year within the walls of the institute only.

Sanbar is now the director of the collection. "We are betting that life will always be stronger," he says. "It is a museum of solidarity. The ambition is not to show Palestinian painters per se, but the work of world artists who are in solidarity, in a world that comes to Palestine, since Palestine is imprisoned. We said, 'Whoever is in solidarity against the occupation gives a work,' and it started like that . . . and since then, donations have been pouring in."

The collection includes many paintings and photographs but also sculptures, comics, installations, and films (Jean-Luc Godard donated his last film a few months before his death). The works have been chosen by the artists themselves. It is telling what has been donated to express support, because in this context, a work of art can no longer be defined by and for itself. It becomes almost automatically a sign, a message—a dialogue, with the Palestinian people, certainly—but above all it questions the viewer: And you, tell me, what are your thoughts, your feelings on the subject? What are you prepared to do, to be *engagé*?

There are works that reflect real-life situations (checkpoints, bombing, confinement, waiting); there are messages of hope; perspectives with openings, doors, windows, holes in the wall, girls jumping over the wall, vanishing point, stairs, mazes.

And then there are tributes to people. The most cited figure is Mahmoud Darwish, the great Palestinian poet, whose main translator was Sanbar. Finally, many of the pieces reveal an inner point of view, a personal feeling, a state of being or not being—and somehow one feels the works are in dialogue with each other.

Sanbar explains, "You have to know that in Palestine, daily life is hell. Not only because of the repression, the annexation of land, the harassment. . . . It is something we can't see. Because the basis of the occupation is to make your life unbearable, impossible, with the idea that at some point, you say 'Okay, you won, we're leaving.' The final goal is expulsion."

Sanbar continues, "The daily life of Palestinians is very, very hard.

This museum must be a public museum, and the responsibility of the state is to put at the disposal of its people 'beautiful' works. It may sound a bit literary, but it's fundamental. I think that beauty and aesthetics, beautiful things, are great levers of resistance. Beauty is a part of the fight.

"Apart from museums, you find an abundance of collections in Palestine, mainly private initiatives or those carried out by nongovernmental associations. Archaeological and heritage collections that safeguard national identity are the first act of resistance against the occupier. A museum of modern and contemporary art is something else again. It is a question of questioning the present in order to look to the future, as most free and sovereign countries around the world do. Tel Aviv has its museum of 'modern and contemporary art,' a magnificent building with light and futuristic lines. The Palestinians do not have one. A simple observation."

Sanbar also explains the importance of the present "museum" collection for exiled Palestinians visiting for the first time, especially for kids and their future prospects, to learn about the existence of a "national" museum of modern and contemporary art in Palestine. This gives the illusion, even the imminent hope, of the legitimacy of a "State of Palestine," which unfortunately still has no real legal recognition, need we remind you?[3] Although, very recently, the Algiers Declaration foresees, by October 2023, elections for the presidency and for the Palestinian Legislative Council, which acts as a parliament for the Palestinians of the occupied West Bank, Gaza Strip, and East Jerusalem. At present, Palestine is recognized as a "nonmember observer state" by 138 countries of the UN. France, the United States, and many European countries are not on this list.

In 2013, the European, British, and French parliaments voted their support for a recognition of the Palestinian state, but this has not been followed up by the governments to date.

However, an extraordinary thing has just happened, a real

---

3   Palestine was officially recognized as a "state" by a majority of United
    Nations member countries on November 29, 2012.

revolution: On November 30, 2022, the UN passed a stunning resolution to commemorate the seventy-fifth anniversary of the Nakba, on May 15, 2023. This is tantamount to declaring that the creation of the State of Israel was a "humanitarian catastrophe," which the Israeli and American delegations did not appreciate.

In this context, when an artist gives a work for Palestine, it's a strong political act, remarkable.

In terms of solidarity with this Palestinian museum in exile, if we look summarily at the nationality of the artists who donated work, we notice that they are mainly of European and Arab origin, with a small but apparently significant share from Latin America. MO.CO. director Numa Hambursin believes that the Palestine collection is known mainly by word of mouth, and that many artists have actually never heard of it. If it is true that the collection was somewhat hidden until now, in its citadel on the banks of the Seine, let's hope that the collection of the Palestinian National Museum of Modern and Contemporary Art will quickly become known, now that it is starting to travel. It is clearly not utopian to imagine donations coming from the US, Russia, Africa, Asia—and even Israel!

Since 2015 the collection has been slowly but surely growing, tucked away behind the photosensitive walls of the Institut du Monde Arabe. The MO.CO. exhibition is in effect a great premiere, here in the south of France, with forty-four works chosen by Hambursin.

"Our goal," he reveals, "was to show the diversity of this collection in terms of media, artistic periods, and the nationality and age of the artists. But more than that, it is one of the rare exhibitions where big names of the art scene rub shoulders with lesser-known artists on the same level. The issues of the collection go beyond the strictly artistic framework and allow us to transcend dogma. Here we abandon any idea of hierarchy between artists."

When you visit *Museums in Exile*, you notice that the part reserved for Palestine is not only underground and in the last rooms before the exit, but also that you are faced with a wall upon arriving. One can hardly ignore the significance of such a symbol—Wailing Wall,

wall of shame, wall of annexation or division, wall of apartheid, how many walls in Palestine already? Here, MO.CO. inaugurates a new kind of wall, that of the sacred and the spiritual, with the work *The Invisible Masters* from Algerian artist Rachid Koraïchi. Decorated with sixty-four lithographs representing the teachings of great Sufi masters such as Jalāl al-Dīn Rūmī, Hafez of Shiraz, or Ibn el-Arabi, the wall carries a message of hope and tolerance for future generations.

٭

With respect to the installation of the works, Hambursin goes on to explain that the aim was to avoid any homogeneous path, in order to lead the visitor astray. Here you enter a closed space, you arrive directly in front of a wall, and you have the choice of going left or right. And if you go around the wall, you come across the fresco *Exile Palestine*, created in 2009 by Jacques Cadet, a pictorial representation of the real wall, the one built day after day in the West Bank. This contrasts with the other two collections, for Chile and Sarajevo, where one enters a space that is open but closed in on itself. There is a beginning and a natural way out, but both these museums are no longer in exile, even if the Sarajevo building hasn't yet been built. Pinochet occupied Chile for "only" seventeen years, and the siege of Sarajevo lasted "only" four years, while millions of Palestinians have been in exile since 1948.

"These two collections remain very homogeneous," observes Hambursin. "The one in Chile reflects the strong politicization of art in the 1970s, while the Sarajevo collection carries the humanitarian dimension of the 1990s. The Israeli–Palestinian conflict has been going on for seventy-five years, and we don't know when it will end. We're all a bit lost when faced with what's going on over there. Here, we're in a less collective adventure, the journey is more a matter of the personal involvement of each artist . . . as each visitor."

The journey proposed by *Museums in Exile*, from beginning to end, its layout and choice of these exceptional collections, the organization of the narrative, its spatiotemporal articulations, both in the use of the museum's structure and in the echo that each piece reflects in the face of current events and in each of us—all this was conceived as a work in its own right. A work that confronts two fundamental questions: How to protect the art from war, from destruction and dehumanization? And how does art in turn protect us?

*

We end our visit to the exhibition in the basement of the museum: we can see in it an allegory of the descent into hell, which is part of everyday life in Palestine, but we can also detect, in this positioning of the collection underground, an unconscious and collective desire not to see, not to know what is happening in this part of the world. After the comfort zones and gentle reminders of the past, the visitor finds herself out of it, disoriented, in the midst of these works that support a cause we have unwittingly forgotten. Then as we leave, we're free, open to all possibilities!

Viewers arrive at their own conclusions but won't be left unmoved by this monumental exhibition.

Translated from the French by **JORDAN ELGRABLY**

December 12, 2022

Mohammad Sabaaneh, *Lines*, January 4, 2019. detail. Engraving and printing, 3 x 4 cm; linocut 30 x 40 cm. Edition 50/50. Courtesy of the artist.

Beirut

AHMAD ALMALLAH

I was كنتُ في بيروت
in Beirut. But of NOW: I AM—*actually/in reality/basically and
other fillers I use and abuse to prove that these English sounds carry
meaning that I'm about to roll on my foreign tongue*—WRITING
THIS (sometime after the fact) in the New York Public Library—I
am forced to write, because the security guy tells me: *no wandering
around for visitors! No pictures!* So I WRITE:

I was in Beirut. The heat. The humid life. Nothing but arguments
and disarray . . . I tell everyone in Beirut . . . there was something
off. I didn't get why he was acting this way. They ignore me. No
one believes me . . . oh crazy old Ahmad with his theories about
his ~~father~~ . . . the big bad wolf! Well finally everyone gets their
way with me . . . because crazy old Ahmad is subdued . . . he's got
theories about everything . . . did his father create the monster in
him?! Most likely! Everyone was scared of his feelings . . . yes he
put everyone on edge, just like his father did to him—but he tells
himself that at least he will get to Palestine with his daughter by his
side! On the way in . . . he wants to make things easy for her . . . he
takes the VIP on the JISR. They forget her American passport in
Jordan. He's there with her . . . on the edge of entering but he can't.
She can't. They are both stuck in-the-real-in-between . . . imagine the real! Well, here it is . . . how the fuck did this happen?!
How did he not ask the driver to check if their passports were
there . . . "you'll have to wait . . . here—[Mr. Nowhere]." And he
waits . . . this is a bad sign. Nut job doesn't believe in signs . . . only

273

the real . . . he sighs! He approached the Israeli VIP girl . . . "*bthib mayeh wella sayem?*" The Arabic comes from her mouth like a pool of blood. "What?!" [SILENCE]

"I'm not fasting . . . I can't . . . I'm traveling." As though he was about to explain it to his father. He wanted to tell her: "Well imagine going through the holocaust . . . and to top it off . . . there is an asshole in the family . . . your father . . . pestering you . . . and making your life a living hell . . . imagine . . . would you like some water? Zamzam? Do you know? They say that water from Mecca is magical" . . . It probably annoys the fuck out of these soldiers that all that these Palestinians want to transport is olive oil and holy water . . . in and out! All the fucking time! It's never allowed . . . but you never fail to see some scene with olive oil spattered all over the place . . . [instead of blood?]. His daughter realizes that something is wrong, and till this day she tells him . . . "but don't forget my passport this time" . . . After a couple of hours in the heat, by the entrance to the passport control . . . someone comes running with a smile . . . he's holding the passport in his hand . . . and what does he think at that moment . . . "should I tip . . . how much?!" Instead, he showers the man with lovely words . . . a panegyric! The man should have paid in gold to receive that praise. Well the drama doesn't end there . . .

May I interrupt with a side note here?! To the edification of our dear and kind readers in the developing and advanced worlds, I promise! You see, that's how Palestinians lose their battles. Their suffering is so detailed and absurd that when they try to tell it to the world, they step into a critical defeat: the overdramatic!

Ah well, here I go, stepping into the overdramatic and talking about myself in the third person . . . there goes nothing as the idiot idiom would have it:

Now he—that's also me, if I may remind you, kind reader—has to ask the Israeli officer not to stamp his daughter's passport for when they have to cross back to Lebanon. "Ah don't worry habibi . . . ~~bas~~ a little stamp right here." Chi-ching! The sound travels like a sword through his brain . . . it's all like the sword . . . like the sword, one! He shouts at him without recourse?! Ahmad brings up the courage to shout in the face of his oppressor . . . "I told you not to stamp the passport . . . we're going to Lebanon after this!" "Relax Habibi . . . bamzah ma'ak . . . not real . . . ~~just~~ stamped the table . . . haha! Do you know Hayfa Wahbi? She's hot! Sallem aliha bi libnan! Say hi to her!" He—that's also me—responds a bit idiotically "Oh yes I guess . . . ah . . . a joke! Yes thanks thanks!" Everything moves like a sword, on the way out of the body, it brushes against flesh and on the way in . . . I must be the *ghimd* . . . what is that word in English? *Ok, not cool . . . I'm not a believer in cultural appropriation . . . bla bla . . .* here I go, I lost the critical battle again! We must be destined for defeat. فلسطين التي

تتراءى في الأفق دون عودة. كنتُ على مرأى من المكان الأوّل دون أن أراه. ولم يبقَ من الزيارة سوى أسبوع وبضعة أيام. قلتُ لنفسي سأكتب بالعربية هنا... في تلك المساحة الضيّقة من الوقت. سأكتب ما سأكتبه من الأم. قريباً من البعيد. أنا هنا واللغة الأم. تلك العربية هنا أيضاً، ليست بين الكتب أو في المكتبات. هي هنا على الوجوه الشاحبة، على آفاق من الملل الممزوج بالقلق. في هذا المكان. في هذا البلد لبنان. بضعة أيام لأسترجع فيها اللغة الأم. بضعة أيام في مكان لا أطلال لي فيه. بضعة أيام... والزمان يضيق مُطبقاً على الاحتمال.

Let's get back to the business of translation. YES: There's something about those sites. The ruins. Everything turning to sand. It must be deserted . . . like this time that wants to contain and flatten . . . you . . . you know . . . the possible/impossible . . . and that nonsense about dichotomy . . . etc.

Note to self: I do not understand this tone?! This constant fishing for irony . . . isn't it exhausting. What you're deflecting is your own emotions. Just a few sentences like the ones you have in Arabic. They say the wrong metaphor for exile is a broken heart. It should be more like TWO HEARTS. Could it be two broken ones? Just like language . . . because when the heart stops pumping the pool of blood to the head, one loses the ability to speak. Biology takes its toll . . . on the language. Just give me a few days to be immersed completely in everything Arabic and I'll start spitting words like broken teeth.

Keys
RAEDA SAADEH

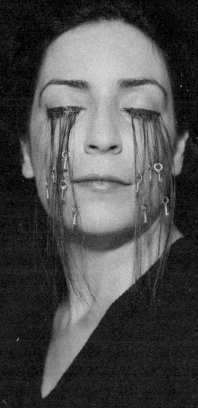

Raeda Saadeh, *Keys*, 2013. Archival pigment print, 90 x 60 cm. Courtesy of the artist.

In her art Raeda Saadeh is an everywoman, as she writes, "living in a world that attacks her values, her love, and her spirit every day. She is in a state of occupation." In self-portraiture and performance, sometimes the separation wall is literally *on* the artist's face; other times she's knitting amid the ruins of a demolished house. The subject matter of *Keys* is both the dreams and the weighty expectations of homeland that effectively tie her eyes shut.

Raeda Saadeh, *Keys*, 2013, detail. Archival pigment print, 90 x 60 cm.
Courtesy of the artist.

Being There, Being Here
Palestinian Writings in the World
MAURICE EBILEENI

In "The Shape of Time: New Palestinian Writing," an online issue of *Words Without Borders*, guest editor, poet, and playwright Nathalie Handal presented a variety of works composed in languages other than Arabic by Palestinians and descendants of Palestinian refugees and immigrants from across the globe. Handal argued that the existence of these literary productions in multiple languages, of different nationalities and cultural influences, as well as of diverse aesthetics, demonstrates the ongoing dynamic and fluid character of Palestinian literature.

Though written in multiple languages, all these works stem from mutual memories and narrations of a lost homeland. I believe, like Handal, that it is by now plausible to ascertain that Palestinian literary productions have surmounted their circumscribed position within the Arab cultural context. The ongoing cultural diversification among displaced Palestinian communities running through several generations since 1948 (and even prior to 1948) has become conspicuous in literature because of the increasing production of Palestinian writing in Hebrew, English, Spanish, Italian, and Danish, among other languages. Up-and-coming—as well as some already established—Palestinian writers or authors of Palestinian descent who may have grown up as second- or third-generation exiles or immigrants in Western countries, or as citizens of Israel, have not, in many instances, enjoyed the choice of writing in Arabic. Rather, as a number of the authors have remarked at some point in their careers, growing up in their respective societies, they have had to write in the language of the majority in their host nations because they were unable to write in their parents' native tongue.

Palestinians writing in the diaspora are bringing their national heritage and personal stories into a variety of languages through different literary media. Depending on lingual and cultural contextualization, their writings engage varied political, social, and aesthetic conditions, contributing to the Palestinian national narrative while also determining its multiple prospective transnational proliferations. For example, the status of Palestinian authors in Israel differs from the status of their counterparts from Europe and the Americas. They are a special case in that they belong not to a migrant community but to the country's indigenous Arab population. They enjoy citizenship under Israeli law. However, while enduring the perils of relative cultural and geographic isolation from their Palestinian counterparts "outside" Israel, they are also generally viewed as culturally and nationally inferior by the country's Jewish majority. In this context, the language of Hebrew Palestinian texts such as Anton Shammas's *Arabesqot* (*Arabesques*, 1986) or any of Sayed Kashua's novels is fueled with these political sensitivities related to both the underprivileged status of Arab citizens since the foundation of the State of Israel and the local mainstream view of these authors' "chutzpah" for making themselves comfortable in a basically Jewish language. Similarly, Anglophone Palestinian writings are inseparable from the instrumental role played by the British (territorial) Empire and the US-led (nonterritorial) powers—since the mid-eighteenth century and World War II—in shaping the history as well as the current conditions of the Israeli-Palestinian conflict, according to long-standing Orientalist discourses. Novels such as Susan Muaddi Darraj's *The Inheritance of Exile: Stories from South Philly* (2007), Randa Jarrar's *A Map of Home* (2008), and Susan Abulhawa's *Mornings in Jenin* (2010) both resist and explore this Anglophone legacy in their respective portrayals of Palestinian displacement.

In comparison, writings from Latin America differ yet again from their counterparts in Europe and North America. The majority of Palestinian communities in Latin America were founded as a result of the waves of Arab emigration from Palestine between 1870 and

1930. Migrants were predominantly Christian merchants from the Bethlehem region, Jerusalem, Taybeh, and Ramallah who wished to escape Ottoman rule. Today's descendants of these migration waves generally belong to middle- and upper-social classes and are well represented among political and business elites (representing, for once, a "successful" Palestinian story). Consequently, they do not easily fit into the national narrative shaped by experiences of exile in the Arab world, dispossession, and life under the Israeli military occupation.

Writings by Palestinian-descended authors in the Spanish language, such as Lina Meruane's *Volverse Palestina* (*Becoming Palestine*, 2014) or Rodrigo Hasbún's *El lugar del cuerpo* (*The Place of the Body*, 2012) cannot be separated from the cultural nuances and sensitivities that have developed over a century since the first waves of immigration from Ottoman Palestine. Furthermore, whereas Palestinian writers residing in Europe and the Americas may generally be defined as exiles or émigrés, they basically belong to historically different waves of migration. Europe and North America variedly host exiles who have escaped either the perils of Israeli occupation or the dire conditions of refugee camps in the Arab countries.

Last, the narratives of recent Danish texts—such as the late Yahya Hassan's two self-titled poetry collections *Yahya Hassan* (2013) and *Yahya Hassan 2* (2019), Ahmad Mahmoud's *Sort Land: Fortællinger fra Ghettoen* (*Black Nation: Stories from the Ghetto*, 2015), and Abdel Aziz Mahmoud's *Hvor Taler Du Flot Dansk* (*How Wonderfully You Speak Danish*, 2016)—cannot be separated from contemporary public discussions on the problems of immigration, assimilation, and the "parallel societies" evolving in certain "ethnic" neighborhoods, such as Nørrebro, in Copenhagen; Vollsmose, near Odense; and Gellerup, at the heart of Århus. My point is that as a result of decades of displacement, the Palestinian story has—within distinct lingual and social environments—proliferated in multiple directions and, as a result, was compelled to grapple with different cultural and political conditions.

The number of Hebrew, Latinate, Anglophone, and Nordic writings by Palestinian authors began to "flourish" between the late 1980s and the second decade of the twenty-first century, following a nearly quarter-century interval since Jabra Ibrahim Jabra's pioneering and sole English novel, *Hunters in a Narrow Street* (1960), and Atallah Mansour's *Deor Hadash* (*In a New Light*, 1966), the first Hebrew-language novel by an Israeli Palestinian writer. Accordingly, if we look beyond the Gaza Strip and the West Bank, or the Arab diaspora, and make an in-depth analysis of literature produced in Israel and the West, it is a sine qua non condition to recognize contemporary artistic expressions of Palestinian experiences presented in languages other than Arabic alongside their Arabic counterparts. Moreover, rather than argue for the prioritization of the Arabic literary branch at the expense of another, I think we need to establish a polylingual category of Palestinian literature that could comprehend the ongoing cultural and literary implications of displacement in the various contexts "inside" and the variety of locations "outside" Israel/Palestine.

The critical move of interlacing literary productions by authors from Israel/Palestine with those works of diasporic writers is necessary in the case of Palestinian literature, since it amalgamates works that represent a diversity of deterritorialized experiences in the absence of a successful nation-building project. Rather than define literary works as Palestinian according to criteria of theme, content, language (Arabic), and the author's identity, I deem it crucial to further problematize the canon by including critical considerations for territoriality and languages other than Arabic as basic factors for the demarcation of liminal spaces of artistic creation among culturally diverse Palestinian authors in the global context.

*

Prior to the events of 1948, the development of Palestinian literature partook in the literary movements that flourished in the Arab world through cultural centers such as Cairo, Beirut, Damascus, and Baghdad. However, it is not to claim that it did not already assume a local character, addressing the political and economic crises reverberating throughout

Palestine during the 1930s. Ghassan Kanafani explains in *Thawrat 36-39 Fi Filistin* (*The 1936-39 Revolt in Palestine*, 1972) that the political repercussions of the peasants' revolt in 1936 also marked a turning point in Palestinian letters. Poets such as Ibrahim Tuqan, Abu Salma, and Abdrahim Mahmoud joined the struggle and became the leading voices in the creation of what Kanafani refers to as a "popular culture," countering the alliance between British imperialism and Zionist settler colonialism as well as the complicit Arab elites. Following the suppression of the revolt in 1939 and the destruction of the multifaceted reality of Palestine in 1948, the generation of new fragmented ones necessitated the invention of new themes, motifs, and techniques. During nearly two decades of collective confusion in these new contexts of displacement, and following the events of 1967 with the revival of a national consciousness across borders, intellectuals took to "arms" again and revived the Palestinian popular culture—this time defying a new world order that had not left room for Palestinians on the map.

Mainstream Palestinian writings assumed an anticolonial tenor and variedly combined representations of a nostalgic craving for the lost homeland and renderings of the apathetic present reality of displacement with a sense of heading toward an uncertain future. On the one hand, poetry composed by distinguished literary figures such as Abu Salma, Salem Jubran, Fadwa Tuqan, Sameeh al-Qasem, and Mahmoud Darwish established a thematic bond, rooted in nature, between people and land. Such literary motifs not only emerged as a result of the exiled poets' need to romanticize their bond to the homeland but were also inspired by a historical relationship between Palestinian peasants and their environment.

Conversely, prose writers such as Kanafani in *Rejaal fil-Shams* (*Men in the Sun*, 1963) and Emile Ḥabiby's *Al-Waqā'i' al-gharībah fi 'khtifā' Sa'īd Abī 'l-Naḥsh al-Mutashā'il* (*The Strange Facts in the Disappearance of Saeed the Ill-Fated Pessoptimist*, better known as *The Secret Life of Saeed the Pessoptimist*, 1974)—a masterpiece of the tragicomic—developed and connected a political consciousness to Palestinians' sense of existential futility and estrangement in the respective contexts of displacement following their historic uprooting. Eventually, such literary productions perpetuated founding principles of the national script for the dispossessed populations and facilitated a literary framework that has since comprehended the production of subsequent texts. During those early years, Palestinians, in their distinct situations of displacement, have craved a token of recognition from the outside world, and literature—particularly poetry—became the medium through which the dispossessed called out to the world as a people.

March 30, 2022

Memoirs of a Militant
The Arrest
NAWAL QASIM BAIDOUN

In late 1986, my village, Bint Jbeil, like all other towns and villages in South Lebanon occupied by the Israeli enemy, was rife with darkness and deprivation, sorrow and misery. Similarly to the rest of the occupied south, Bint Jbeil was continually ravaged by waves of relentless, merciless terrorism. Each day, the Israeli state and its Lebanese collaborators tightened the noose around the necks of the people in these villages in any and every way they could. This included mass arrests of anyone they suspected of having ties to the resistance, or even of people who frequented places of worship. They also increased taxation on raw materials and other commodities that some merchants managed to bring into the region by obtaining specific permits to cross over from outside the occupied zone. On top of all of this, there was the forced military recruitment of every boy who had reached thirteen years of age to contend with. If families refused, they would find themselves faced with two options—condemn their sons to jail or banish them from home, to go live outside the occupied areas.

It wasn't safe anywhere, neither on the streets nor at home. No one could ever relax. Someone might even jump out of bed late at night, all aquiver, because of a terrifying pounding on the door: it would be the collaborators, ordering the owner of the house to hurry up and open the door. The collaborators would regularly head to a specific address because they were on the prowl for one of the members of the family living there. And this is how it came to be that in our town, as in so many others, it was difficult to find even one household without at least one family member in prison. Further, any person who so much as grumbled or muttered something that Israeli collaborators might find suspicious would simply be picked up and locked away. This is how Khiam prison and others filled with hundreds of innocent victims—righteous people.

The prison became a cemetery. The Israelis and their local collaborators made it into something whose name alone still has the power to strike fear in anyone who hears it. As the saying goes, "He who enters is lost, but he who comes out is reborn."

Despite all this harassment and abuse, many young people in town still managed to find ways to secretly work with the resistance against the occupation.

On April 19, 1988, a Wednesday afternoon to be exact, the target Husayn Abdel-Nabi and two of his agents—Abdel-Nabi Bazzi, nicknamed Al-Jalbout, and Fawzi al-Saghir, both from Bint Jbeil—arrested K.Z. at her place of study in town. They also arrested F.Y. at her home. A strange feeling I'd never experienced before washed over me, but I didn't do anything or react in any way that showed I was worried, or even that I knew either one of them.

Time passed slowly. All day, the only thing I could think about was getting home, but I had to wait for the last school bell to ring. I finally returned home, thinking about what had happened to my comrades and what would happen to me. My siblings, who were already there, noticed that something was bothering me. But I insisted that nothing was going on and that I was perfectly fine. The whole time, I kept thinking about what had happened and what would follow—how and why had the two of them gotten arrested? Had the local Israeli collaborators figured out what we were up to? Would K.Z. and F.Y. be released if nothing were found? Or would I end up joining them? So many questions were swirling around in my head. The following day, I went to school and kept up appearances. I was surprised that the teaching staff had heard news of the arrests and was outraged.

One of the women workers at the school said: "The people of the village should all stand together against this, religious clerics should condemn these arrests, there should be a sit-in at the town square. Has the world gone mad? Has it come to this, locking up the girls in town? And why? They've taken all the boys, so now they're coming for the girls!"

These words, which she voiced out loud with no reservations, still resonate with me today. This working woman had a political position that not one of my colleagues on the teaching staff would dare show openly at school.

Somehow the school day ended, and I managed to make my way back home. The incident had paralyzed me, but I tried to act completely normally for fear that my siblings might notice something. Then my time was up: the moment I had been waiting for arrived—that is, the moment of my arrest.

It happened at six fifteen in the evening, on Thursday, April 20, 1988—the fifth day of Ramadan. I was busy preparing for the iftar. Just five minutes before the breaking of the fast, I heard wild knocking on the door to the house. I could feel my heart beating stronger and faster than the pounding at the door. I hurried to see who was there, and I was shocked to find three collaborators with the Israeli occupying army standing there: Husayn Abdel-Nabi, aka Enemy-Nabi; Kamal Salih, from Ayta al-Shaab; and Fawzi al-Saghir, from my town, Bint Jbeil.

I asked them, "What is it? What do you want? There is no one here but my brother, who is not even thirteen years old, and my two sisters, younger than me." It seemed that my turn had come. Husayn Abdel-Nabi just looked down at his hand and said to me, "Are you Nawal Qasim Baidoun?"

"Yes," I replied, "What do you want?" It turns out that my name was written on the palm of his hand.

"Come with us to town, we'd like to ask you some questions. It won't take long and then you can come back home," he told me.

"What do you want from me? What do you want to ask me about?"

"Come with us. You will soon know everything there is to know."

At this point, Fawzi al-Saghir interrupted saying, "We would like to clarify a few things with you. It will only take five minutes. Don't worry. This may all turn out to be a simple misunderstanding."

But this was neither a misunderstanding nor would it take five minutes. Wasn't this what they always said, though it typically led to years of detention in an Israeli prison?

Entrance Procedures

The car stopped outside of a room from which a tall, dark-skinned agent emerged, weapon slung over his shoulder. This was at exactly seven o'clock in the morning. I knew what time it was because I'd heard the news broadcast begin in the car.

Fawzi al-Saghir ordered me to get out of the car and go into a room that had doors on either side, leading to more rooms. As soon as I climbed out, the guard carrying the weapon asked me: "So what's up—did you finish law school?" I stared at him and wondered how he knew I was studying law. Mere seconds later, I found myself inside a large room where a tall, dark man wearing civilian clothes was waiting for us. I found out later that it was the interrogator named Wael, or at least that's what they called him—they didn't use their real names.

A few seconds later he asked me my name, and I gave it to him. He ordered me to take off my jewelry and then went to make a phone call. I could make out only a bit of what he was saying. "Come down here and bring handcuffs and a bag with you." Moments later, two young women wearing civilian clothes entered the room. One was a full-figured, boxy blonde; the other one, who was rather thin with jet-black hair, was holding iron handcuffs in one hand and something black in the other. She asked me to hold out my hands, and I was shocked that she spoke to me in Arabic with a Lebanese accent. At first glance I'd assumed they were Israelis and would speak Hebrew. She then put a black bag over my head.

I couldn't bear it, so I tore it off. This lady collaborator reprimanded me loudly, "Don't ever do that again." She put it back on and tied a blindfold of the same color over my eyes. I couldn't see anything and felt as if I were suffocating. She tugged the edge of my sleeve and told me to follow her. I asked, "Where to?" She retorted sarcastically, "To the cinema! . . . Now walk and don't ask questions."

Blindfolded, I was afraid of bumping into something, so I followed close behind her.

We walked a few steps and she told me to stop. After this I heard the click of a lock turning, and then the creak of a metal door opening. She ordered me to lift one foot and then the other so I could enter the room. She unlocked my handcuffs and ordered me to remove the bag from my head and untie my blindfold. I did both. I found myself in a room that was barely a meter or two long and half a meter wide. "So this is the place you imagined," I thought. Then she told me to put my hands behind my back. She locked handcuffs on them and did the same with my feet. She propped me up on the ground and said, "Don't move." Then she left, locking the cell door on me. The top of the metal door had a peephole of scratched-up glass that was difficult to see through.

As I took in my surroundings, I felt like someone was putting their hands around my neck. I looked around and thought, "Where am I? What is this?" The first thing I noticed were the words written on the cell walls and scratched into the door. They were the names of young women and men, their dates of incarceration, and also words about their families, their mothers especially, and the homeland. There were also Qur'anic verses. At that moment, I found myself unable to concentrate on any specific thought. I felt dazed, as if I were sleepwalking. Suddenly a very clear image of my family appeared to me—I could see my parents and siblings. My mind was plagued by so many questions about their reaction to my arrest and what would happen to them. Only after this did I find myself thinking about what was in store for me in this place.

I was in Khiam prison.

Translated from the Arabic by **MICHELLE HARTMAN** and **CALINE NASRALLAH**

October 15, 2021

Vera Tamari, *Woman at the Door*, 1994, detail. Clay relief and engobe colors, 33 x 17 x 1.5 cm. Courtesy of the artist.

Pledging Allegiance
NOOR HINDI

I am tired of language. I don't want to make metaphors. About olive trees. About wearing a keffiyeh. About About About. The dream has not ended. My grandma is back in Jordan. She loves her passport. What does it mean to love? A country? A book? A people? To say "I absolutely and entirely renounce and abjure all allegiance and fidelity to any foreign prince, potentate, state, or sovereignty," while thinking about Palestine. While holding the key to your father's first home. While While While. The news keeps screaming. The headlines chew at our eyes. A bald eagle burdens its wings with suitcases, then drops them in another land.

*

The language isn't enough.

Here—an image of homeland. The word *colonization*, a photo of a fruit so bloodied. I hold a beam of light to a wall, make shadows of Palestine I try to catch. Olive tree, Israeli soldier, a metaphor of Palestine as a woman.

In a workshop, a white classmate says *some of us celebrate diversity*. Someone wants to talk about hummus and falafel (pronounces them both wrong, then asks me for the labor of forgiveness).

I'm supposed to be feeding them whatever is the opposite of guilt. I want to move beyond. Where?

There are bodies. And then there are fewer bodies. This is the formula.

Ask me about a two-state solution. About caring for a world that does not love you back. About holding a knife and tearing into a map. But oh—

There's the cliché again. But the deaths. But the deaths. But the deaths. Have they, too, become a cliché? A transgender Palestinian teen is stabbed. Israa Ghrayeb is dead. Gazan families continue to face an electricity crisis.

And still—*I didn't even know any of this was happening. // Thank you for educating me. // Do you like living in America? // But what about those terrorists? // When you say Palestine, do you actually mean Pakistan?*

What comes after awareness? And then what? There's a bird. No, it's a drone. My tax dollars pay for the bombs that kill my people.

*

I'm locked out of my home. No, I can't recognize my home. I grabbed the wrong keys. The house has been painted a different color. There is music inside but I don't understand the words. There is smoke inside, but nothing is burning.

All I do is wait. I peer in from the windows. The house is inhabited by ghosts. They recognize my face but not my tongue. I try to find where it hurts.

*

The ghosts laugh. Their laughs end with a sharp pang of grief; it sounds like a fist, or a hand around my throat. I reach for them, begging to be let in. When I ring the bell, no one answers. I draw letters on the outside of the door.

Shoreless Sea

TAYSEER BARAKAT

Tayseer Barakat, *Shoreless Sea* #11, 2019. Acrylic on canvas, 50 x 70 cm.
Courtesy Zawyeh Gallery.

Tayseer Barakat grew up by the sea, in Gaza. His series *Shoreless Sea* is a meditation on the large numbers of Arabs becoming refugees and crossing the perilous Mediterranean while the world watches on, indifferent to their tragedy. The artist acknowledges how the monotone tones of his paintings "reflect the hardships of our time and our present life. I think the pressure on us makes us use dark colors."

Tayseer Barakat, *Shoreless Sea #11*, **2019, detail. Acrylic on canvas, 50 x 70 cm. Courtesy Zawyeh Gallery.**

Israel's Intimate Separations
JENINE ABBOUSHI

On the morning of the second day of the Eid of the Sacrifice, I stepped out of a service taxi into Hebron's deserted streets. Though guided by no road signs, the driver knew the way to our destination, through zigzagging turns and, to me, unfamiliar Israeli urban expansion. We passed by Hebron's vineyards, which I conflated with the southern reaches of Tyre, Lebanon, as well as with parts of the Moroccan oases. The landscapes of harsh, forgotten poverty bring these worlds together.

From the top of the hill, I walked down to an empty, forsaken market strewn with holiday debris. A lone shop selling parakeets and flowers was open. There was also a fellow making falafel, busy slicing tomatoes and arranging fuchsia-colored pickled turnips on a long-board table in front of his shop. An old man wearing a *dishdasha*, who told me he had lived in the old city all his life, appeared and was intent on leading me further into the barricaded *souq*. Instead of turning the corner to get from the mosque to the cemetery, he pointed out that funeral processions must now circle the town for five kilometers to reach the cemetery, which is next to the settlements. He instructed me where to climb up high in this Old City, sometimes maneuvering through barbed wire, to get a view of the riches seized by the Israeli settlements. For decades now, settlers have built a ghetto by their own hand, quite literally confining themselves and everyone else with over one hundred barricades and eighteen checkpoints in the small area of the Hebron souq, which is an ancient trade center, and was recently made a UNESCO world heritage site. Israel confiscated a large percentage of Hebron's land, subjecting destitute townspeople to captivity and daily abuse in their historical homes and lands.

The medieval Ibrahimi Mosque, built on what the Israelis believe is the burial site of the patriarchs, is now barricaded from the inside, having lost 60 percent of its interior to Israeli settlements. The Israelis have seized entire homes. And it is these Israeli-occupied Palestinian homes and businesses in Hebron's Old City that best showcase the neurotic nature of Israel's colonization—that is, if only the nature of these brutal arrangements were properly communicated to the world. In one part of the souq, families have to enter their homes through their windows (hoisting groceries and small children), as the Israelis have long sealed off access to these houses' front doors. Indeed, the Palestinians of Hebron are hidden, left for generations now at the mercy of the Israelis surrounding them. Last month, Israelis danced inside the Ibrahimi Mosque, boots on rugs. Following this disgraceful frolic, they burned the mosque's Qur'ans, discarding the charred pages and bindings. The willful deception of limiting blame to settlers and "Israeli extremists" for Israel's systemic brutality and theft is exposed yet again by Netanyahu's appointment of Itamar Ben Gvir, resident of Kiryat Arba, a large Israeli settlement in Hebron, as the country's national security minister.

Much of the world seems to grant Israel freedom from historical irony, thereby supporting and sustaining its annihilation project against Palestinian society. Israeli expansion and rule in Hebron, cut off from the world by both physical and virtual (media) blockades, is not an exception, but rather the model of Israeli policy in Palestine. And the Israelis are creating many more Hebrons. Benefiting from the near absence of international concern, the Israelis busy themselves sequestering the Palestinians into tiny, densely populated territories, seizing most of the land of Palestine and its water, but all the while failing to develop a workable way to get rid of its people.

＊

The next day I headed to Nablus and the north. Nablus and Sebastia are particularly coveted by the Israelis, as certain locations in these towns figure in Jewish religious texts and lore. The north is hidden from international view, deliberately so, as the Israelis wish to secure a secret playing field where they can commit war crimes by their methods in forcibly quelling Palestinian resistance movements in Jenin camp—which has grown to cover 30 percent of the town—and in Nablus, where the latest homegrown resistance movement, the Lion's Den, has taken root. Al Jazeera's Shireen Abu Akleh was executed (with simultaneous attempts on her colleagues' lives) as a warning to any journalists who attempt to shine a light on what the Israelis are doing to Palestinians in Jenin camp and in the north in general.

Israeli assassinations of Palestinians in the north in particular take terrifying forms. Friends from Arraba took me to see the internationally funded restoration of beautiful historical buildings. The idea to reroute pilgrims and visitors from the Jerusalem-Bethlehem area and into the north strikes me as a potentially brilliant way of rendering this region less hidden from international view. Along the way, my companions showed me the most important sites of all—and they were ones I could not see. We got out of the car just outside of Arraba. "It was just there," my companion said, pointing to the side of a road with agricultural fields and low mountains in the background, gesturing as if something were there. We gazed at the scene as he explained: "On the fourth day of Ramadan, a civilian car stopped here—right here!" He said this while advancing to a point on the asphalt. "Two Israeli agents got out of the car," he continued, "assassinated two *shabab*, young Palestinian men, strolling together on this road, and took their bodies with them in the car." What I could not see that day haunts me today.

All over the West Bank, Gaza, and Jerusalem, the Israelis steal the bodies of assassinated Palestinians, refusing to return them to their families. The Israelis admit to keeping them in their cemeteries of numbers, and in fact in 2018 they passed legislation making it "legal" to retain Palestinian corpses, against international humanitarian laws and the Geneva Conventions, according to Al-Haq.[1] The Israelis started this practice in the 1970s against the Palestinian liberation movement, supposedly to use corpses as barter and inflict punishment on Palestinian families, who cannot mourn or even fully believe their children were killed because they never buried them. In the past, Palestinian doctors noticed that organs were missing from Palestinian martyrs' bodies that were returned to their families. In 2009 Israel admitted to having extracted organs from Palestinian corpses, but claimed that it had stopped this practice in the 1990s.[2]

If Zionism creates "cancerous" bodies without organs in terms of its accelerated production of divisions, hierarchies, and barriers—like the one that philosophers Deleuze and Guattari envision in *A Thousand Plateaus: Capitalism and Schizophrenia*—the Israeli state also creates literal bodies without organs. Activist Palestinians, families with their children's cadavers stolen by the Israeli army, founded organizations, like the Association founded by Mohammad Alawan from Beit Safafa (whose son's body was held by the army for a year and a half). The Association organizes legal action to demand the return of Palestinian bodies, and the number of names they publish of stolen Palestinian martyrs is in the hundreds (Al-Haq cites over 265 bodies).

And it so happens that Israel has the biggest skin bank in the world, the Israel National Skin Bank, founded by the army. The harvested skin is sold and exported, but the bank's founding and main purpose is to graft it onto wounded Israeli soldiers. This in a country with dominant religious practices that require the physical integrity of the deceased upon burial. There are marginal challenges in Israel to this religious law—requests to religious authorities to make exceptions if Jewish lives can be saved by organ donations. But exceptions to this law are rare.

In a video report, two well-known left-wing Israeli reporters, Guy Meroz and Orly Vilnai, walk into the Israel National Skin Bank and

---

1   "Newly Adopted Law to Withhold the Bodies of Palestinians Killed Breaches International Law, Must Be Repealed," Al-Haq, March 14, 2018.
2   Associated Press, "Israel Harvested Organs in '90s without Consent," NBC, December 21, 2009.

ask what percentage of the Bank's "donated" skin is Israeli. The woman working there at first protests that they ask a "strange" question, and one of the journalists retorts, "Is the question strange or is the answer strange?" Then she admits that most of the skin harvested for the bank is non-Israeli. This makes sense, given the interdiction of Jewish law. So where could all that harvested skin be coming from? This question begs further investigation, but while Palestinians have no access to the resources in Israel needed to conduct this research, *Haaretz* and B'Tselem do.

Early Sunday morning, after my trip to the north of Palestine, I returned to Jerusalem and visited the new Museum of Tolerance (also named the Museum of Human Dignity), which is built on Mamilla, a historic Palestinian Muslim cemetery. *Haaretz* calls it an "ancient Muslim" cemetery, which it is (with a glorious historical registry of Sufis, Amirs, and notables, from Crusader to modern times, including, it is said, several of the *sahaba*, the companions of the Prophet Mohammad)—but this language obscures the fact that Mamilla is Palestinian, part of Jerusalem's historical record, and also that it was a "living," in-use cemetery until recently. "The bulldozing of historic cemeteries is the ultimate act of territorial aggrandizement: the erasure of prior residents," says archeologist Harvey Weiss, of Yale University, adding that "the desecration of Jerusalem's Mamilla Cemetery is a continuing cultural and historical tragedy."[3]

Palestinians from Jerusalem are buried here, many from prominent historical Palestinian and regional families. My friend Ruba walked through with a friend from the Dajani family who pointed out her relatives' graves. The Islamic Waqf and Al-Aqsa lost their suits in the High Court against the museum's desecration project, and hundreds of Palestinians' tombs were dug up to accommodate this Israeli Museum of Tolerance, which was built literally into Palestinian graves and

---

3   "Archaeologists Worldwide Urge Halt to 'Museum of Tolerance' Construction on Ancient Muslim Cemetery," Center for Constitutional Rights, Press Release, October 20, 2011.

on Palestinian land, mocking human rights, international law, and justice. This not only passes unnoticed, but the Israeli violations also continue to receive the approval of world celebrities. The then governor of California, Arnold Schwarzenegger, for instance, participated in the cornerstone celebration, and architect Frank Geary only stepped down due to financial disputes.

I visited Mamilla with a friend. We came upon a down-and-out Palestinian lying next to the now derelict historical mausoleum—our people's last night guard, it seemed, of Jerusalem's history. Groups of Israeli thugs regularly pass by, smashing and damaging the tombstones and axing off parts of the beautiful *Kebekiyeh*, where the emir Aidughdi Kubaki was buried in 1289, as they maraud gleefully through a path of tombs, shrubbery, and old trees that links two streets of West Jerusalem. The tombs farther afield, which I reached on my second visit there before leaving the country (making my way through high dead grass and thistles) still have inscriptions, and some are even mostly intact. It is easy to deface and destroy tombstones, as the Israelis can claim that time and weather are the culprits (but specialists can readily identify the vandalism—that is, if only someone from the international community of archaeologists would bother to do so).

On that Sunday morning of my second visit to Mamilla, I looked through the openings to the Museum of Tolerance that is not yet open. I observed the walkway leading up to the main door, with luminous placards of famous faces accompanied by texts, like that of South African Nobel laureate Nadine Gordimer. I circled the museum to the back, where Mamilla's tombstones—lots of tombstones— reach up to and against the museum's wall. It saddened me to imagine that Israeli society and visitors to Israel have dehumanized the Palestinians to the point of not questioning this scandalous scene of desecration and erasure of historical artifacts and memory. Many will enter through the front only, just as they are instructed to never enter the West Bank, meaning that most will not stroll through this park of historical annihilation.

*

I took my return flight the next day. The jet out of Tel Aviv was full of Israelis returning to the US, many of them ultra Orthodox. Jerusalem is heavily ultra Orthodox, and much of the real estate is purchased at astonishingly high prices by American Jews who benefit from Israel's ten-year tax break. Jerusalem is full of empty apartment buildings of owned apartments, trophies of Israel's legal money laundering of sorts (which is in fact similar to Beirut's empty skyscrapers of purchased apartments—as in the Raouche area, which helped create offshore wealth and local poverty in Lebanon).

The Hasidic Jews on the plane did what they wanted, mingling, standing up, opening suitcases, changing places, passing food across seats and other passengers, at any and all times—but in a mild-mannered, socially insular way, oblivious to airplane regulations. The staff looked desperate, having spent the flight begging and cajoling the unruly passengers. Next to me sat a woman with conservative clothing, seemingly from another era and world, and a wig. She struck up a conversation. I learned that she was born and raised in Detroit, and I mentioned that I too was born in Detroit. We discovered we were born in the same hospital, that we were the same age, and that both of us had two children nearly the same ages, a girl and a boy, with the older one in both instances a lawyer.

Soon, the woman started to look worried. When she asked me my name and I answered, she looked confused, saying she didn't remember my family from Detroit. Then she asked me if I was Jewish. I said no, and she repressed her surprise when I said that I was Palestinian. The coincidences were astonishing; the overlap of our lives stunned her. But when I told her about my trip and impressions, she said that she had never heard such things before, that she had no idea about the Palestinians behind the wall. She said that what I described was terrible. I too had never spoken at length with anyone from her community. I felt lucky to have met and learned from her. We are as different as possible, yet moving, it seems, along parallel paths.

The idea that if only "the two sides" meet and get along personally, "peace" would be possible has always been so tiresome. We can find friendly, personable people in any group. The problem is the ideas and practices of Zionism, and complicity with its crimes, which have caused so much death, destruction, and loss. That and Israeli state greed. Consequently, there must first be post Zionism recognition of historical injustice, followed by reparations. As long as Zionism is still in operation and receiving lots of help, the Palestinians will remain bone-tired of silent "friends."

And yet the way dehumanization and violence works is *always* through separating people, including social classes and children in segregated neighborhoods and schools. Who will allow me, as a Palestinian, to buy an apartment in Israeli Jewish neighborhoods of Jerusalem, Tel Aviv, or Haifa (if any decent ones were affordable) and mix my generations with theirs?

December 5, 2022

Fida'i

HEBA TANNOUS

Heba Tannous, *Fida'i*, 2022. Digital illustration. Courtesy of the artist.

Heba Tannous's illustration *Fida'i* is named after the eponymous Palestinian national anthem. The lyrics urge the people of an occupied land, inspired by sacrifice, to rise up and revolt. An architect, Tannous incorporates her professional expertise into her artistic practice. Her drawings often feature aerial views of refugee camps and street scenes, to capture the essence of Palestine's built environment.

Heba Tannous, *Fida'i*, 2022, detail. Digital illustration. Courtesy of the artist.

The End of the Palestinian State?
Jenin Is Only the Beginning
YOUSEF M. ALJAMAL

Thanks to the Iraqi army, the Palestinian city of Jenin was not captured in 1948 when Israel was created. The Iraqi army was able to retake the city, and the dozens of graves in the Iraqi Army Martyrs' Cemetery bear witness to the battle that took place there against armed Jewish militias, which were routed. But in 1967, Jenin was captured when Israel "finished the job" and occupied the West Bank, the Gaza Strip, Sinai, and the Golan Heights in the Six-Day War.

Just outside the city of Jenin, a refugee camp was built in 1948 and became home to thousands of Palestinian refugees who were expelled at gunpoint when Israel was created. In 1967, more Palestinians were driven from Jenin into Jordan, becoming refugees for a second time. *Mornings in Jenin* is a novel by Palestinian writer Susan Abulhawa that tells the story of a Palestinian family from the village of Ein Hod, near Haifa, who became refugees in Jenin in 1948. The scenes of Palestinians leaving the refugee camp en masse on July 4 were a stark reminder of the Nakba.

Jenin is more than a Palestinian refugee camp. It is a symbol of the refugee issue and of the defiance in the face of Israel's expansion; in 2005 Israel withdrew from the Hermesh settlement, near Jenin, at the same time as it decided to withdraw from the Gaza Strip. Three years previously, in 2002, the right-wing Israeli coalition, led by Benjamin Netanyahu, decided to legalize the settlement as part of its drive to expand settlements and annex parts of the West Bank, namely Area C, which makes up 60 percent of the territory. In the eyes of Israel's most right-wing government, the 2005 disengagement from Gaza and parts of the northern West Bank was a strategic mistake that needed to be reversed.

For this reason, and to pave the way for Israel's plans to annex Area C of the West Bank, the Israeli army has launched a campaign targeting the Jenin refugee camp in the West Bank. Throughout 2023 Israel has carried out repeated incursions into the refugee camp, killing dozens of Palestinians. For Israel, the crushing of any Palestinian resistance is a precondition for its annexation plan. For the first time since 2002, when Israeli infantry, commandos and assault helicopters attacked the Jenin refugee camp , the Israeli army used drones and helicopters to demolish dozens of Palestinian homes, calling the incursion Operation Home and Garden.

Ironically, Operation Home and Garden left many Palestinian homes and gardens in Jenin in ruins. Israeli bulldozers deliberately destroyed roads, targeted media and medical crews, and forced thousands of Palestinian refugees out of the camp after threatening to bomb their homes. In this manner, Israel announced the start of the second phase of the operation in which it plans to target every single house and capture or kill Palestinian armed men inside the crowded refugee camp. So far the Israeli operation in Jenin has killed twelve Palestinians and injured one hundred others, twenty of whom are in critical condition.

The Israeli army will extend its operations to other towns and refugee camps in the West Bank—Jenin is just the beginning. The Israeli government is determined to confiscate more Palestinian land, demolish more Palestinian homes, and give the green light to Israeli settlers to carry out more pogroms against Palestinian towns, as happened recently in the West Bank towns of Huwara and Turmus Ayya.

*

International Silence

As we have seen in the past, Israeli violations in the West Bank and Jerusalem are unlikely to remain there: Gaza will join the escalation, threatening another Israeli war in the coastal enclave. In fact, Palestinians have begun protesting at Gaza's eastern borders in solidarity with Jenin, burning tires and demanding action to end the Israeli incursion into the refugee camp. Palestinian factions in Gaza are likely to target Israel, and other Palestinian cells in the West Bank are expected to target Israel, Israeli settlers, and the Israeli army in response to the events in Jenin, leading to further escalation on the ground.

Without international intervention to stop the Israeli escalation in Jenin, another war is in the making this summer, just like what happened in May 2021 and May 2023. The US and UK governments see Israeli actions as part of "Israel's right to defend itself," while a number of Arab and Muslim countries are content with issuing statements of condemnation, reducing the pressure on the Israeli government, which enjoys total impunity. Speaking in numbers, Israel has killed 193 Palestinians since the beginning of 2023.

The Palestinian Authority says it has stopped security coordination with Israel, a move that was announced repeatedly in the past, in response to what is happening in Jenin, but the Israeli government claims security coordination is ongoing. Nowadays, the vast majority of Palestinians have lost all hope that peace talks with Israel could lead to the establishment of a Palestinian state. Indeed, Netanyahu has never been clearer that Israel will do everything in its power to prevent the establishment of a Palestinian state, and that allowing the Palestinians to have a state is a strategic threat. Netanyahu recently declared that Israel must "crush" Palestinian statehood ambitions.

Jenin Is Only the Start

Palestinians on the ground know only too well that Israel will never leave the West Bank and will only expand there. They also knew back in 1993, when the Palestine Liberation Organization and Israel agreed to establish a Palestinian state "within five years," that it was simply a trap and that Israel would never have allowed the Palestinians to have their own sovereign and independent state. All the Palestinians can aspire to is a couple of mayorships outside Area C of the West Bank, without any political representation or rights. The Israeli invasion of the Jenin refugee camp, and probably other West Bank towns, is proof of this.

In Israel's eyes, Palestinians are merely cheap laborers that can build Israeli cities and settlements, and granting them full rights is out of the question. For Palestinians with Israeli citizenship, who make up 20 percent of Israel's population, all that is in store for them is more violence and crime that will eventually force them to leave, without the Israeli police ever intervening to make any arrests. What is certain, sadly, is that there are worse days ahead for the Palestinian people and that their conditions will only get worse under Israel's continuing military occupation. Jenin is only the beginning.

July 10, 2023

Jenin's Freedom Theatre
Survives Another Assault

HADANI DITMARS

The Freedom Theatre, headquartered in northern West Bank's Jenin refugee camp, is nothing if not a crucible for the Palestinian experience. Up against grinding poverty, occupation, religious extremism, and, more recently, aerial bombardment from the Israeli Defense Forces during a July 2023 assault and a raid and arrests in December of 2023, the theater miraculously survives.

In July, a few days after the IDF occupied its offices and the ceiling of its old British mandate-era building, cracked from the impact of bombing, staff and supporters were busy cleaning up the rubble and making plans for a new season. After a show of solidarity by a wide range of Palestinian artists, theater makers, and intellectuals from across the occupied territories who staged a "cultural protest" in the theater's courtyard—a community gathering place—discussions were underway for a series of drama-therapy workshops intended for traumatized children (five were killed during the IDF incursion) and health care workers (who were shot at by the IDF as they tried to reach the injured). At the time of the attack on the camp, TFT was planning a feminist-theater festival and in rehearsal for a play by Charles Mee called *Big Love*, based on Aeschylus's *The Suppliants*, which explores gender politics, love, and domestic violence.

Many TFT staff, like the other fifteen thousand occupants of Jenin refugee camp, bore the brunt of the unrelenting forty-eight-hour military campaign that killed twelve people, injured 143, and displaced hundreds of families. In fact, the drama of living in Jenin rivals the plots of the plays performed by TFT since its inception, in 2006. These range from a reenvisioned *Alice in Wonderland*, about a girl who refuses to marry the man her family has chosen for her, to Athol Fugard's apartheid-era drama *The Island*. In the face of everyday events in Palestine, TFT productions transform into hyperreal metatheater.

Staff and Students Killed, Injured, Arrested

Fourteen-year-old Sadeel Naghniyeh, a young participant at the theater and the niece of TFT's chief technician Adnan Torkoman, was killed by the IDF. Just two weeks later, Torkoman, who lives in a residential complex that abuts the theater, was arrested and held for four days by the Israeli army. His home was also damaged.

As many of TFT's staff and students live in Jenin refugee camp, some had to flee the camp as the invasion took place. According to a press release, "Some of the team [members] were forced to stay in their homes and were used as human shields and others refused to leave at all."

These included Isra Awartani, TFT's accountant, who "hastily created a safe space within her home to shield her three daughters from harm," and Rania Wasfi, a past member of the theater who "frantically tried to reach her mother and sister after news that their house was bombed."

Ahmed Tobasi, the theater's artistic director, "found himself face-to-face with an armored vehicle stationed right outside his house, its barrel aimed at his window." His twice-daily video diaries on his Facebook page became a riveting cinema verité during the forty-eight-hour siege, when the camp was virtually closed to the outside world and journalists attempting coverage were shot by the IDF (the same soldiers who killed renowned Palestinian American journalist Shireen Abu Akleh (1971–2022) while she was covering a raid on Jenin).

On a July 9, 2023, emergency Zoom call for the theater's supporters that drew hundreds of participants from around the world, Tobasi said, "It was just like 2002"—the so-called Battle of Jenin that killed fifty-two Palestinians—"only they somehow managed to inflict more damage in two days than they did in two weeks."

Then, just as the theater was getting back on its feet, it was raided by the IDF on December 12 and 13, 2023, as the war on Gaza spread to the West Bank. Soldiers spray-painted the Star of David on the wall of an interior film-screening room, while graffiti depicting the Star of David and a menorah defaced an exterior wall. At the time, Tobasi told *Democracy Now!*: "They stormed in. They broke everything, any electronic stuff, any glass ... the children were screaming, crying." That same day a drone strike in the camp killed four young Palestinians. Tobasi was handcuffed, beaten, and arrested and then made to wear an IDF uniform and pose for humiliating photos with the soldiers. He was blindfolded and forced into a truck, taken to a checkpoint, and thrown into the muddy street. He was released after fourteen hours, but theater manager Mostafa Sheta remained in detention in the Megiddo military prison in northern Israel.[1]

Tobasi later said in an online statement, "To be released by the army and to find our friends and colleagues around the world had demanded my freedom made me feel I have family in all these countries who care for me."

"We have many challenges," explained Tobasi, who spoke of high-tech military tactics and drones being used to attack the densely populated refugee camp. "The conservative culture, the religious people, the Israelis, the political situation, funding—but when we see this kind of support, it helps us to go on and to continue with Juliano's legacy."

The legendary Israeli Palestinian founder of the theater, who is referred to by his first name by friends in Jenin, has become a kind of secular saint among his supporters. A martyr to the cause who famously said, "The Third Intifada will be a cultural one," Juliano Mer-Khamis founded the theater in 2006, together with Zakaria Zubeidi, a former military leader of the Jenin al-Aqsa Martyrs Brigades; Jonatan Stanczak, a Swedish Israeli activist; and Dror Feiler, a Swedish Israeli artist.

In 2011, Mer-Khamis was murdered in front of the theater by a masked Palestinian gunman. Four months later, masked Israeli

---

[1]   As of January 26, 2024, Mostafa Sheta was still imprisoned in Megiddo prison.

soldiers attacked TFT in the middle of the night, and a year later Israeli authorities arrested artistic director Nabil al-Raee and cofounder Zubeidi on various trumped-up charges, including terrorism and involvement in the murder of Mer-Khamis. The story of the actor, director, filmmaker, and activist was told in a recent piece of theater produced by TFT based on actual interviews with Palestinian artists. But his tale is as much Greek tragedy as verbatim theater.

Juliano was born to Arna Mer-Khamis, a Jewish former combatant in the Palmach (a Mandate-era Zionist military organization) who became a Communist after participating in operations to drive Bedouins out of the Negev, and Saliba Khamis, a Palestinian Christian and one of the leaders of the Israeli Communist Party in the 1950s. Juliano himself was stationed in Jenin as a member of the IDF's Paratroopers Brigade. He soon became disenchanted with his role when he saw the violence and humiliation inflicted on a captive population. As he said in the 1991 film *Deadly Currents*, he identified as a Jew in his youth because he was raised by a free-thinking Jewish mother, but when he joined the IDF he realized that "this wasn't my mama—it was fascism!" He was eventually sent to prison for punching a commanding officer after refusing an order to frisk an elderly Palestinian man.

After his release he went to theater school and spent a year in the Philippines taking magic mushrooms, later declaring, "I lost all my identities. I said to myself, you have a gift, you are not only consciously unnationalized, you are inside yourself divided. Use it!"[2] While his response to the First Intifada was to perform street theater in Tel Aviv nude and covered in blood, his mother Arna started a children's center in Jenin refugee camp and asked her son to teach drama therapy.

After the Second Intifada broke out and two of his former students became suicide bombers—one after witnessing the death of a young girl killed by an IDF bombing—he returned to Jenin a month after the 2002 Battle of Jenin began. Hosted by a former student who was the

---

2   See "Juliano Mer-Khamis—Street Show," April 10, 2021, online: https://youtu.be/ESoPWbqe6pM?si=DZ_Jmr5CECaoZxZg; edited original footage from the documentary *Deadly Currents* (1991), dir. Simcha Jacobovici.

leader of the al-Aqsa Martyrs Brigade, he met future theater cofounder Zubeidi and later made a film about the experience called *Arna's Children*, released in 2004. Although he said in an Israeli radio interview in 2009 that he was "one hundred percent Palestinian and one hundred percent Jewish," in reality he trod on dangerous terrain, slipping between identities in Jenin and Tel Aviv.

In addition to Israeli/Palestinian issues, Jenin was a hotbed of conflicting interests and loyalties to Fatah and Hamas, rife with rumors and realities about corruption and collaboration. Juliano's murder, which occurred shortly after he pulled the plug on a production of *Spring Awakening* that offended local socially conservative sensibilities, has still not been solved, and both the Palestinian Authority and the Israeli government have been reluctant to provide answers. As he once famously said, "They think that if you replace the Israeli occupation with the Arafat occupation, it's going to be better, and I say no, fight both of them!"

Sieges, Poetry, and International Tours

TFT's current artistic director, Ahmed Tobasi, has had no less of a dramatic life narrative. In fact, his story of going from armed resistance to acting and his journey as a refugee from the West Bank to Norway and back again are the subjects of TFT's production *Here I Am*. The play is based on the famous verse by Mahmoud Darwish: "I am from there. I am from here. / I am not there and I am not here / I have two names, which meet and part and I have two languages. / I forget which of them I dream in." *Here I Am*, written by Hassan Abdulrazzak and directed by longtime TFT associate Zoe Lafferty, toured the UK as well as Jenin and the West Bank.

Although TFT produces a variety of international plays, its strength lies in its portrayal of Palestinian reality. A compelling example is 2015's *The Siege*, created by Raee and Lafferty, about the thirty-nine-day siege of Bethlehem's Church of the Nativity, in 2002, which played out at the same time as the siege of Jenin. The drama moves back and forth between the historical event and the present, drawing from interviews with surviving combatants, who were exiled in Europe.

Now, as residents of Jenin recover from yet another Israeli siege, one recalls Darwish's words:

> In the state of siege, time becomes space
> Transfixed in its eternity
> In the state of siege, space becomes time
> That has missed its yesterday and its tomorrow.

TFT draws on the many layers of Palestinian memory and trauma to produce poignant and powerful emotional truths as well as drama therapy for the residents of Jenin. But it is the theater's international productions, such as *Here I Am* and *The Siege*, that serve to "humanize the Palestinians," points out Gary M. English, an American drama professor who was TFT's artistic director from 2012 to 2013. As he wrote in the 2020 book *Theater in the Middle East*:

> Narratives portraying Palestinians as human, complex, caring, deliberate, and thoughtful, or simply taking on the task of daily life roles, are often decried as propaganda. When it comes to any representation of the Palestinian-Israeli conflict in particular, theater that takes a humanistic and complex look at Palestinian resistance invokes accusations of anti-Semitism and is regularly deemed dangerous.[3]

*

Interviewed at his home in Connecticut, English relates that TFT plays two key roles. One is that "it provides children and youth of the camp a way to think about who they are in the world. It's an educational alternative to the conservatism of the camp and offers a way for them to imagine themselves as something other than martyrs—to think about themselves as creative individuals who think for themselves."

---

3   Gary M. English, "Artistic Practice and Production at the Freedom Theatre: The Interpenetration of the Personal and the Political," in *Theater in the Middle East: Between Performance and Politics*, ed. Babak Rahimi (Anthem Press, 2020).

"Like Juliano always said," notes English, "TFT was about being independent of social forces that would define you—so it's very much about ending the psychological occupation."

An equally important role, he says, is to offer a counternarrative in the "rhetorical war of negative stereotypes" through international tours, where "audiences have to contend with the humanity of the Palestinian actors on stage."

Beyond the important educational aspect for foreign audiences, the ability to produce theater about the Palestinian experience and tour it, he says, "contradicts the Israeli narrative that Palestinians are 'barbarians.'"

Paraphrasing bell hooks, he contends that "the act of taking something from the margin and putting it into the mainstream is itself a radical act."

How to Help the Theater

For now, as TFT rises once again from the ashes, there is much work to be done. The courtyard area outside the theater where children used to play was severely damaged and is littered with the burnt-out husks of cars. The level of structural damage after the bombing that cracked the ceiling is still being evaluated. "It could be a simple fix, or we might need to rebuild it completely," says a theater spokesperson. The IDF also raided the Freedom Theatre Guesthouse, shattering windows and damaging the exterior of the building.

To add insult to injury, TFT lost 80 percent of their funding from the EU in 2020 after rejecting conditions that stipulated they must depoliticize their work.

However, there are practical ways for supporters to help. In addition to a call for donations, TFT is encouraging allies to program Palestinian plays and films and to perform or create an event around their verbatim theater work *The Revolution's Promise*. Created by TFT and *Artists on the Frontline*, the project is billed as "a collection of testimonies from artists across Palestine, celebrating cultural resistance and highlighting censorship and attacks on artists."

"We are inviting friends, activists, and artists worldwide to join this collaboration by telling these stories in the community you live, work, or organize in," says TFT's website.

Paradoxically, the recent assault on Jenin refugee camp has brought home what Lafferty describes as "Juliano's mission—to bring the story of Jenin camp to the world."

In spite of everything that has transpired, she says, "TFT has absolutely triumphed in that mission. Juliano would be proud."

One can only imagine that recent events will once again find their way into TFT productions as they continue to spin the straw of Palestinian experience into theatrical gold.

July 24, 2023

Homeland
SLIMAN ANIS MANSOUR

Sliman Anis Mansour, *Homeland*, 2010. Charcoal and acrylic on canvas, 188 x 233 cm. Courtesy of Ramzi and Saeda Dalloul Art Foundation.

As of 2024, a Palestinian passport allows Palestinians to travel visa-free to only 14 countries—as opposed to an Israeli passport, which allows Israelis to enter 136 countries visa-free. Since Israel's 2007 siege of Gaza, Palestinian professionals, artists, athletes, and students, among others, have been stopped from traveling abroad. Also, Palestinians are unable to move freely between the occupied territories of the Gaza Strip, the West Bank, and East Jerusalem without the necessary ID cards, permits, or visas. These, granted by the Israeli authorities, are often not recognized by Israeli soldiers manning the checkpoints. According to 2023 statistics published by OCHA (United Nations Office for the Coordination of Humanitarian Affairs), Israeli military authorities controlled 645 checkpoints, roadbocks, and barriers in the West Bank, an area slightly smaller than Delaware.

Homeland, by Sliman Anis Mansour, captures the penning of Palestinians waiting to cross from Gaza into Israel through the Erez checkpoint. The artwork also intimates the travel restrictions placed on Palestinians in the West Bank: the settler-only roads closed to them and the continual denied access to East Jerusalem. They are a people caged in plain sight since the Nakba, a year after the artist was born, in 1947.

A Response to *Gaza: Mowing the Lawn*, an exhibition by Jaime Scholnick, 2014–15

TONY LITWINKO

Jaime Scholnick, *Gaza: Mowing the Lawn*, 42, 2014. Mixed media on panel, 7.5 x 11 in. Artwork appears courtesy of the artist.

You cannot go there now, and when you were there in 2009 it was too brief to take it all in. Barely twenty-four hours. Yet the first impressions are still strong. The broken American International School, the demolished cement plants, the apartment buildings with their folded floors and rubble sliding into the streets as if from a scoop, a plastic tent covering a family, the administrative building with the burned windows on the third and fourth floors, its blackened walls where the missile had entered precisely. The divided boulevards with the donkey-drawn wagons with auto tires, the vista down to the Mediterranean. When you were in Gaza six months after Operation Cast Lead, the rubble was still there, the holes in the stucco, and yet: you could stand on that boulevard separated by a dusty divider with broken trees and imagine what peace might bring—a seaside vacation spot with thriving tourism, the beach down below the hotel looking out over a rebuilt tiny harbor like the one in Jaffa, the fisherman casting for an unpolluted dinner. But now all you can remember—no, because of pictures you imagine—are children playing soccer on the beach in 2014 then struck by shells from offshore and torn apart.

In the gallery where the artist placed her exhibit, your first impression was that these are so small, so dwarfed by the wall on which they hang, double rowed, leading to and around the far corner, so that you have to approach and zoom in as if you were on Google Maps, to drill down and look hard at these images, barred and threaded and strung instruments of grief, the screams and wails silent, the fierce steadfastness, roads to nowhere passing between disintegrating rubble. Dead children, dead mothers, the screaming fathers, the dead children.

But go closer. These taut threads of color keep you from seeing the images in their journalistic mode, truly the size of the news photos they are built on, providing only the slimmest of narratives for this most recent of Israel's vicious attacks on the Palestinians enclosed in Gaza since 1994. Haven't you had enough of those photos by themselves? Haven't you seen, since the Vietnam War, the naked torment of a running girl scorched in a napalm flash? Or some other version of her? Of the father holding his dead child in a pink bathrobe in Baghdad, her spindly leg dangling from a tendon? And for us, the empathizers, seeing their inner pain of loss?

When you stand back you see them as photos no longer, but you know the stories are behind the bright primary colors, the way reality is behind the images. The way death is immediate in the arms of the loving survivor in pain, or the fear of another death that brings the scalpel in the white-gloved hands of a surgeon excising shrapnel from a child's gut.

*

For almost all Americans, these fifty-one images have evaporated in time. A picture for each day of the war, now hidden by fast currents of the news—so here, says the artist, here, work into your commitment, struggle with it, because you must know that only those who feel the empathic pain, that is, only we Americans who have rejected the clichés of the media ("terrorism," "the right to defend themselves") are coming to this gallery to experience the grief of these condemned and brutally ignored victims and defiant steadfast Gazans. It seems at moments like these that only those who know want to know more, want to see how someone else knows, how an artist knows.

Ironic, is it not, that all of us who have come to see these images understand and assume that it is not a member of the American Israel Public Affairs Committee next to us shaking his head in grief. We know that Hillary Clinton will not be here. We know that Haim Saban will be off electronically transferring funds to the Friends of the IDF. They will not be looking at the images of Jaime Scholnick, although we wish they were.

These photographs bear witness to the violence against this concentration of ill-nourished and captive people, classified by their prison administrators as if they are vegetation, growing and growing until "the lawn must be mowed." The Israeli thug who first used the phrase "mowing the lawn" has dehumanized the Gazans as if they were a cosmetic nuisance for a slumlord who wants to keep things neat and trimmed and manageable, who does it with machinery, blades of shrapnel, Weedwackers with wings, and missiles supplied by his US benefactors.

Operation Rainbow (2004). Operation Days of Penitence (2004). Operation Summer Rains (2006). Operation Autumn Clouds (2006). Operation Hot Winter (2008). Operation Cast Lead (2008–2009). Operation Pillar of Cloud (2012). Operation Protective Edge (2014),

aka Operation Strong Cliff ("Miv'tza Tzuk Eitan"). Nine years after
Israel bused out the illegal settlers to help reinforce the occupied West
Bank settlements; stationed its Gaza occupation soldiers around the
Gaza border fence, its marines out in the Mediterranean, its helicopters
and drones and American-supplied fighter and bomber jets in the air
above the destroyed Gaza Airport (and then insisted that it was not
"occupying" the Gaza Strip)—nine years after that withdrawal, Israel
launched its last and most vicious infiltration, "mowing the lawn"
of the 27.4-square-mile Gaza Strip—including, of course, the almost
half-kilometer-wide killing strip inside the fence that nullifies a good
deal of Gaza's best agricultural land; that is to say, the soil farthest
away from the encroaching salt water of the sea.

*

Come with me, my fellow Americans; come with me for a tour of this
proscribed acreage. You won't as a private citizen enter Gaza easily.
I know. I have friends who have been patiently waiting for years. So
let us enter Gaza as a photograph, courtesy of Google. You can find
the perimeter fence easily, and then see how the perimeter road runs
on the Israeli side, how the land to the west looks spotty and grayed,
with some patches of green. But to the east, observe the Israeli farm-
land: green, blue-green, and yellow-green butting right up against
the perimeter road. Observe the difference in action. Patchwork fields
like in the American Midwest or all over the world, and an occasional
irrigated circle. Observe them from Sderot in the northern edge to Kfar
Aza, Alumin, Kfar Masrion, Be'eri, Re'Im, Kissufim, Nirim, Magen,
Yedea, Ein Ha'Besor, Yesha, Nir Yitzhak, Holit—down to the Egyptian
border, all these settlements or villages created since 1948, or having
been occupied, renamed—and you will see that the land within the
fence could be very productive for all. Could be feeding Gazans. Could
be producing exports to the European Union. Rolling agricultural land.

Please observe how Google gives us bonus photos, ironically usually
without people, since landscape images seem more serene without them.

Does this remind you? Click on Nir Yitzok to see the photo of a purple iris in front of a field of mustard and trees in the distance, as if this were a pastoral. Scan the "Phoenician-Style Modern-art Colonnade," with greening hills in the distance covered with trees from the New Israel Fund. Check out the "Wonderful World of Beery Vale," filled with idyllic grass. Or the "Green Road Border of Gaza." Click and you will see cultivated land on the Israeli side. Is this not wonderful scenery?

And in the same exercise observe how you can safely hop over the fence without an entry permit to see a plume of evil smoke issuing from a fire near the Gaza power station. Could this be from the July 29, 2014, tank attack on the fuel depot near the plant? (Google Maps never says.) That was the attack that in turn disabled the water-treatment facilities for Gaza. The plume is ugly, thick, and black. The shadows of the smokestacks fall on the ground. There are patches of plowed land within the Gaza confines—as far away from the encroaching polluted sea as can be and edging right up and into the no-man's-land where brave farmers and belligerent, frustrated, shouting youth are shot for their livelihood or their defiance. And as more than one person has commented, notably Noam Chomsky, the no-man's-land could have been placed on the eastern side of the border fence. The no-man's-land is a systemic encroachment that drives us nuts when we know the reality. In Sara Roy's revised edition of *The Gaza Strip: The Political Economy of De-development*, she reprints a warning from the Israeli "Defense" Forces and a rough translation: "To the People of the Strip: The Israel Defense Forces repeat their warning about the danger of approaching within 300 meters of the borderline. Henceforth, the Israel Defense Forces will take all necessary measures to eliminate anyone who gets close to the zone. If necessary the IDF will open fire without hesitations. No excuses will be accepted now that you have been warned."

Google Maps will show the detail but not the motion and life needed to understand the texture of ruin and rubble, death and pain, defiance and terror. We can only go so far into the pixels of the image or the pointillist graphics of a news photo. One pixel equals a smashed bedroom.

So let us return to the gallery of the chosen scenes of Gaza.

The artist emphasizes the borders of empathy and has deliberately added to the limits of visualization, reminding us that you have to be there to understand the 2014 onslaught on Gaza, reminding us, showing us what we will see when we zoom in—the anguished father's eyes clenched tight while his clenched fists rend his *jalabiyah*; a father tenderly carrying the corpse of his eight-year-old; mourning families; anger and frustration; blackened corpses lying in sheets; a screaming father near the drawers of a morgue that hold his wife and children. Is there not enough sadness? Then think of the children. The children. And then there is too much sadness.

If in those fifty-one days of terror, of "mowing the lawn," some religious people of conscience will recall Isaiah 40:68—"All flesh is grass and all its loveliness is like the flower of the field. The grass withers and the flowers fade when the breath of the Lord blows upon it"—then no doubt well-read partisans of self-defense will see in this most recent mowing of the lawn that the Israeli onslaught was like the "breath of the Lord." Perhaps that will be the military title of the next mowing . . . Operation Breath of the Lord.

Because, you know, the lords of the land, as they have been called, appear in Scholnick's last picture element, which she has made to stand alone on its own wall. Apart. Distant. But always there.

And by this means of separation the artist makes the final commentary on the lords of that constricted land. She shows Israelis enjoying the show as if they were on a hill above a Fourth of July celebration in this city. We zoom in and see the calm figures of Israeli photographers and sightseers on the hill outside of Sderot, looking down on the plumes of smoke and destruction but at a safe distance, lords of the land looking down on the out-of-sight flesh as if it were grass, being whipped and shrapneled to blood and entrails, far, far off in the distance, where the explosions are immediate and lethal but the blast is heard much later. Please note the seconds of silence between smoking reality and sound. Observe how you never, never hear the screams of the children.

July 14, 2021

The Art of the Poster
NADINE ARANKI

During the assaults on Gaza, an art form born out of conflict and strife has been experiencing a resurgence. The Palestinian political poster has always been intimately connected to the country's politics. The Nakba of 1948 had been "a radical rupture" in the lives of Palestinians. Hence, visual art and graphic productions were hugely affected as Palestinians were uprooted from their homes and land. Hundreds of thousands were expelled during the creation of the state of Israel, becoming refugees in neighbouring countries or internally displaced within historic Palestine. It was not until 1955 that a distinctly visual Palestinian identity began to reemerge, with silk-screening in Beirut.

The golden age of Palestinian political posters flourished between the early 1960s and 1982, with the later years including the initial phase of the Lebanese Civil War (1975-1990). Today, art collectives, such as Art Commune, started by Palestinian artists, and Artists Against Apartheid, with international artists, maintain open-access poster drives online. This new generation of Palestinians and non-Palestinians stands together in solidarity, making their artwork available to the public at a time when Palestinian cultural voices in art and literature have been canceled in the US and Europe. For example, in Germany, alignment with BDS by signature on a petition can be deemed legally "antisemitic" and effectively destroy a creative career.

In its evolution, the Palestinian poster has become more than a tool of political propaganda; it is art. The *Posters for Gaza* exhibition at the Zawyeh Gallery, Dubai (January 26-April 21, 2024) featured work by established Palestinian artists, such as Hazem Harb, Vera Tamari, Nabil Anani, Sliman Mansour, Tayseer Barakat and Rana Samara, among other cultural figures not known for producing visual art, like the renowned Lebanese revolutionary singer Khaled El Haber. He has written and produced songs for Palestine, and his poster in the exhibition takes its title from one of his songs: *We Are Doing Fine in Gaza . . . What about You?!*

Palestinian digital artist in the United Arab Emirates Dyala Moshtaha captures a troubled history in her poster *Freedom in Bloom*, with a collage that addresses Palestinian heritage and the right to return. The oranges represent stolen land; the old man in a keffiyeh alludes to a generation that experienced the Nakba and has always longed for return. In effect, the artist is passing the struggle from one generation to another.

Artist Haneen Nazzal belongs to Art Commune. Her poster, *Against*, was included in the Zawyeh exhibition. The artist took the poster's title from a poem by Palestinian American poet, journalist, and UN correspondent Rachid Hussein (1936-1977), the translation of which she has provided:

"Against a child / any child / Becoming a hero at ten / . . .
Against the rosebeds / Becoming trenches / And yet /
After the burning of my land / my comrades, and my youth /
How can my poems not become guns?"
The last two lines appear on the poster, in Arabic.

Meanwhile, Victoria García, a member of Artists Against Apartheid, has been influenced by archival photographic iconography. Her posters dare to make the promise: freedom for Palestine.

February 26, 2024

Khaled El Haber, *We Are Doing Fine in Gaza . . . What about You?!,* 2024. Fine art archival paper, 310 gsm, 75 x 55 cm. Courtesy of Zawyeh Gallery.

Dyala Moshtaha, *Freedom in Bloom*, 2023. Fine art archival paper, 310 gsm, 75 x 55 cm. Courtesy of Zawyeh Gallery.

Haneen Nazzal, *Against*, 2022. Fine art archival paper, 310 gsm, 75 x 55 cm.
Courtesy of the artist and Zawyeh Gallery.

Victoria García, *Freedom for Palestine*, No. 2, 2023. Series of five posters, high-res PDF, 11 x 17 in (each). Courtesy of the artist.

Disrupting the Colonial Gaze
Gaza and Israel after October 7th
IVAR EKELAND and SARA ROY

The Gaza experiment is ongoing, and it is taking the world further than any of us would have thought possible. In our article "The New Politics of Exclusion: Gaza as Prologue,"[1] published more than two years ago, we claimed that Israel had turned Gaza into a human laboratory where entirely new conditions were artificially created. A society numbering over two million people found itself cut off from the world, confined by fences and walls to a small sliver of land and kept under constant surveillance, deprived of every right except the right to what Italian philosopher Giorgio Agamben calls a "bare life"; that is, a life reduced to the mere biological dimension of eating and reproducing. They were even deprived of the means to exercise that right, since they were almost entirely dependent on the outside world for food, water, medicine, and fuel, like animals in a cage. We claimed that this experiment was a portent of things to come, that Western countries were creating mini-Gazas around the world to park unwanted people, mostly nonwhite migrants (Ukrainians are welcome in Europe, Africans are not), and we were wondering where this terrible state of affairs would lead us.

Now we know. The end of the Gaza experiment is no longer to ensure separation or repudiation but elimination through genocidal slaughter, or, more euphemistically, "forced" or "voluntary" emigration to other lands largely unwilling to accept them. At a conference held in Jerusalem on January 28, 2024, entitled Conference for the Victory of Israel – Settlement Brings Security: Returning to the Gaza

---

1   Ivar Ekeland and Sara Roy, "The New Politics of Exclusion: Gaza as Prologue," *Markaz Review*, October 15, 2021.

Strip and Northern Samaria, the participants, who numbered in the thousands and included several government ministers and Knesset members, called for the resettlement of the Gaza Strip and the transfer of Palestinians who live there. Shlomo Karhi, Israel's minister of communications, explained what he meant by "voluntary emigration" in times of war: " 'voluntary' is at times a state you impose [on someone] until they give their consent."[2]

As this conference shows, the goal of "exterminating the brutes" and the racism underlying it are no longer concealed but openly justified and valorized. This is what Israel has long proclaimed, repeatedly and consistently, from top to bottom—from the prime minister and other members of government calling the Palestinians "animals" and "wild beasts" to soldiers on the ground in Gaza chanting and dancing in the ruins to the tune of "there are no innocent Palestinians," as South Africa's brief to the International Court of Justice has convincingly documented. For Israel, furthermore, Palestinians are not only guilty but also criminal. Israel's President Herzog stated it thus: "It's an entire nation out there that is responsible. This rhetoric about civilians not aware, not involved, it's absolutely not true. They could've risen up, they could have fought against that evil regime."[3] That is, Palestinians are not only responsible for their own justifiable deaths but also guilty of not struggling against Hamas to protect Israelis. They exist either to protect Israel or to destroy it.[4]

This points to another critical dynamic of the post-October 7 world: the criminalization of context and the abandonment of history. History did not begin on October 7, as Israel argued when it claimed that the attack was unprovoked. Yet the attempt to historicize and contextualize Israel's repression of Palestinians and the damage it has wrought on Palestinian life over seven decades is treated as

---

2   Nir Hasson, "Netanyahu Ministers Join Thousands of Israelis in 'Resettle Gaza' Conference Calling for Palestinians' Transfer," *Haaretz*, January 28, 2024.

3   Chris McGreal, "The Language Being Used to Describe Palestinians Is Genocidal," *Guardian*, October 16, 2023.

4   Ruba Salih, "Can the Palestinian Speak?" *Allegra Lab*, December 2023.

justification for the horrific murder of Israeli men, women, and children, and therefore morally reprehensible and illicit. Rather, the devastation that occupation imposed at the individual and societal level was not only ignored over the last fifty-six years but also deemed necessary and justifiable by Israel and the West. As we argued in our original piece, Israel's aim—until October 7—was not the "death of the 'Indigenous other'—as it is now—but his nullification, along with the countermemories and counterclaims that otherness naturally embodies. In this way, Israel . . . redefined the colonial distinction between self and other, the space that Israelis and Palestinians inhabit. In this redefined space, there [could] be no approach or nearing, let alone engagement . . . reciprocity or redemption. . . . Palestinians [were] erased from Israel's emotional and political landscape, precluding contestation and complexity, and restoring to Jewish Israelis a knowable, unambiguous, easily interpretable clarity."[5] It is this clarity that October 7 destroyed.

Consequently, the philosopher Judith Butler argues, Palestinians are "deprived of life before they are killed, transformed into inert matter or destructive instrumentalities . . . To kill such a person, indeed, such a population, thus calls upon a racism that differentiates in advance who will count as a life and who will not. . . . Under such conditions, it becomes possible to think that ending life in the name of defending life is possible, even righteous."[6] It is this very argument that Israel now uses to justify its shredding of Gaza and the destruction of its people.

Hence, it is only Israeli life that is valid and consequential, innocent and civilian. Palestinians exist either as the "guardian of Israeli life or colonized subject. . . . Whether Palestinians are worthy of merely living or dying depends thus on their active acceptance or refusal to remain colonized."[7] Any possibility of living through a shared experience has

---

5   Sara Roy, "I Wish They Would Disappear," *Postcolonial Studies* 21, no. 4 (December 2018), 531.
6   Judith Butler, *Frames of War: When Is Life Grievable?* (London: Verso, 2009), xxix-xxx.
7   Salih (December 2023).

been extinguished. The question remains: why is the destruction of Palestinian life met with such "calm uninterest and lack of remorse, reflecting what the historian Gabriel Kolko termed the 'absence of a greater sense of abhorrence'"?[8] So repudiated, Palestinians have long failed to enter our consciousness, let alone our conscience, until now, but only when Israeli lives were destroyed.

Another point related to the barring of context is the failure to connect the everyday nature of oppression with Palestinian actions, including military escalation—a failure to account for the lived experiences of Palestinians and the misery that so deeply defines it.[9] This failure sees Palestinians as something separate and distant, impenetrable, unable to approximate the Other as us. Deprived of any claims based on justice, Palestinians continue to remain absent in Israeli eyes. "The real threat, therefore, lies not in acts of Palestinian violence against Israel but in understanding that those acts are responding to injustice and dehumanization . . . in making Palestinians intimate, in seeing the world through their eyes . . . in rejecting any endeavor that would treat them as indeterminate and notional, or consign them to abstraction."[10] Or, as professor Ghassan Hage has argued, "In the war/siege society, social explanation can disrupt the way both self and society are invited to define and stabilize themselves against an other that has to remain different and unknowable. Social explanation can threaten the warring self with disintegration, which is why it sometimes unleashes such passionate response. Social explanation is not merely rejected. The threat of the humanized other it carries with it is affectively feared."[11] Hence, it must be understood that evil resides in the conditions, not in the people—what other scholars have termed "structural sin."[12]

---

8   Roy (December 2018), 534.
9   Some of these points appear in Sara Roy, "Gaza: Can You Hear Us?" *Cambridge Journal of Law, Politics and Art* (forthcoming).
10 Roy, *Postcolonial Studies*, 532.
11 Ghassan Hage, " 'Comes a Time We Are All Enthusiasm': Understanding Palestinian Suicide Bombers in Times of Exighophobia," *Public Culture* 15, no. 1 (2003), 87.
12 Hage, *Public Culture*, 89.

As far as Israel and the West are concerned, the siege, including in its current genocidal form, was accepted and unquestioned, in effect telling Palestinians in Gaza: this is how you must live, and this is the violence you are expected to endure even if it means the eradication of your way of life.

Consequently, social and political problems, which arise from poverty, dislocation, and destruction and the efforts of Palestinians to address them, have consistently been treated as a threat, even as a form of terrorism. Privation remains unexamined and unfamiliar and disconnected from action and understanding, where justice is removed from and irrelevant to context. Consequently, Israel's struggle against Gaza, which is also a struggle against Palestine, must be sustained and unbroken no matter the cost, as we see in Gaza today.

The level of inhumanity that is revealed is unprecedented since the Holocaust and the colonial wars. The Gaza experiment has now reached the point where Palestinians are removed from not only human society but also history, deprived of the only right left to them: the right to a life, however "bare." How then are we to think of Gaza? As a place of nonlife? Where does this leave any of us? "Once again," writes the historian Jean-Pierre Filiu, "what is happening in Gaza goes far beyond this ravaged enclave."[13]

The declarations by Israeli government officials and the massacres they lead to are even more terrifying against the complete indifference with which they are met by Western governments and media—an indifference and neglect that have a long history in this conflict. In 2019, Michael Lynk, who was then the UN Special Rapporteur on the situation of human rights in the Palestinian territories, occupied since 1967, captured the essence of Western disregard:

> The . . . Israeli occupation of the Palestinian territory—Gaza and the West Bank, including East Jerusalem—is a bitter illustration of the absence of international accountability in the face of the systemic violations of Palestinian rights

---

13 Jean-Pierre Filiu, "American Christian Zionists Crusade against Palestinian 'Evil,' " *Le Monde*, January 30, 2024.

under human rights and humanitarian law. . . . Israel, a relatively small country in terms of geography and population and with a particular dependence on the international community for both trade and investment and diplomatic cooperation, could not have sustained such a prolonged and repressive occupation in clear violation of international law without the active support and malign neglect of many in the industrialized world. While the international community has issued numerous resolutions and declarations critical of the unending occupation by Israel and its steady designs for annexation, such criticisms have rarely been matched with any meaningful consequences. . . . *It is therefore necessary to ask whether it is simply to be accepted that, with this occupation, international law is closer to power than it is to justice.*[14] (emphasis ours)

The question posed by Mr. Lynk reveals a position on the part of the international community that legitimizes Israel's occupation as long as there is no collective agreement to end it. The recent interim ruling issued by the International Court of Justice in South Africa's case against Israel for its horrifying assault on Gaza repudiates, at its core, Western acquiescence to Israeli violence against Palestinians. The court found "plausible evidence that Israel has the intent to commit genocide; and . . . plausible evidence that Israel is committing genocide" and ordered Israel "to stop committing those acts that appear to be genocidal, and to preserve any evidence that bears on this matter, obviously for the trial ahead."[15] To our knowledge, this is one of very few legal decisions to hold Israel accountable for its crimes, challenging the impunity with which it has consistently violated the rights

---

14 Michael Lynk, *UN General Assembly, Report of the Special Rapporteur on the Situation of Human Rights in the Territories Occupied by Israel since 1967, A/74/507* (October 21, 2019), 10, 21.

15 John J. Mearsheimer, *Israel's Day of Reckoning*, January 27, 2024.

of Palestinians.[16] Unsurprisingly, Israel's Western allies, notably the US, have condemned the Court's decision. Even before the ruling was made, the US found the charge "meritless, counterproductive and without any basis in fact whatsoever."[17]

Another striking example of Western disdain concerns the United Nations Relief and Works Agency for Palestine Refugees in the Near East (UNRWA). On the same day as the ICJ ruling was handed down, Israel provided UNRWA with information about the alleged involvement of twelve of its employees (out of a workforce of around thirteen thousand in Gaza alone[18]) in the abhorrent October 7 attack in Israel. In response, UNRWA immediately terminated the contracts of these individuals and launched an investigation to determine the truth. Yet, in the absence of any investigation and in clear violation of the principles of due process, several Western countries, including the United States, Britain, Germany, Italy, the Netherlands, Switzerland, New Zealand, Finland, Australia, and Canada,[19] froze their funding to UNRWA (amounting to around $700 million) at a time of desperate need, when the entire population of Gaza is at imminent risk of famine.

In fact, according to the Integrated Food Security Phase Classification (IPC) assessment, Gaza's entire population of over two million people are "estimated to be acutely food insecure [meaning they are facing acute food shortages], while a quarter of its population faces catastrophic hunger and starvation, [which] is unprecedented. No IPC analysis has ever recorded such levels of food insecurity anywhere in

---

16 The others are the 2004 ICJ advisory opinion on the illegality of the separation wall (and Israeli settlements) and the 2009 Goldstone report that accused Israel of various war crimes and referred to the criminality of the blockade. See Norman Finkelstein's comments in: https://www.youtube.com/watch?v=Kj7mqGVg554&list=RDCMUCUsMkDtVyel9USjCTaM42r-w&start_radio=1.

17 "US Rejects 'Meritless' South Africa ICJ Case Against Israel," Foundation for Defense of Democracies, January 5, 2024.

18 Of this, 3,000 have reported to work during the war. Over 130 UNRWA employees have been killed in the war. The agency employs a total of 30,000 people regionwide.

19 Japan and the European Union also froze their funding, but Norway and Ireland did not, drawing a needed distinction between possible criminal activity of individual staffers and UNRWA itself.

the world."[20] Of the total world population facing famine, 80 percent are now found in Gaza.[21]

Against this reality of acute need created in large part by Western support for Israel's assault on Gaza, the denial of funding to UNRWA is as appalling as it is devastating. According to Philippe Lazzarini, the UNRWA commissioner-general, "These decisions threaten our ongoing humanitarian work across the region including and especially in the Gaza Strip. It is shocking to see a suspension of funds to the Agency in reaction to allegations against a small group of staff, especially given the immediate action that UNRWA took by terminating their contracts and asking for a transparent independent investigation."[22]

The decision to temporarily suspend funds on the part of Western governments reveals their contempt for Palestinian suffering, and for the ICJ, given its ruling that called for the provision of urgently needed humanitarian aid, in which UNRWA plays the dominant role. Does the withholding of funding therefore make the West complicit in plausible acts of genocide? Furthermore, the unwillingness of Arab governments, particularly Saudi Arabia and the United Arab Emirates, to increase their funding of UNRWA—because it is accused of having links to Hamas—is similarly shocking given the regional instability that UNRWA's collapse would precipitate.

Subsequent statements by Israeli officials expose the real purpose behind the attack on UNRWA, which has long been the object of Israeli assault—to shutter and eliminate the agency and ensure it

---

20 "Gaza: Joint Statement by High Representative Josep Borrell and Commissioner for Crisis Management Janez Lenarcic on the Risk of Famine," European Commission, December 22, 2023.

21 Sharon Zhang, "80 Percent of Global Famine Is Currently in Gaza, UN Expert Warns," Truthout, January 3, 2024; and Isaac Chotiner, "Gaza Is Starving," *New Yorker*, January 3, 2024. Also see "Israel: Starvation Used as a Weapon of War in Gaza," Human Rights Watch, December 18, 2023; and Leanna First-Arai, "Famine in Gaza Is a Culmination of Israel's Long War on Palestine's Food System," Truthout, January 10, 2024.

22 Philippe Lazzarini, "UNRWA's Lifesaving Aid May End Due to Funding Suspension," United Nations Relief and Works Agency for Palestine Refugees in the Near East, January 27, 2024. Also, "More Countries Pause Fund for UN Palestinian Agency," Reuters, January 27, 2024.

has no role in postwar Gaza. In so doing, Israel (and the West) aims to undermine Palestinian refugee status, refugee rights—especially the right of return—and remove the refugee issue and any attendant demands, such as compensation from future discussions. And as the analyst Jonathan Cook critically points out, "Uniquely, [UNRWA] is the sole agency unifying Palestinians wherever they live, even when they are separated by national borders and Israel's fragmentation of the territory it controls. UNRWA brings Palestinians together even when their own political leaders have been manipulated into endless factionalism by Israel's divide and rule policies."[23] UNRWA has long acted as a defense against Israel's persistent efforts to eliminate the rights of Palestinian refugees. The growing demands of Israeli government officials to expel Palestinians from Gaza reflects Israel's desire to have them integrate into other countries, forever suspending the question of the right of return, among other claims.

According to Israel's foreign minister, Israel Katz, "We have been warning for years: UNRWA *perpetuates the refugee issue* [meaning that it helps refugees reproduce?], obstructs peace, and serves as a civilian arm of Hamas in Gaza."[24] (emphasis ours) Yet, it is not UNRWA that perpetuates the conflict, as Katz would have us believe; it is the conflict that perpetuates UNRWA.[25] What then is the alternative to UNRWA? Will Israel or the Arab states be willing to assume responsibility for over two million refugees in Gaza and the West Bank and millions more beyond, providing them with food, education, health care, housing, and employment?

Despite Western derision, Gaza has powerfully disrupted the colonial gaze. Gaza is evidence of a future that is already here, bereft of humanity, law, and human rights. We are at a crossroads where, as Antonio Gramsci

23 Jonathan Cook, "In Waging War on the UN refugee Agency, the West Is Openly Siding with Israeli Genocide," January 30, 2024, http://jonathancook. substack.com.
24 Mehul Srivastava and Neri Zilber, "UN Chief Urges Countries Not to Pull Funding over Israel Attack Allegations," *Financial Times*, January 28, 2024.
25 Marilyn Garson, "With Gazans Starving and Freezing, the US Wihholding Funds from UNRWA Is Unconscionable," *Forward*, January 30, 2024.

states in *The Prison Notebooks*: "The crisis consists precisely in the fact that the old is dying and the new cannot be born; in this interregnum a great variety of morbid symptoms appear."[26] In Gaza, this morbidity speaks to gross insecurity, famine, disease, economic disintegration, physical destruction, displacement, and ecological collapse.

If Israel, with Western support, achieves its aims in Gaza, it will constitute the end of fellowship among inhabitants of this planet, forcing a confrontation between the rules-based international order, in which the West predominates and prioritizes its own interests, and international law "which has governed the behavior of states for over 500 years."[27] It will be clear to everyone that Western societies, meaning the US and its allies, consider themselves apart and exceptional, where rules they apply to others do not apply to them, and where advocacy of democracy and the rule of law is no more than a means to preserve their historic hegemony, no matter the cost. Global institutions, such as the UN, which were created after World War II to foster diplomacy over force, peace over war, will fall into disrepute and irrelevance.

The global south and large segments of public opinion in the Western world see the danger and are organizing to pressure Israel, the US, and Europe to recognize that the Gaza experiment has failed, that it is immoral and unacceptable. This brings to mind something the American writer James Baldwin once said about being Black in America, and it has particular resonance for Israelis and Palestinians: "Every white person in this country . . . knows one thing: they may not know . . . what I want but they know they would not like to be Black here. If they know that, they know everything they need to know. . . . We are all, in any case, here."[28]

February 1, 2024

---

26 There are many references to the popular statement. See, for example, Gilbert Achcar, "Morbid Symptoms: What Did Gramsci Really Mean?" *Notebooks: Journal for Studies on Power*, February 14, 2022.

27 John Dugard, "The Choice before Us: International Law or a 'Rules-based International Order'?" *Leiden Journal of International Law* 36 (2023), 224.

28 James Baldwin, "Reflections," speech, University of California, Berkeley, January 15, 1979.

Habibti Ghazal

HALA ALYAN

Nineteen's slow violence. Your arm a tusk slicing the air—whoa, habibti—
for that first Jack-and-Coke. Here we go, take it slow, habibti.
Soon, you'll become an emergency: I.V. bag and emerald bruise.
First love hammering your door, but you're no habibti,
no bait turned proposal. On the third page of an old journal,
the same question in pale ink: *Can I be my own habibti?*
You glaze-eyed. You lit like a county fair. The long twine
of a decade, hold the tattoo needle to skin and sew *habibti*.
Even the sea rots here. This prop city with its prop heart.
The hot-eyed men whistling the streets: Hello, habibti.
Hello, cream. Hello, daughter of men. Hello, almost-wife.
I can't teach you about metaphor; I'm stuck in the future. O, habibti,
I want to see those legs running. There's the oncoming headlight of boy:
Ribcage. Fist. War. It's time, habibti. Please, habibti. *Go*, habibti.

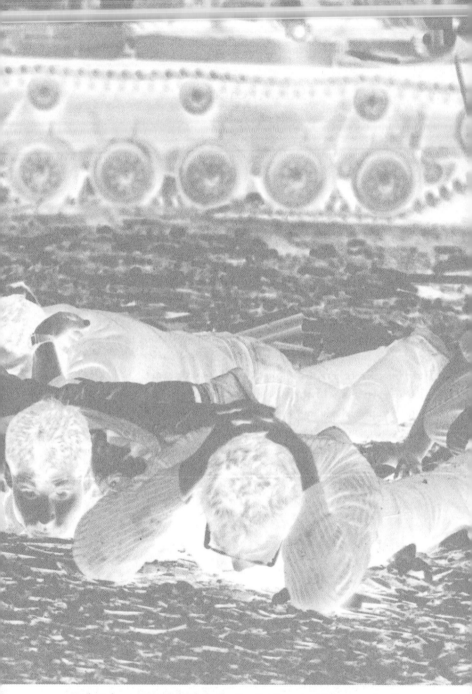

Rula Halawani, *Untitled VI* from the *Negative Incursion* series, 2002, detail.
Archival print, 90 x 124 cm. Courtesy of the artist and Ayyam Gallery.

Contributors

Jenine Abboushi is a Palestinian American writer, freelancer, and traveler. She lived for many years in the US, Palestine, Morocco, and Lebanon and now makes her home in Marseille, France. She has written for the *Times Literary Supplement* (TLS) and the *Markaz Review*, where she is a senior writer.

Maya Abu Al-Hayyat is a Beirut-born Palestinian poet and novelist living in Jerusalem. She is the author of four collections of poems, including *You Can Be the Last Leaf* (Milkweed, 2022), translated by Fady Joudah; four novels; and numerous children's stories. Her work has appeared in *A Bird Is Not a Stone: An Anthology of Contemporary Palestinian Poetry* (Freight Books, 2014). She is also the editor of *The Book of Ramallah: A City in Short Fiction* (Comma Press, 2021).

Mosab Abu Toha is a Palestinian poet, scholar, and librarian who was born in Gaza. He is the founder of the Edward Said Library, Gaza's first English-language library. His debut collection of poems, *Things You May Find Hidden in My Ear* (City Lights, 2022), won an American Book Award, a 2022 Palestine Book Award, and was named a finalist for the National Book Critics Circle Award in Poetry, as well as the 2022 Walcott Poetry Prize. His poems have been published in *Poetry*, the *Nation*, the Academy of American Poets' Poem-a-Day, *Poetry Daily*, and the *New York Review of Books*, among others. His latest poetry collection, *Forest of Noise*, has been published by Knopf in 2024.

Rahaf Al Batniji is a self-taught photographer and visual artist from Gaza City. Her first solo exhibition was in the backyard of her home. Recent exhibitions include Institute Du Monde Arabe, Gulf Photo Plus Dubai, and a group show at the Navy Officers' Club, Arsenale, Biennale Venice, with Cité international des arts, Paris. Her work has been published extensively, including in *Le Monde diplomatique*. Until recently she was training young adolescents in Gaza City in photography and drawing.

Layla AlAmmar is a writer with a PhD in Arab women's fiction and literary trauma theory. Her debut novel, *The Pact We Made* (Borough Press, 2019), was longlisted for the Authors' Club Best First Novel Award. Her second novel, *Silence Is a Sense* (Borough Press, 2021), was shortlisted for the William Saroyan International Prize for Writing. She has written for the *Guardian*, *TLS*, *New Lines Magazine*, *LitHub*, *ArabLit Quarterly*, and the *New Arab*, among others.

Yousef M. Aljamal is from Al-Nuseirat refugee camp in the Gaza Strip. He holds a PhD in Middle Eastern studies and is coauthor of *A Shared Struggle: Stories of Palestinian and Irish Hunger Strikers* (An Fhuiseog, 2021). His articles have been published in *Politics Today*, *Electric Intifada*, and *Mondoweiss*. He is also the translator of *Dreaming of Prison: Palestinian Child Prisoners Speak* (2019) and *The Prisoners' Diaries: Palestinian Voices from the Israeli Gulag* (2013).

Ahmad Almallah is a Palestinian poet. His poetry collections include *Border Wisdom* (Winter Editions, 2023) and *Bitter English* (Phoenix Poets Series, University of Chicago Press, 2019). He is the recipient of the Edith Goldberg Paulson Memorial Prize for Creative Writing, and his set of poems "Recourse" won the Blanche Colton Williams Fellowship. His poems and other writing have appeared in *Jacket2*, *Track//Four*, *All Roads Will Lead You Home*, *Apiary*, *Supplement*, *SAND*, *Michigan Quarterly Review*, *Making Mirrors: Righting/Writing by Refugees*, *Cordite Poetry Review*, *Birmingham Poetry Review*, *Great River*

Review, *Kenyon Review*, *Poetry*, and *American Poetry Review*. He has been published in Arabic in *Al-Arabi Al-Jadid*. He is artist in residence in creative writing at the University of Pennsylvania.

Hala Alyan is an award-winning Palestinian American poet, writer, and clinical psychologist. Her poetry collections include *The Moon That Turns You* (Ecco Press, 2024); *The Twenty-Ninth Year* (Ecco Press, 2019); *Hijra* (Southern Illinois University Press, 2016), winner of the Crab Orchard Series in Poetry; *Four Cities* (Black Lawrence Press, 2015); and *Atrium* (Tree Rooms Press, 2012), winner of the 2013 Arab American Book Award in Poetry. She is the author of the novels *The Arsonists' City* (Harper Perennial, 2022) and *Salt Houses* (Houghton Mifflin Harcourt, 2017) and the recipient of a Lannan Foundation fellowship.

Zeina Azzam is a Palestinian American poet, writer, editor, and community activist. Her books include the collection of poems *Some Things Never Leave You* (Tiger Bark Press, 2023) and the chapbook *Bayna Bayna, In-Between* (The Poetry Box, 2021). She is the poet laureate of the City of Alexandria, Virginia, for 2022–2025.

Tayseer Barakat was born in Jabalia refugee camp, in Gaza. After finishing his art education in Alexandria, Egypt, he moved to Ramallah, where he has lived since 1983. He has worked in a variety of media and experimented with wood, metal, and glass but remains devoted to painting. Barakat has held many solo exhibitions and has participated in numerous group exhibitions in Japan, the US, Brazil, Europe, and across the Arab world. He is a founding member of Al Wasti Art Center in Jerusalem and the International Academy of Art Palestine.

Taysir Batniji is an artist who was born in Gaza, in 1966. His multimedia practice includes drawing, installation, photography, video, and performance. His artworks have been shown in Europe, the Middle East, Australia, the US, and Brazil and have been collected by the Centre Georges Pompidou, Paris; Victoria and Albert Museum, London;

Kunsthalle Wien, Vienna; Jameel Arts Center, Dubai; Zayed National Museum, Abu Dhabi; and Mathaf, Doha, among others. He was awarded the 2012 Abraj Capital Art Prize and in 2017 the Hermès-Aperture Immersion, a French American photography commission and residency.

Chloé Benoist is a French journalist, editor, translator, and photographer who has spent more than a decade working in and on the Middle East, mostly focusing on political and social issues related to Palestine, Lebanon, and France's relationship with immigration and Islam. She worked as a journalist in the occupied West Bank city of Bethlehem for Palestinian and international news outlets from 2016 to 2018.

Adam Broomberg is an award-winning South African photographer, art educator, and activist. He is the cofounder and coordinator of the NGO Artists + Allies x Hebron, with Palestinian activist Issa Amro. In his work, Broomberg often explores themes of conflict, power, and the representation of truth in contemporary society. In a long, distinguished career, he remains committed to challenging existing power structures and using art as a means of fostering social change. His most recent book, with Rafael Gonzalez, *Anchor in the Landscape* (Mack Books, 2024), documents majestic olive trees and their locations in Palestine.

Hadani Ditmars is the author of *Dancing in the No-Fly Zone: A Woman's Journey through Iraq* (Arris Books, 2001) and a former editor at *New Internationalist Magazine*. She has been reporting from the Middle East for three decades. Her writing and photographs have been published in the *New York Times*, Al Jazeera, the *Guardian*, the *San Francisco Chronicle*, and *Haaretz*, and her work has been broadcast on CBC, BBC, NPR, and RTE. Her book in progress, *Between Two Rivers*, is a travelogue of ancient sites and contemporary culture in Iraq.

Maurice Ebileeni is a faculty member of the English literature and language department at the University of Haifa. His books include *Being There, Being Here: Palestinian Writings in the World* (Syracuse University

346 *Contributors*

Press, 2022) and *Conrad, Faulkner, and the Problem of Nonsense* (Bloomsbury Academic, 2017). He analyzes fatalistic tropes in Palestinian sci-fi, in "Palestine 2048 in Inertia: False Utopias, a Dwindling Nation, and the Last Palestinian," *Interventions*, September 23, 2023.

Ivar Ekeland is a former president of the Paris Dauphine University and a former Canada Research Chair in mathematical economics at the University of British Columbia. He is a member of the Royal Society of Canada and of the Academia Europea.

Khaled El Haber is a pioneering singer renowned for his political songs in Lebanon and the Arab world. He began his artistic career in 1974, as a solo singer accompanied by guitar. By 1975 he founded Al-Firqah (the Band). Most of his songs, which he composes, feature poetry by Mahmoud Darwish, Samih Al-Qasim, Tawfiq Ziad, Joseph Harb, and others. El Haber continues to tour and remains a staunch advocate for human rights and the oppressed, with a focus on Palestine.

Mohammed El-Kurd is an internationally touring and award-winning poet and writer from Jerusalem, occupied Palestine. His debut collection of poetry is *Rifqa* (Haymarket Books, 2021). He has been featured in numerous international outlets such as the *Guardian*, the *Nation*, the *Washington Post*, MSNBC, the *New York Times*, CNN, and elsewhere. El-Kurd is also a visual artist and printmaker.

Saeed Taji Farouky is a Palestinian Egyptian British filmmaker, educator, and curator. His documentary *A Thousand Fires* won the Marco Zucchi award for most innovative documentary in the Directors Fortnight of the 2021 Locarno Film Festival. A previous documentary *Tell Spring Not to Come This Year* premiered at the Berlinale 2015 and won the Audience Choice Panorama Award and the Amnesty Human Rights Award. He runs the Radical Film School in London, a free film course for participants from backgrounds underrepresented in the film industry.

Victoria García is an artist and designer from Doraville, Georgia, and organizer with the Buford Highway People's Hub. Her upbringing, along Buford Highway, has led her to focus on the intersection of art and activism as it pertains to immigration, diasporas, and gentrification. Passionate about the arts, cultural preservation, local and oral histories, storytelling, and working-class solidarity, she has been documenting her rapidly changing neighborhood through analog photography and collage.

Yonatan Gher is the Israeli CEO and co-executive director of Combatants for Peace. He was formerly the executive director of Amnesty International Israel, Greenpeace Mediterranean, and the Jerusalem Open House for Pride and Tolerance.

Jo Glanville is a journalist, editor, broadcaster, and BBC radio and podcast producer. She is the editor of *Looking for an Enemy: Eight Essays on Antisemitism* (W.W. Norton, 2022) and *Qissat: Short Stories by Palestinian Women* (Saqi Books, 2006). Formally the editor of *Index on Censorship* and the executive director of English Pen, she has written for the *Guardian*, *London Review of Books*, the *New York Times*, and *Financial Times*, among others.

Rafael Gonzalez is a lens-based artist living and working between Berlin and New York. In 2021 he worked for André Viking, and between 2022 and 2023 for Adam Broomberg. Gonzalez is a founding board member of Artists + Allies x Hebron, since 2023.

Saleem Haddad is a novelist and writer. His critically acclaimed novel, *Guapa* (Europa Editions, 2016) was awarded both a Stonewall Honour and the 2017 Polari First Book Prize. He also writes nonfiction and short stories, and his story for the Palestinian sci-fi anthology *Palestine +100* (Comma Press, 2019) was selected as one of the best sci-fi stories of 2019. His directorial debut, *Marco*, premiered in 2019 and was nominated for the 2019 Iris Prize for Best British Short Film. He is currently based in Lisbon, with roots in London, Amman, Beirut, and Palestine.

Rula Halawani is an artist from occupied East Jerusalem. Her work captures the many aspects of living under a protracted political conflict—from the tedious moments of attempting to perform daily tasks under the restrictions of military occupation to the cyclical onset of violent siege that transforms Palestinian neighborhoods, towns, and cities overnight into war zones. Her photographs have been collected by the Centre Georges Pompidou; Victoria and Albert Museum; British Museum, in London; and the Khalid Shoman Foundation, in Amman, among others. In 2021 she was awarded the Sheikh Saoud Al Thani Project Award.

Hazem Harb is a visual artist who has lived in Gaza, Rome, and the UAE. His art combines photographic collages and drawings. Inspired by academia, architecture, and European art traditions, he takes his subject matter from the heritage and power dynamics of Palestine and the complexities of memory—selective, lost, and false. His work has been collected by the British Museum; Sharjah Art Foundation; Centre Georges Pompidou; the Oriental Museum Durham University; Salsali Private Museum, in Dubai; and A.M. Qattan Foundation, in Ramallah and London; among others. He has curated many solo exhibitions and participated in numerous international group exhibitions, art fairs, and art biennials.

Samir Harb is an architect and cartoonist who has been working in the fields of architecture and landscape planning in the West Bank since 2006. His artistic practice merges strong graphic forms—mapping, storytelling, illustration, and animation—with his architectural research in order to critically explore the processes of territorial transformation that have been taking place in the occupied Palestinian territories. His work has been featured in exhibitions in Rome, Oslo, and Amman.

Noor Hindi is a Palestinian American poet. Her debut collection of poems, *Dear God. Dear Bones. Dear Yellow.* (Haymarket Books 2022) was an honorable mention for the Arab American Book Award. Her poetry has been published by *Poetry* magazine, *Hobart*, and *Jubilat*. Her essays have appeared in *American Poetry Review*, *Literary Hub*, and the *Adroit Journal*. She was a 2021 Ruth Lilly and Dorothy Sargent Rosenberg Poetry Fellow.

Fady Joudah is a Palestinian American physician, poet, and translator. His most recent collection of poetry, *[. . .]*, was published in 2024. His previous collections include *The Earth in the Attic* (2008), which won the 2007 Yale Series of Younger Poets competition; *Alight* (2013); *Textu* (2014)—each poem exactly 160 characters long and written on a cell phone; and *Footnotes in the Order of Disappearance* (2018). In 2014 he was a Guggenheim Fellow in poetry. Poems by Mahmoud Darwish, translated by Joudah, have won both US and UK translation awards. His translation of Ghassan Zaqtan's *Like a Straw Bird It Follows Me* (2012) won the Griffin International Poetry Prize in 2013.

Fadi Kattan, the Franco-Palestinian chef and hotelier, is the voice of modern Palestinian cuisine. His Bethlehemite family cultivated a francophone culture on the maternal side and a British culture, with passages to India, Japan, and the Sudan, on the paternal side. His cuisine and savoir faire combine worldly influences and a passion for the local terroir, a philosophy he maintains in his restaurants, Fawda in Bethlehem and akub in London. Kattan's debut cookbook is *Bethlehem: A Celebration of Palestinian Food* (Hardie Grant, 2024).

Karim Kattan is a writer born in Jerusalem. His books, in French, include the novel *Le Palais des deux collines*. His writings, in English, have appeared in the *Paris Review*, the *Markaz Review*, the *Baffler*, the *Magazine of Fantasy & Science Fiction*, *Strange Horizons*, *+972 Magazine*, the *Funambulist*, and more.

Brett Kline is a journalist who has worked in print, online, radio, and television. A frequent visitor to Israel/Palestine, he is closely involved with people on both sides of the Green Line. Formerly a reporter for

France Télévisions, he has been published in *Haaretz*, the *Times of Israel*, *Globes*, and the *Jerusalem Post*.

Tony Litwinko is a writer, poet, and teacher. After a career in the field of insurance and risk management, he retired in 2006. He became an activist in the peace and justice movement, traveling in the Middle East and Europe and studying modern history.

Hossam Madhoun is an artist and theater-maker. In Gaza, he is cofounder of Theatre for Everybody, with Jamal Al Rozzi. Because of the constant Israeli aggression against Gaza, the theater is closed. Madhoun has been working with traumatized children as a project coordinator for the local nonprofit Ma'an Development Agency, in Rafah.

Sliman Anis Mansour is a Palestinian painter, sculptor, author, and cartoonist, born in Birzeit. Considered a leading figure among contemporary Palestinian artists, he is known for his 1973 work *Camel of Hardship*, which depicts an old porter carrying Jerusalem on his back. During the first Intifada against Israeli occupation (1987-1993), he and other artists in the New Visions art movement boycotted supplies from Israel. Mansour used local materials like mud and henna in his work. He has drawn inspiration from the olive tree and focused on the theme of land since 1970. His recent work has been centered on the individual and differing states of anticipation or loss, resulting from living under continual, unrelenting occupation.

Ahmed Masoud is a writer and director who grew up in Palestine and moved to Britain in 2002. His debut novel, *Vanished: The Mysterious Disappearance of Mustafa Ouda* (Rimal Books, 2015), which won the Muslim Writers' Award, was followed by *Come What May* (Victorina Press, 2022). His theater and radio credits include *Application 39* (WDR Radio, Germany 2018); *Camouflage* (London, 2017); the still-touring *The Shroud Maker* (London 2015); *Walaa, Loyalty* (London 2014); and *Escape from Gaza* (BBC Radio 4, 2011). Masoud is a founding member of the PalArt Collective, which aims to increase Palestinian voices in the arts and media.

Dyala Moshtaha is a Palestinian artist who specializes in digital art and art direction. In homage to her roots, Moshtaha employs Palestinian symbolism to great effect in her colorful and lively collages and digital illustrations. Her work has been published in *Haya* magazine and *Jamalouki*. Through art, she aims to inspire others to engage emotionally and intellectually with Palestine.

Lina Mounzer is a Lebanese writer and translator. She has been a contributor to many prominent publications including the *Paris Review*, *Freeman's*, the *Washington Post*, and *The Baffler*, as well as in the anthologies *Tales of Two Planets* (Penguin 2020), and *Best American Essays 2022* (Harper Collins 2022). She is Senior Editor at the *Markaz Review*.

Haneen Nazzal is a visual artist based in Palestine. In work that focuses on the role of art in liberation movements and Indigenous identity, her multidisciplinary art practice combines illustration, calligraphy, animation, poster art, and experimental design. Through initiatives and collaborations with community organizations, she actively advocates for decolonization, social justice, and human rights to encourage a comprehensive understanding of the Palestinian cause.

Nora Ounnas Leroy is a Franco-Algerian photojournalist of Egyptian and Italian heritage based in Montpellier. She is also a director, screenwriter, and composer.

Ilan Pappé is one of Israel's New Historians. He has been rewriting the history of Israel's creation since the release of pertinent British and Israeli government documents in the 1980s. He was a senior lecturer in political science at the University of Haifa (1984-2007) and chair of the Emil Touma Institute for Palestinian and Israeli Studies in Haifa (2000-2008) before he left Israel in 2008, after he was condemned in the Knesset and received death threats. Pappé is a professor of history and director of the European Centre for Palestinian Studies at the University of Exeter, in the UK.

Protest Stencil is an anonymous collective of artists, writers, and political activists. Described as "London's most prolific *subvertiser*," the collective has made headlines with its political interventions in the bus shelters of the British capital. The collective's euphonious book (Dog Section Press, 2019) brings together the group's most iconic posters, in situ, with timely advice on public art interventions for activists intent on changing the cityscape.

Nawal Qasim Baidoun is a militant and activist in Bint Jbeil, South Lebanon, from a Palestinian refugee family. She was "detained on suspicion of involvement in an Islamic resistance plot to assassinate [an] Israeli collaborator and agent," as Malek Abisaab, the editor of *Memoirs of a Militant: My Years in the Khiam Women's Prison* (Olive Tree Branch, 2023) writes in the book's introduction. Qasim Baidoun graduated from law school and after her incarceration worked as a teacher and became the principal of the high school in Bint Jbeil. She is a founding member of the Lebanese Association for Prisoners and Liberators. Her first book, *Memoirs of a Militant*, was translated by Michelle Hartman and Caline Nasrallah.

Eman Quotah is the author of the debut novel *Bride of the Sea*, which won the Arab American Book Award for fiction. She grew up in Jeddeh, Saudi Arabia, and Cleveland Heights, Ohio. Her writing has appeared in the *Washington Post*, *USA Today*, the *Toast*, the *Establishment*, *Book Riot*, *Literary Hub*, *Electric Literature*, and the *Markaz Review*, among other publications.

Fadi Quran is the Middle East and North Africa campaigns director for Avaaz, a global web movement, with community campaigns in seventeen languages. Quran, who lives in Ramallah, is the vice president of operations of Riah Al-Istiklal (Independent Wind) Company, which develops and operates projects in the wind-energy sector. He is also the chief business officer for iWind.

Khalil Rabah is a Palestinian conceptual artist born in Jerusalem. He cofounded the Al-Ma'mal Foundation for Contemporary Art, Jerusalem, in 1998, and the Riwaq Biennial, in 2005. He has had numerous solo exhibitions and participated in group shows worldwide. His artwork, which, according to Darat al Funun, "reflects on themes of displacement, memory, and identity, examining the relationship between humans and their surroundings, as well as the nature of global human condition," has been acquired by MACRO, Rome; the British Museum; the Guggenheim, Abu Dhabi; Mathaf, Doha; Kunsthaus Zurich; and the Sharjah Art Foundation.

Sara Roy is a senior research scholar at the Center for Middle Eastern Studies, Harvard University. Her books include *Unsilencing Gaza: Reflections on Resistance* (Pluto Press, 2021); *Failing Peace: Gaza and the Palestinian-Israeli Conflict* (Pluto Press, 2006); and *Hamas and Civil Society in Gaza: Engaging the Islamist Social Sector* (Princeton Studies in Muslim Politics, Princeton University Press, 2013).

Raeda Saadeh is an artist born in Umm Al-Fahem, Palestine, in 1977. Gender and oppression are at the core of her self-portraits, installations, video, and performances. In 2000 she was the recipient of the first Young Artist of the Year Award by A. M. Qattan Foundation. She has participated in exhibitions in Europe, the Middle East, and the US. Her photographs are in the permanent collections of Victoria and Albert Museum; Fonds Régional d'Art Contemporain de Lorraine, Metz, France; and Le Magasin–Centre National d'Art Contemporain, in Grenoble, France.

Mohammad Sabaaneh is a Palestinian painter and caricaturist whose work has been exhibited around the world. A cartoonist since 2002, he has been published in *Aletihad*, *Al-Quds Al-Arabi*, *Al-Ghad*, and

Al-Akhbar, and has a daily cartoon in the Palestinian newspaper *Al-Hayat Al-Jadida*. Sabaaneh is the recipient of numerous awards and the author of *Palestine in Black and White* (Saqi Books, 2018) and *Power Born of Dreams: My Story Is Palestine* (Street Noise Books, 2023).

Steve Sabella was born in Jerusalem. An award-winning artist, writer, and public speaker based in Berlin, he uses photography and photographic installation to focus on the genealogy and archaeology of the image. Sabella received the Ellen Auerbach Award from the Akademie der Künste Berlin by nomination, leading to a published monograph covering twenty years of his art. His award-winning memoir, *The Parachute Paradox* (Kerber Verlag, 2016), received international recognition, winning two awards for best memoir. The artist's life and art have been the subject of several documentaries, and his art has been exhibited internationally and is held in private and public collections, including those of the British Museum, in London; the Institute du Monde Arabe, in Paris; and the Mathaf: Arab Museum of Modern Art, in Doha. In 2014 the International Center for Photography Scavi Scaligeri, in Verona, held Sabella's first major retrospective, *Archaeology of the Future*.

Rana Salman is the Palestinian CEO and co-executive director of Combatants for Peace. A translator and writer, she has spent much of the last decade leading international groups on alternative tours and fact-finding missions in the region.

Jaime Scholnick is a visual artist working in a variety of mediums and forms. After a five-year expatriation to Japan to study papermaking, Scholnick returned to Los Angeles in 1999. Her work has been exhibited in galleries and museums nationally and internationally; at PS1 Long Island City, PØST, Angles Gallery, CB1 Gallery, UCLA Hammer, the Torrance Museum of Art, Barnsdall Municipal Art Gallery, and in LAX Terminal One.

Diane Shammas received her PhD in international and intercultural education from the University of Southern California. Her regional focus is on the Middle East and North Africa, while her research centers around ethnoreligious and transnational identity, interethnic and interfaith relations; Arab Americans and Muslim Americans post-9/11 and the diaspora in US and Europe; indigeneity; settler colonialism; and comparative analysis of African American and Palestinian liberatory struggles.

Raja Shehadeh is a lawyer, writer, and founder of the pioneering Palestinian human rights organization Al Haq. He is the author of several acclaimed books published by Profile Books including the Orwell Prize–winning *Palestinian Walks: Notes on a Vanishing Landscape* (2008), as well as *Strangers in the House (2009); Occupation Diaries* (2003); *Language of War, Language of Peace; A Rift in Time (2015); Where the Line Is Drawn* (2018); *Going Home: A Walk through Fifty Years of Occupation* (2020); and his most recent book, *We Could Have Been Friends, My Father and I: A Palestinian Memoir* (2023), a finalist for the National Book Award. He lives in Ramallah, Palestine.

Olivia Snaije is a journalist and editor based in Paris. She is a contributing editor to *New Lines Magazine* and the *Africa Report* and has written for a variety of magazines and newspapers covering culture, the Middle East, and the book industry. She worked as a commissioning editor at Saqi Books in London, co-edited the book *Keep Your Eye on the Wall: Palestinian Landscapes* (Editions Textuel/Saqi Books, 2013) and translated Lamia Ziadé's *Bye Bye Babylon* (Jonathan Cape, 2011). She has written several books on Paris published by Dorling Kindersley and Flammarion.

Deni Takruri is an award-winning journalist who has reported extensively on the Israeli occupation of Palestine, Europe's refugee crisis, tensions on the Korean peninsula, and other global struggles. Raised in the US, she is the daughter of Palestinian immigrants, who spent many summers in Palestine. Takruri is a senior presenter and producer at AJ+ and has previously worked for *HuffPost Live* and Al Jazeera Arabic.

Vera Tamari is one of Palestine's leading artists. She established the first ceramics studio in the West Bank, in Al-Bireh, near Ramallah. She was a founding member of the Al Wasti Art Center in Jerusalem, and the New Visions art group, with Sliman Anis Mansour and others. She is a member of the League of Palestinian Artists and Khalil Sakakini Cultural Center. Tamari lectured on art at Birzeit University, where she founded the Virtual Gallery. She also created the Founding Committee for the Development of Cultural Heritage. In 1989 she coauthored, with Suad Amiry, *The Palestinian Village Home* (RIWAQ, second edition, 2003). She has held solo exhibitions in Ramallah and Jerusalem and taken part in international group exhibitions.

Ahed Tamimi is a Palestinian student activist from the village of Nabi Saleh in the occupied West Bank. As a child, she rose to global prominence for repeatedly confronting Israeli soldiers during weekly demonstrations in her village, which resulted in violent attacks on her family and her imprisonment at the age of sixteen. She is widely regarded as a symbol of Palestine's youth movement. Tamimi is studying international law at Birzeit University.

Heba Tannous is a Palestinian artist with a background in architecture and urban planning. Employing ink and watercolor, her abstract forms document and represent the organized chaos of urban Palestinian street life. The principal theme in her art explores the intersection between urban morphology and the life of the space.

Ahmed Twaij is a practicing doctor and multimedia journalist and film director. He has worked as a humanitarian medic in war zones. His audio and visual reports have been featured in the *Independent*, the *Guardian*, the *New York Times*, CNN, Vice, and BBC. He also curates Everyday Iraq, a social media platform dedicated to shedding light on the daily life of Iraqis and providing a new narrative for the country.

Visualizing Palestine creates visual stories for social justice for Palestine. A nonprofit based in Canada, the organization is made up of a compact, multidisciplinary team that collaborates remotely from the Middle East and North Africa to North America. VP has published approximately two hundred original Creative Commons infographics and has created four educational platforms, including Visualizing Palestine 101, Palestinian Journeys, Growth of a Movement Timeline, and Palestine Open Maps. Over the past twelve years, these platforms and visual stories reflect and contribute to significant narrative shifts in regard to international public opinions and perceptions about Palestine.

Taline Voskeritchian is a writer and translator. Her articles and cotranslations, from Arabic and Armenian into English, have appeared in the *Los Angeles Review of Books*, the *London Review of Books*, the *Nation*, *Bookforum*, *Words without Borders*, the *Journal of Palestine Studies*, and many other publications. She has taught at Boston University and American University of Armenia and conducted translation workshops in Palestinian universities.

TRANSLATORS

Michelle Hartman is a professor of Arabic and francophone literature at McGill University in Montreal, and a research associate at the Simone de Beauvoir Institute at Concordia University. She is the translator of several memoirs and novels from Arabic.

Caline Nasrallah is a literary translator, editor, and researcher with a focus on language as a feminist tool. In her editing and translation of fiction and nonfiction, she endeavors to put language at the service of liberation in her projects.

EDITORS

Malu Halasa is a Jordanian Filipina American writer. *Woman Life Freedom: Voices and Art from the Women's Protests in Iran* (Saqi Books, 2023) is her latest book as editor. Her coedited anthologies include *Syria Speaks: Art and Culture from the Frontline* (2014), *The Secret Life of Syrian Lingerie: Intimacy and Design* (2008), *Transit Tehran: Young Iran and Its Inspirations* (2008), *Kaveh Golestan: Recording the Truth in Iran* (2005), *Transit Beirut* (2004), and *Creating Spaces of Freedom: Culture in Defiance* (2000). She was managing editor of the Prince Claus Fund Library, a founding editor of *Tank* magazine, and editor at large for *Portal 9*. She has written for the *Guardian*, the *Financial Times*, and the *Times Literary Supplement*. Her debut novel, *Mother of All Pigs* (Unnamed Press, 2017), is a fictionalized family memoir. She is the Literary Editor of the *Markaz Review*.

Jordan Elgrably is a Franco-American and Moroccan writer and translator whose stories and creative nonfiction have appeared in numerous anthologies and reviews, including *Apulée*, *Salmagundi*, and the *Paris Review*. Editor-in-chief and founder of the *Markaz Review*, he is the cofounder and former director of the Levantine Cultural Center/the Markaz in Los Angeles (2001–2020). His work on behalf of the arts and cultures of the Middle East and North Africa have won many awards and major grants, including the Rachel Corrie Conscience and Courage Award from the American Arab Anti-Discrimination Committee. Elgrably is the editor of *Stories from the Center of the World: New Middle East Fiction* (City Lights, 2024). He is based in Montpellier, France, and California.

Nadine Aranki is a Palestinian curator and cultural researcher based in London. She earned her master's in cultural studies from Goldsmiths University and her bachelor's in journalism and politics from Birzeit University. Aranki works as a research fellow at De Montfort University, in Leicester. With a focus on culture and human rights, she has volunteered for many heritage, educational, and social justice initiatives. She co-curated, with Meg Peterson, *The Many Lives of Gaza*, a 2024 touring exhibition that featured photographs, drawings, videos, and posters from the Palestinian Museum, Birzeit.

Khaled El Haber, *We Are Doing Fine in Gaza . . . What about You?!,* 2024, detail.
Fine art archival paper, 310 gsm, 75 x 55 cm. Courtesy of Zawyeh Gallery.

Credits

Hossam Madhoun, "Messages from Gaza Now." Copyright © 2024 Hossam Al Madhoun. Published by arrangement with Jonathan Chadwick, Az Theatre, London.

Lina Mounzer, "Palestine and the Unspeakable" was first published in the *Markaz Review*, October 16, 2023. Published here by arrangement with the author.

Khalil Rabah, *Palestine Philistine*, 1997, *Oxford Desk Dictionary, Thesaurus*, and nails, 10.5 x 26 x 19 cm, Edition 4/4 + 1AP. Published by arrangement with Ramzi and Saeda Dalloul Art Foundation.

Mosab Abu Toha, "Palestine A-Z" from *Things You May Find Hidden in My Ear: Poems from Gaza*. Copyright © 2022 by Mosab Abu Toha. Reprinted with the permission of the Permissions Company, LLC on behalf of City Lights Books. citylights.com.

Ilan Pappé, "Culture and Resistance in *Imagining Palestine*," originally published as "The Agency and Resilience of the Palestinians Shines: On Imagining Palestine: Cultures of Exile and National Identity by Tahrir Hamdi" in *Janus Unbound: Journal of Critical Studies* 2, no. 2 (July 15, 2023), 69-79. Published here by arrangement with the author.

Taysir Batniji, *Watchtowers*, 2008. Series of twenty-six black-and-white photographs, inkjet prints on FineArt Pearl paper, 50 x 40 cm (each). Published by arrangement with the artist and Sfeir-Semler Gallery, Hamburg/Beirut.

Karim Kattan, "At the Threshold of Humanity: Gaza Is Not an Abstraction" first appeared in the *Baffler*, October 31, 2023. Published here by arrangement with the writer and the *Baffler*.

Olivia Snaije, "The Past Is Being Destroyed in Palestine—As Well As the Present" was first published by *New Lines Magazine* in 2023. Published here by arrangement with the writer and *New Lines Magazine*.

Hazem Harb, two artworks from the series *Gauze #22*, 2023; *Dystopia Is Not a Noun #14*, 2023; *Dystopia Is Not a Noun #16*, 2023; and *Watermelon* (1917) II, 2024. Published here by arrangement with the artist.

Ahmed Twaij, "Gaza versus Mosul from a Medical and Humanitarian Standpoint" was first published in the *Markaz Review*, November 27, 2023. Published here by arrangement with the writer.

Ahmed Masoud, "Application 39" was originally commissioned for *Palestine + 100*, edited by Basma Ghalayini, Comma Press, 2019. Published here by arrangement with Comma Press. commapress.co.uk.

Noor Hindi, "Fuck Your Lecture on Craft, My People Are Dying" and "Pledging Allegiance" from *Dear God. Dear Bones. Dear Yellow*. Copyright © 2022 Noor Hindi. Used with permission of Haymarket Books. haymarketbooks.org.

Samir Harb, *Rafah*. Published here by arrangement with the artist.

Jordan Elgrably, "They Kill Writers, Don't They?" Published here by arrangement with the writer.

Yousef M. Aljamal, "The End of the Palestinian State? Jenin Is Only the Beginning" was first published in *Politics Today*, July 5, 2023. Published here by arrangement with the writer.

Hadani Ditmars, "Jenin's Freedom Theatre Survives Further Assault" was first published by the *Middle East Institute*, July 14, 2023. Published here by arrangement with the author.

Sliman Anis Mansour, *Homeland*, 2010, charcoal and acrylic on canvas, 188 x 233 cm. Published here by arrangement with the Ramzi and Saeda Dalloul Art Foundation.

Tony Litwinko, "A Response to *Gaza Mowing the Lawn*, 2014–15" was first published in the *Markaz Review*, July 14, 2021. Published here by arrangement with the writer.

Jaime Scholnick, *Mowing the Lawn, Gaza, 42*, 2014, mixed media on panel, 7.5 x 11 in. Published here by arrangement with the artist.

Nadine Aranki, "The Art of the Poster" is an abridged version of a longer essay, "New Palestinian Poster Art Responds to War and Apartheid," first published in the *Markaz Review*, February 26, 2024. Published here by arrangement with the writer.

Dyala Moshtaha, *Freedom in Bloom*, 2023, fine art archival paper, 310 gsm, 75 x 55 cm. Published here by arrangement with Zawyeh Gallery.

Haneen Nazzal, *Against*, 2022, fine art archival paper, 310 gsm, 75 x 55 cm, and *We Will Never Leave*, 2021, digital illustration, 36 x 51 cm. Both posters appear by arrangement with the artist.

Khaled El Haber, *We Are Doing Fine in Gaza . . . What about You?!*, 2024, fine art archival paper, 310 gsm, 75 x 55 cm. Published here by arrangement with Zawyeh Gallery.

Ivar Ekeland and Sara Roy, "Disrupting the Colonial Gaze: Gaza and Israel after October 7." Published here by arrangement with the writers.

Hala Alyan, "Habibti Ghazal" was first published in the *New Yorker*, January 29, 2024. Published here by arrangement with the poet.

Acknowledgments

The *Markaz Review* would like to thank its generous supporters over the years, first and foremost Dr. Diane Shammas, of the Shammas Family Trust, and Dr. Linda Jacobs, of the Violet Jabara Charitable Trust, as well as Rowan Storm, Tony Litwinko, Mark Amin, India Radfar and the A & A Fund, and Bana and Nabil Hilal. We also wish to acknowledge the visionary support we have received from the Open Society Foundation, Hawthornden Foundation, Andrew W. Mellon Foundation, the Community of Literary Magazines and Presses (CLMP), and the Jan Michalski Foundation.

Sumūd: A New Palestinian Reader would not have been possible without the contributions of its many writers, poets, artists, and activists or the *Markaz Review* managing editor Rana Asfour, and senior editor Lina Mounzer, who initially assigned some essays and discussed ideas included in the book. For their advice and support, we also thank Steve Sabella; Venetia Porter; Wafa Roz, at the Ramzi and Saeda Dalloul Art Foundation, Beirut; Ziad Anani and Anna Rodionova, at Zawyeh Gallery, Ramallah and Dubai; Rose Issa; Jonathan Chadwick; Lawrence Joffe; Lydia Wilson and Danny Postel, at *New Lines Magazine*, and Nupu Press. Seven Stories Press's editors Dan Simon and Tal Mancini immediately recognized the imperative of producing a Palestinian reader during the war on Gaza, and, with copyeditor Kristen Steenbeeke and designer Stewart Cauley, were instrumental in its swift publication.

Sumūd is dedicated to the generations of people—some are with us and some are not—who have believed in and worked toward the creation of a Palestinian homeland.